TRADITION HISTORY AND
THE PSALMS OF ASAPH

SOCIETY OF BIBLICAL LITERATURE

DISSERTATION SERIES
J. J. M. Roberts, Old Testament Editor
Charles Talbert, New Testament Editor

Number 88

TRADITION HISTORY AND
THE PSALMS OF ASAPH

by
Harry P. Nasuti

Harry P. Nasuti

TRADITION HISTORY AND THE PSALMS OF ASAPH

Scholars Press
Atlanta, Georgia

TRADITION HISTORY AND THE PSALMS OF ASAPH

Harry P. Nasuti

Ph.D., 1983
Yale University

Advisor:
Robert R. Wilson

© 1988
Society of Biblical Literature

Library of Congress Cataloging-in-Publication Data

Nasuti, Harry Peter.
  Tradition history and the psalms of Asaph.

  (Dissertation series / Society of Biblical
Literature ; no. 88)
  Bibliography: p.
  1. Bible. O.T. Psalms L–Criticism,
interpretation, etc. 2. Bible. O.T. Psalms
LXXIII-LXXXIII–Criticism, interpretation, etc.
3. Asaph (Biblical figure) I. Title. II. Series:
Dissertation series (Society of Biblical Literature ;
no. 88.
BS1430.2.N37   1987   223'.2066   86-25232
ISBN 0-89130-970-5 (alk. paper)
ISBN 0-89130-971-3 (pbk. : alk. paper)

Printed in the United States of America

Contents

Acknowledgments vii

Chapter 1: Tradition History and *Traditionsgeschichte* 1
    Traditionsgeschichte: Some Initial
        Methodological Considerations 1
    The Tradition-Historical Systems of Steck and Huber 7
    Conclusions 18

Chapter 2: Tradition History and the Psalms of Asaph 25
    Illman and his Predecessors: Methodological Considerations 25
    Illman's Use of Tradition History 38
    Illman's Analysis of Characteristic Common Content
        in the Psalms of Asaph 40
    Illman's Alternate Search for Tradition in the Psalms of Asaph 45
    Critique of Illman 49
    A New Tradition-Historical Study of the Psalms of Asaph 54

Chapter 3: A Linguistic Analysis of the Psalms of Asaph 59
    Psalm 50 59
    Psalm 73 63
    Psalm 74 66
    Psalm 75 71
    Psalm 76 75
    Psalm 77 78
    Psalm 78 81
    Psalm 79 94
    Psalm 80 97
    Psalm 81 102
    Psalm 82 108
    Psalm 83 111
    Conclusions 115

Chapter 4: A Form-Critical Analysis of the Psalms of Asaph 117
    The Collective Laments 118
    The "Prophetic" Psalms 127

Excursus: Form-Critical and Tradition-Historical Implications
of the Phrase, "I am the LORD Your God" 136
Other forms 149
Psalm 73 149
Psalm 76 151
Psalm 77 154
Psalm 78 155
Conclusions 157

Chapter 5: Asaph and the Asaphites: A Tradition-Historical
Analysis of the External Evidence............................... 161
Conclusions 186

Chapter 6: Conclusions 193
Tradition-Historical Conclusions...................................193
Methodological Conclusions 195

Bibliography...199

Acknowledgments

As I reflect upon this final act of formal studenthood, I am struck by how much I owe to those whose talents and generosity are but dimly mirrored here. First and most obvious is my debt to my advisor, Robert R. Wilson, both for the stimulation of his scholarship and for his guidance in this work and throughout my doctoral studies. In a more general way, thanks are also due to the biblical faculties of Yale University, Union Theological Seminary (New York), Oxford University, and Fordham University, all of whom have given me many valued gifts. Of these I mention in particular Raymond E. Brown, S. S. and Brevard S. Childs, who by their teaching and example have helped to shape my understanding of what it means to spend one's life in the study of the Bible.

Special thanks are due my friends and fellow graduate students, Tim Polk, Bob Robinson, and Pam Johnson Scalise. By adopting me into their year they increased the fruitfulness of my graduate studies beyond measure.

Many thanks are also due the students, faculty, and administration of Le Moyne College, Syracuse, New York. Their support, encouragement, and forbearance during the final stages of this dissertation were essential to its completion. Equally essential and appreciated was the great effort of my typist, Mrs. Joyce Bell. Her efficiency with a difficult manuscript and her patience with its author were more than could have ever been expected.

I close by recalling the continuous support of my family, especially that of my wife, Jane-Louise. Her sustaining love has made this dissertation possible. May she find joy in its long-awaited completion and in her husband's deep and sincere gratitude.

1
Tradition History
and *Traditionsgeschichte*

In recent years, biblical studies have been increasingly concerned to isolate both the general theological background and the specific historical circles out of which the various parts of the Bible developed. The discipline by which this enterprise is carried out is usually known in English as tradition history. As is well known, however, this general English term includes within itself a number of more specific German disciplines, each devoted to more or less the same end but employing different means.

This work is intended as both an exegetical and a methodical contribution to the tradition-historical study of the Hebrw Bible. On the exegetical level, it will offer a tradition-historical analysis of a series of biblical texts, namely, those twelve psalms which share the superscription *lĕ'āsāp* (Psalms 50; 73-83). On the methodological level, it will use this analysis to examine certain aspects of the contemporary discipline of tradition history itself. More specifically, it will focus on the most recent methodological developments in the field, those connected with the name *Traditionsgeschichte*. To this end, the first chapter will consider the latter method in some detail, while the chapters which follow will turn to a tradition-historical study of the Asaphite psalms and its implications for both *Traditionsgeschichte* and tradition history in general.

TRADITIONSGESCHICHTE:
SOME INITIAL METHODOLOGICAL CONSIDERATIONS

The fact that *Traditionsgeschichte* is an increasingly important aspect of biblical studies may be seen from its inclusion in several of the most recent xegetical handbooks in the field.[1] As the name would imply, *Traditionsgeschichte* has perhaps been most appreciated among German-speaking scholars, although there are indications that its influence has begun to be felt in the rest

---

[1] Especially to be noted here are Hermann Barth and Odil Hannes Steck, *Exegese des Alten Testaments: Leitfaden der Methodik* (Neukirchen-Vluyn: Neukirchener, 1971) 70-80; Georg Fohrer et al., *Exegese des Alten Testaments* (Heidelberg: Quelle & Meyer, 1973; 2d ed. 1976) 99-116. Compare the treatment in Gottfried Adam et al., *Einführung in die exegetischen Methoden* (München: Kaiser, 1975) 47-48.

of the scholarly world as well.² Nevertheless, despite the recent attention received by the method, there still persists some degree of uncertainty as to its exact boundaries and even as to its central features. The present work is concerned with an examination of this uncertainty, a discernment of its possible causes, and the exposition of an alternative, or at least a modified, approach.

The confusion surrounding the discipline begins with the term *Traditionsgeschichte* itself and, more specifically, with the problem of how to distinguish it from the semantically similar term *Überlieferungsgeschichte*. One may indeed justifiably question the necessity for making such a distinction, both with respect to most past and current usage and with respect to the many theoretical difficulties in separating the two disciplines.³ Nevertheless, since this work is primarily concerned with the terms and concepts of those scholars who do distinguish between the two disciplines, such a distinction will be observed here. In an effort to avoid the stylistic awkwardness which would result from repeated reference to these German terms, this work will use the capitalized term Tradition history to refer to *Traditionsgeschichte* and the somewhat makeshift term transmission history to refer to the alternate discipline of *Überlieferungsgeschichte*. The uncapitalized term tradition history will be used to refer to the more general English usage which includes both of these disciplines.

Along these lines, one may note that the two foremost exponents of the method distinguish Tradition history from transmission history in a similar way. Thus, according to Odil Hannes Steck, Tradition history is concerned with the traditional content of a text rather than with the history of a textual unit itself (transmission history or redaction history) or such questions as the effects that a text might have (*Wirkungsgeschichte*).⁴ Similarly, for Friedrich Huber, Tradition history is not concerned with the changes that a unit undergoes in the course of its history but rather with the historical development and transformation of traditions, as defined in terms of fixed meaning complexes (*geprägte Bedeutungssyndrome*).⁵ In both of these theoretical discussions, the concern of Tradition history is not so much with the history of the text itself (as in transmission history) as with a phenomenon which turns up in the individual text but which leads its own life before, during, and afterwards in certain tradition centers.⁶ The description of the development of such a phenomenon is seen to contribute to the understanding of the text which contains it, as well as to the larger theological history of ancient Israel.⁷

The phenomena which are the subject matter of Tradition history are variously described, even by the adherents of the method. For Huber, Tradition

---

² One might mention the notice taken of the method in Douglas A. Knight, *Rediscovering the Traditions of Israel* (Missoula: Scholars, 1975) 23, 187–192.
³ See Adam, *Einführung*, 47–48, and Knight, *Rediscovering*, 21–25.
⁴ Barth/Steck, *Exegese*, 70.
⁵ Friedrich Huber, "Motiv- und Traditionskritik," in Fohrer, *Exegese*, 116.
⁶ Barth/Steck, *Exegese*, 70.
⁷ See Huber, "Traditionskritik," 102.

history deals with such fixed meaning complexes as motifs, fixed themes, fixed features, and traditions.[8] Although Steck also uses some of these in his discussion of Tradition history, he speaks more often of "notions" (*Vorstellungen*) which are capable of being combined into notion complexes (*Vorstellungskomplexe*) or traditions, and eventually into tradition spheres and tradition streams.[9] Some of the differences between Huber and Steck are noteworthy and will be discussed below. Nevertheless, it is important to emphasize that both are concerned with those elements which they feel allow one to discern the theological and historical background of a text even though these theological and historical dimensions are not apparent in the history of the text itself.

It is readily apparent that most of the analytical terms used by Huber and Steck have a prior history within biblical studies, as well as antecedents within the larger sphere of the humanities in general. Biblical scholarship since Gunkel has used the term "motif," a word mediated through folklore studies, and has considered motif research a useful tool in assessing folkloric material in the Bible.[10] Similarly, "theme," a term with both folkloric and wider literary critical antecedents, has also been taken over into biblical studies, especially since the work of Martin Noth.[11] Terms such as "tradition" and "notion" are, of course, widespread in the humanities and capable of flexible usage there. Nevertheless, as its name implies, it is especially with transmission history and Tradition history that tradition receives its most intensive use in biblical scholarship. Similarly, it is in Steck's Tradition-historical use of notion that that term carries its largest significance in the field.

---

[8] Ibid., 101–116. In the second edition of this work (1976), Huber includes the term "image" in this list and uses the term motif in a somewhat different way. On this see further below, especially in note 46.

[9] See Barth/Steck, *Exegese*, 70–73; also Odil Hannes Steck, "Das Problem theologischer Strömungen in nachexilischer Zeit," *EvT* 28 (1968); and Steck, "Theological Streams of Tradition," in *Tradition and Theology in the Old Testament*, ed. by Douglas A. Knight (Philadelphia: Fortress, 1977) 183–214. The translation of *Vorstellung* by notion follows the usage of Steck, "Streams" and Knight, *Traditions*, 188–192.

[10] For a consideration of Gunkel's use of the term motif, see Robert C. Culley, "An Approach to the Problem of Oral Tradition," *VT* 13 (1963) 113–125. Also see his *Studies in the Structure of the Hebrew Narrative* (Philadelphia: Fortress, 1976) for a consideration of the term in folklore studies. That the term does not ultimately originate in folklore studies may be seen in Elisabeth Frenzel, *Stoff-, Motiv-, und Symbolforschung* (Stuttgart: J. B. Metzlersche, 1963) 44, where concern for the discernment of motifs is already to be seen in Lessing.

[11] For the use of the term theme in folklore studies, see Robert C. Culley, *Oral Formulaic Language in the Biblical Psalms* (Toronto: University of Toronto, 1967) 17–20. For its less technical use in literary criticism, see Wolfgang Kayser, *Das Sprachliche Kunstwerk* (Bern: Francke, 1968) 62. The most prominent biblical usage is that of Martin Noth, as found in his *Überlieferungsgeschichte des Pentateuch* (Stuttgart: W. Kohlhammer, 1948).

As is the case with its analytical terms, many of the central methodological features of Tradition history were also at least foreshadowed in the earlier scholarship of biblical studies and the humanities in general. Thus, for example, the close analysis of "antecedent materials" which then appear in biblical texts has a long history within the discipline, with scholars perhaps being especially concerned with the Israelite usage of "foreign" materials.[12] Tradition history continues this analysis of how such materials are used in specific texts. However, it also adds to this a deeper search for the means by which such appearances take place. In such a way, it has a specific interest in the historical tradents of the antecedent materials. Further, in Tradition history the search is no longer pursued mostly in terms of an Israelite/non-Israelite dialectic. Rather, there is a greater appreciation of the complexity of the theological and cultural situation within Israel itself and, with this, an increased realization of the need to apply such comparative methods to the inner-Israelite evidence of biblical texts.[13]

In all of these areas, the most recent predecessors of Tradition-historical scholars are to be found among the proponents of transmission history. This is especially the case when the latter have gone beyond the purely textual concerns which adherents of Tradition history assign to transmission history and have touched upon what might be seen as pre-textual "antecedent material." Thus, for example, von Rad's analysis of ancient credos pointed to the existence of certain centers where both Sinai and exodus/conquest traditions already existed prior to the specific textual formulations of the credos.[14] This Tradition-historical aspect of von Rad's work was further broadened by Martin Noth with his analysis of the five different Pentateuchal "themes" and their ramifications for the history of earliest Israel.[15] From a Tradition-historical point of view, it is significant that these themes are not to be equated with specific texts but are rather indicative of antecedent materials and the centers which were responsible for them. It is precisely this search for pre-textual materials and their socio-historical connections that is embraced and broadened by the advocates of Tradition history.

Despite the fruitfulness of these forerunners of Tradition history, it is significant that their views have not been accepted by the entirety of biblical scholars. In particular, a large number of English-speaking, as well as some German-speaking, scholars have had their difficulties with either the methods employed

---

[12] Perhaps the classic example of this basically *religionsgeschichtliche* approach is Hermann Gunkel, *Schöpfung und Chaos in Urzeit und Endzeit* (Göttingen: Vandenhoeck & Ruprecht, 1895). It is, however, a common approach for other aspects of studies in the Hebrew Bible (such as those concerning apocalyptic), as well as for NT studies.

[13] See especially Steck, "Problem" and "Streams."

[14] Gerhard von Rad, *Das formgeschichtliche Problem des Hexateuch* (BWANT IV/26; Stuttgart: W. Kohlhammer, 1938). E. T. "The Form-Critical Problem of the Hexateuch" in von Rad, *The Form-Critical Problem of the Hexateuch and Other Essays*, trans. by E. W. Trueman Dicken (Edinburgh and London: Oliver & Boyd, 1966).

[15] Noth, *Überlieferungsgeschichte*, see esp. pp. 48–49.

or the conclusions expounded.[16] Moreover, it appears that many of these difficulties touch upon what might be seen as the transfer from transmission-historical to Tradition-historical models. Thus, although von Rad was credited with underlining the striking omission of Sinai material from his credos, critics tended to dispute the more Tradition-historical aspect of his argument that this omission pointed to originally distinct traditions which existed in separate historical circles.[17] Noth's isolation of his five Pentateuchal themes, together with the historical conclusions drawn from this isolation, met with similar opposition.[18] In this connection, it is important to note that while von Rad's basic analysis was a form-critical study of certain texts, Noth's argument was in its fundamentals Tradition-historical, since his isolation of Pentateuchal themes was not based on any existing textual units. This makes the critical response to Noth's analysis even more interesting from a Tradition-historical point of view.

While there have been numerous responses to Noth, some of the most forceful have come from the English-speaking scholarly world.[19] These scholars have taken special issue with Noth's historical conclusions. In this, they argue that while Noth's approach explains the existence of the individual aspects of the Pentateuch, it leaves the question of the ultimate unity of these aspects (and of Israel itself) fundamentally without answer.[20] In their attempt to address such issues, some of the critics have appealed to what they contend are early units of Israel's poetry.[21]

This is not the place for yet another review of this important scholarly discussion about Israel's earliest history. What is of interest here is the underlying methodological discussion as it relates to Noth's moves in a Tradition-historical direction. This discussion may be focused on Noth's use of "theme." In this respect, it is interesting to note that Noth at times uses the term almost synonymously with the term "tradition," even to the point of combining the two terms into a single entity.[22] Thus, with von Rad, he can speak of the Sinai

---

[16] For an overview of such criticism with a good bibliography, see Knight, *Rediscovering*, 193-213.

[17] See, among others, Leonhard Rost, *Das kleine Credo und andere Studien zum Alten Testament* (Heidelberg: Quelle & Meyer, 1965) and Artur Weiser, *The Old Testament and Its Formation*, trans. by Dorothea Barton (New York, Association, 1961) 84.

[18] See, among others, John Bright, *Early Israel in Recent History Writing* (Chicago: Alec R. Allenson, 1956).

[19] See again Bright, *Early Israel*, and also George Ernest Wright, "Archaeology and Old Testament Studies," *JBL* 77 (1958) 39-51, among others.

[20] Bright, *Early Israel*, 84. See Knight, *Rediscovering*, 210 and the works cited there.

[21] So, for example, David Noel Freedman, "Early Israelite History in the Light of Early Israelite Poetry" in Hans Goedicke and J. J. M. Roberts, ed., *Unity and Diversity* (Baltimore: Johns Hopkins Press, 1975) 3-35.

[22] For the term *Überlieferungsthema*, see Noth, *Überlieferungsgeschichte*, 49.

tradition as representing a separate theme and the taking possession of the Palestinian arable land as representing an independent tradition-theme.[23] Nevertheless, he can also speak of the "Pentateuchal tradition" of which these themes are a part.[24] This ambiguity, along with the rest of his discussion, suggests that for Noth theme already implies in itself the presence of a group responsible for its continued existence. This implication is of crucial importance both for Noth's critics in the Pentateuchal debate and for the modern adherents of Tradition history.

For the critics of Noth's position, the crucial question has been not whether these themes point to separate groups, but whether they point to separate historical events. Thus, the tendency has been to move from the assumption of an "actual historical memory" of a sequence of events[25] to the question why these events are dealt with separately in individual cases.[26] History thus is seen as that which alone is able to account for the very unity of Israel which Noth was unable to explain.[27] This connected history, however, would appear to demand the presence of at least one group which experienced it and which would be ultimately responsible for the original account of that history. Thus, it would seem that Noth's critics do not see his isolation of separate "themes" as having any independent historical value in terms of the ability of those themes to indicate the existence of separate groups who are responsible for them.

Methodologically, this is a crucial issue — for Tradition history even more than for transmission history. In what way is a theme (or an aspect similar to it) capable of an historical reference? The critical response to Noth has focused on one side of this question, that of whether such themes do indeed mirror Israel's formative historical events and whether their separation entails the separation of those events from each other.[28] Nevertheless, most of this criticism has only secondarily been concerned with the crucial methodological issue of how these — and any other — themes relate, not to the events themselves, but to the groups which bore them. Here, the question is not so much that of whether the events themselves are to be seen as separate by virtue of the initial separation of themes, but rather whether such separate themes imply separate tradition groups.

Although, in at least one case, Noth himself would seem to argue against

---

[23] Ibid., 49.

[24] Ibid., 48.

[25] Frank Moore Cross, Jr., "The Divine Warrior in Israel's Early Cult" in *Biblical Motifs: Origins and Transformations*, ed. by A. Altmann (Cambridge, MA: 1966) 16. Also see Bright, *Early Israel*, 122, and Siegfried Hermann, "Mose," *EvT* 28 (1968) 326.

[26] Bright, *Early Israel*, 105. Also see Weiser, *Old Testament*, 84f. which makes the same point.

[27] Again see Bright, *Early Israel*, 84.

[28] See Ibid., 42-43, which speaks of "separate history" and "separate existence" without, however, explicitly posing the question in terms of separate tradition *groups* — perhaps because of its preference for the unity of both tradition and tradition group.

this view,[29] the response to this issue is only implied by Noth's critics. As noted above, there has been concern to demonstrate that the separate themes do not necessarily imply separate historical events—the implication of this being, of course, that such unified events demand a unified group of participants in those events who were then responsible for the unified account. While this position appears reasonable in terms of the relationship of the biblical material to the groups responsible for such material, the approach is similar to that of Noth himself. American critics, in particular, in their arguing from early poetic texts to the unified events behind them,[30] and thus by implication to the group responsible for them, also argue from material to group. There is a certain difference, of course, in the fact that these critics are arguing from a text rather than a theme. However, to the extent that even these texts can be considered composite or datable to a time after the themes had already come together, the individual themes may be seen as preceding the texts and the same "separation problem" arises. Form criticism could address the composite argument, though it has for the most part not been so employed by these critics, perhaps because of the nature of the poetry considered.[31] Further, attempts to date the texts early enough to rule out any pre-existent themes (that is, contemporaneous with the events themselves), while impressive, have by no means entirely carried the field.[32]

The methodological issues raised above must be faced squarely. To what extent may historical judgments concerning the groups responsible for biblical materials be deduced from the existence of such phenomena as theme and those aspects related to it? On the answer to this question depends much of the justification for the discipline of Tradition history. It is thus with this question in mind that the various terms and approaches of Tradition history must now be considered.

THE TRADITION-HISTORICAL SYSTEMS OF STECK AND HUBER

The first exponent of a specifically Tradition-historical method to be considered here is the above mentioned Odil Hannes Steck. Steck has written widely on the methodological issues involved[33] and may perhaps be considered the

---

[29] Namely that of the "guidance out of Egypt" which he sees as having an all-Israel orientation from the very beginning. See Noth, *Überlieferungsgeschichte*, 54.
[30] So Freedman, "History."
[31] Since a large part of such poetry is taken up with an enumeration of historical events, it is difficult to see how appeal could be made to formal guarantees to safeguard the integrity of the parts within such an enumeration itself.
[32] See Frank Moore Cross, Jr., *Canaanite Myth and Hebrew Epic: Essays in the History of the Religion of Israel* (Cambridge, MA: Harvard University, 1973) 112-144.
[33] See especially Barth/Steck, *Exegese*, Steck, "Streams" and *Problem*, as well as his *Israel und das gewaltsame Geschick des Propheten* (WMANT 23; Neukirchen-Vluyn:

foremost advocate of the method. For him the basic element of the Tradition-historical enterprise is that of the notion (*Vorstellung*).³⁴ In keeping with the concerns of the method, the notion is to be identified with neither a text nor a genre, but is rather the most fundamental conceptual unit which allows itself to be isolated. When a notion occurs in various places in the Bible which have no possibility of literary dependence on each other, such occurrences must instead have a living historical tradition (*Überlieferung*) as their stage of mediation (*Vermittlungsinstanz*). Both groups and places are examples of such mediation stages.³⁵ In such a way, Steck's isolation of a notion is similar methodologically to Noth's isolation of a theme. Neither notion nor theme is bound to any one text or genre, and both are seen as able to point to an historical referent in the group or location responsible for their origin or continued existence. This is not to say, however, that notion and theme are interchangeable terms. In Steck's usage, notion is a much more basic conceptual element than Noth's "theme," which itself covers many smaller conceptual units.³⁶ Nevertheless, the methodological dynamics are similar in each case.

Despite its essential role in the Tradition-historical enterprise, the notion is for Steck only the ground floor in that enterprise. In order fully to pursue the historical connections of a notion, one must press beyond the individual notion to the more comprehensive notion complex which utilizes the notion in a particular way. This step towards greater comprehensiveness leads to Steck's use of the term "tradition."³⁷

For Steck, a tradition is recognized by its thematically centered association of notions. More specifically, one can distinguish the tradition by means of its set linguistic field, characteristic formulatory structure, specific notional contour, and typical line of assertion (logic of material).³⁸ Defined in these terms, tradition is to be considered as a unit of the *traditum* (that which is handed down), as were notion and notion complex.³⁹ Tradition is, however, more comprehensive than at least the former of these latter elements.

Neukirchener, 1967), esp. pp. 18–19 and p. 107 n. 4, and his *Überlieferung und Zeitgeschichte in den Elia-Erzählungen*, (WMANT 26; Neukirchen-Vluyn: Neukirchener, 1968), esp. p. 103 n. 3.

³⁴ See Barth/Steck, *Exegese*, 71, where it is noted that the method could also be called "*Vorstellungsgeschichte*."

³⁵ Ibid., 72; see also 73 and 75.

³⁶ See Noth, *Überlieferungsgeschichte*, 67–68, where he speaks of themes being "filled out" with further less comprehensive "tradition materials," such as motifs and schemes. Noth's theme would probably be equivalent to Steck's tradition. See further on this below.

³⁷ It is unclear whether Steck means to equate *Vorstellungskomplex* with *Tradition*. The two would seem to be quite closely related. See *Exegese*, 73, where *Vorstellungszusammenhänge* is juxtaposed with traditions.

³⁸ Ibid., 74. Again the translation of these terms follows that of Knight, *Traditions*, 189.

³⁹ Ibid., 74. Also see Steck, *Geschick*, 18.

Given its definition in terms of a thematically centered association of notions, a tradition would seem to be distinguished on the basis of content rather than on the basis of form.[40] As such, it is one element in a series of content units which encompass varying degrees of complexity and comprehensiveness. Thus, on the one side, a tradition is more comprehensive than a notion and may contain several of these within itself. On the other side, a tradition itself belongs in turn to a comprehensive conceptual design which by virtue of its encompassing a more extensive intellectual sphere is known as a sphere of tradition.[41] When this sphere is extended over time it becomes what Steck calls a tradition stream. As the most comprehensive element of Steck's series, the stream of tradition is not constituted simply by the appearance of individual notions or even individual traditions, though these do point to such streams in whose current they can remain alive. As do notions, these streams indicate the existence of the groups and places which mediate such extensive intellectual movements.[42]

Despite the fact that the conceptual content of the *traditum* remains the primary feature which determines the elements of this series, Steck is nevertheless concerned to include form in some way. Thus, on one level, traditions are seen to have a certain formulatory structure, though this does not appear to be the equivalent of a genre.[43] However, spheres or streams of tradition are not only constituted by "structures of expression" (in addition to pregnant concepts, semantic fields, thrusts of affirmation, and distinctive movements of thought), but they also "above all" have their own special genres in which they express their message in appropriate form.[44] Still, the isolation of the form does not seem to be the primary concern of Tradition history, as it is of form criticism. Rather, such formal concern seems to serve the establishment of the basic conceptual units outlined above.

Before commenting on these elements of Steck's methodological system, it might be well to outline the similar elements of the other theoretical exponent of Tradition history mentioned above, Friedrich Huber. As was the case with Steck, Huber outlines a series of elements which are tied neither to a specific form nor to a particular text yet which are still distinct entities able to be isolated within a literary work. Huber calls these entities fixed meaning complexes (*geprägte Bedeutungssyndrome*) and has distinguished four classes of them.[45]

Huber's initial unit is the motif.[46] As with the other elements of his system,

---

[40] Nevertheless, as will be noted below, Steck *is* concerned to include formal elements in his method in some way.
[41] Steck, "Streams," 193-195.
[42] Ibid., 197-198.
[43] See for example, question B on p. 74 in Barth/Steck, *Exegese*, where what is at issue seems more narrowly defined than a genre would be.
[44] Steck, "Streams," 194-195.
[45] Huber, "Traditionskritik," 101-116.
[46] Ibid., 102-106. In the 1976 edition of Fohrer, *Exegese*, Huber uses the term motif in a somewhat different way. There motif has become the general term which includes under

a motif is for Huber a fixed meaning complex, whose fixed quality is usually indicated by its occurrence in at least two independent literary units. However, unlike these other elements, a motif is distinguished by its referential character. The motif thus is able to evoke certain larger associations by its own powers and not simply by virtue of its use in the larger unit. In accordance with these referential powers, a motif is also distinguished by its lack of self-sufficiency within the larger unit. Unlike a theme, a motif usually occurs in connection with another meaning complex. Finally, unlike a tradition, a motif is not the focus of a transmission interest of a circle of tradents responsible for handing it on.

The next element in Huber's schema, the fixed theme,[47] does not exhibit the referential character of the motif. Rather, it refers only to itself and not to something beyond itself. Nevertheless, like a motif, a theme is not as independent as a tradition, since it too is not the focus of a transmission interest of a circle of tradents.

Closely related to the fixed theme is the fixed feature (*geprägter Zug*).[48] Like the theme, the feature neither has a referential character nor is the focus of a transmission interest of a circle of tradents. Nevertheless, the feature differs from the theme in terms of its "weight," since it serves only for the arrangement of details.

The final element in Huber's series is that of the tradition,[49] which, as implied above, is a fixed meaning complex in which a circle of tradents has a transmission interest. Traditions are independent grammatical products which could exist by themselves, although they are almost always bound up with other themes and features. This independent nature does not, however, rule out the possibility of a tradition's being used in combination with other units and even assuming the role of themes or motifs in these units.[50]

It is instructive to consider how Huber determines the classification of a Tradition-historical unit.[51] Once it is established that a fixed meaning complex is present, one first seeks to determine if the unit is the focus of a transmission interest of a circle of tradents. If so, it can be classified as a tradition. If it does not have such a transmission interest, one next seeks to determine if it has a

---

itself fixed images (*Bild*), themes and features. In spite of this change in terminology, Huber's overall system remains much the same, since the new images seem to perform the same as the motifs of the first edition. Since it is the terminology of the first edition that is found in the main work to be considered in the following chapter, that terminology will be presented here. Where appropriate, however, the page numbers of the second edition will also be noted.

[47] Ibid., 107–108; 2d ed., 105–107.
[48] Ibid., 107–108; 2d ed., 105–107.
[49] Ibid., 108–110; 2d ed., 108–109.
[50] See Ibid., 109, where the same flexibility is also seen as possible for the other members of this series.
[51] Ibid., 112; 2d ed., 111–112.

referential character. If it does, it can be classified as a motif. If it has neither a transmission interest nor any referential character, and if it also has a non-independent and non-dominant function, it is to be seen as a feature. Whatever is left may be classified as a theme.

From the above brief outline of Huber's system, it becomes evident that, in spite of its general similarity to that of Steck, there are some important differences. First of all, it can be noted that the basis for differentiating the elements of the system is in some ways different for Huber. For Steck, the series notion, tradition, tradition sphere or stream was one based on increasing comprehensiveness and complexity.[52] This also plays some role in Huber's system, though Huber is inclined to speak more of "independence" or transmission interest than of complexity as that which differentiates an element such as a tradition from one such as a motif.[53] In addition, Huber also introduces such criteria as referentiality to distinguish certain elements—for example, to distinguish a motif from a theme.[54]

Another difference from the system of Steck is evident in Huber's treatment of motif. In fact, while Steck does refer to motifs as the smallest thematic building blocks in texts, he cautions against *Motivgeschichte* as an exegetical method.[55] Such a study of motifs, Steck claims, is always in danger of uniting essentially dissimilar and historically unconnected elements under themes which have been "drawn together" (*herantragenen*). Further, by such an inadmissible isolation of themes, one tends to cross over to constitutive "sense" relations. The basic problem is one of how to understand the historical mediation of a motif which is "lively" and occurs in a number of different places.[56]

In contrast to the "lively" motif, Steck reaffirms the *feste* notion or notional elements which stand in indissoluble sense relations to greater notional relationships.[57] These notions are handed down in a certain framework and they preserve in this association a characteristically formulated sense and contour. Part of the Tradition-historical task is to address the problem of how individual notional elements occur in new relationships and contexts.

---

[52] See above and Steck, "Streams," 197.

[53] Huber, "Traditionskritik," 108 and passim. It is not clear how closely Huber wishes to tie such independence to the tradition's being the focus of a transmission interest of a circle of tradents, since it is possible for the other elements of his system to attain the former without the latter. On the difficulties of whether Huber is making a "literary" or a socio-historical distinction here, see further below.

[54] Ibid., 102–112; 2d ed., 102–112.

[55] Barth/Steck, *Exegese*, 75–76.

[56] Ibid., 76. For Steck, the appeal to the unconscious to explain the presence of similar motifs over widely separated areas is more a sign of the problem than any real solution. On this, see Noth, (*Überlieferungsgeschichte*, 67–68) who sees motifs in terms of the common experience of everyday life.

[57] Barth/Steck, *Exegese*, 76.

Along these lines, it is instructive to note how Steck and Huber differ in their description of the one term that both include in their system — namely, tradition. As noted above, tradition is seen by Steck as a thematically centered association of notions, more comprehensive than the latter but not as comprehensive as a tradition sphere or a tradition stream. It presumably has a mediation stage, such as a group or a place responsible for its continued existence, though this is not stated consistently in Steck's theoretical work and must be implied from the fact that notions and tradition spheres and streams have such stages of mediation.[58] For Huber, on the other hand, such a reference to the *traditio* or process of handing down, is fundamental to the very definition of a tradition, since the latter can only be separated from other elements by reference to its having a transmission interest for a circle of tradents.[59] It may be that this difference in emphasis is a function of the relative place of tradition in each theorist's series. For Steck, tradition occupies an intermediate step between notion and tradition sphere/stream, and it is in terms of the latter that the most complete reference to the *traditio* is made.[60] On the other hand, tradition is the final element in Huber's system and as such it provides for the most complete access to the *traditio*.[61]

Some other differences between Steck and Huber are potentially important and should be noted here. Their comments on the use of language in the isolation of Tradition-historical units are especially interesting. As noted above, a characteristic verbal field and linguistic world are seen by Steck as part of what makes up a tradition or a tradition sphere.[62] While such verbal elements play a role for Huber as well, he specifically maintains that one must reckon with the possibility that fixed meaning complexes utilize none of the same words but only equivalent word classes.[63] It may be that this possibility is also envisioned by Steck with his reference to similar "semantic" fields.[64] Nevertheless, it is significant that, at least for Huber, the object of Tradition history ultimately does not depend on the presence of the same words.

Huber's position would seem to be similar with respect to form. Whereas the repeated appearance of formulae, forms, and genres can lead to the identification of motifs and traditions, they would not appear to be essential elements of the latter.[65] Steck, of course, is concerned to include form as a Tradition-

---

[58] See Ibid., 72-73 and Steck, "Streams," 197-198. Compare his "Problem," 446-447.
[59] Huber, "Traditionskritik," 108; 2d ed., 108.
[60] See Steck, "Problem," 447-448, for the comments on tradition stream there.
[61] Indeed, for Huber, it is only in the tradition that the transmission interest of a circle of tradents is to be found. See Huber, "Traditionskritik," 108.
[62] Barth/Steck, *Exegese*, 74; Steck, "Streams," 194.
[63] Huber, "Traditionskritik," 111; 2d ed., 110.
[64] See Steck, "Streams," 194, though the limits of this term are not clear here.
[65] See Huber, "Traditionskritik," 111 (2d ed., 110), where it is noted how this may "possibly" lead to the identification of such elements.

historical element, even as a pre-eminent element, even while his system is ultimately based on the same non-formal grounds as that of Huber.[66] Once again, this difference in emphasis may be seen to have potentially important consequences, as will be further shown below.

The above comparison of Steck and Huber is interesting not only in itself but even more because of what the similarities and differences between the two theorists show about the nature of Tradition history in general. Thus, for example, one may take note of the conceptual nature of the Tradition-historical enterprise in both systems. Both Steck and Huber have by definition not taken either text or form as their primary criterion, since theirs is an attempt to move beyond both text and form to the historical and theological background which gave rise to these in the first place. In this, they are expanding on the theoretical work of Martin Noth discussed above. However, in doing so, they face theoretical difficulties similar to those of Noth. Chief among these difficulties is the criterion by which one is able to isolate those elements which belong together and which are capable of indicating a socio-historical background. This difficulty may be illustrated further by an examination of how Noth's crucial term "theme" is used in the Tradition-historical work of Steck and Huber.

As noted above, theme has a definite place in Huber's system of Tradition-historical elements, where it is seen as neither referential like a motif nor consistently "independent" like a tradition with its transmission interest for a circle of tradents.[67] However, the question of what a theme actually "is" is never detailed beyond its status as a "fixed meaning complex." Thus, the emphasis in defining a theme would appear to fall on the "fixed" nature of the unit involved. The discovery of this unit, it should be remembered, while aided by a repetition of language and form, is in the last resort dependent on neither.[68] What distinguishes a theme is the fixed nature of its content or concept.

Nevertheless, such a criterion raises a major dilemma, since something can never be fixed in itself but only for a certain audience. The real question which underlies Huber's isolation of a theme is one of whether he has isolated some thing which is not only fixed for a modern historian, but which actually had a fixed status for ancient Israel. If this is not the case, it is at best questionable whether any historical conclusion about the theological background of such "fixed units" in ancient Israel can be considered valid.[69]

[66] Again see Steck, "Streams," 194-195.
[67] Huber, "Traditionskritik," 107.
[68] Ibid., 111; 2d ed., 110.
[69] One may perhaps note here the opinions of Wolfgang Richter, *Exegese als Literaturwissenschaft* (Göttingen: Vandenhoeck & Ruprecht, 1971), who is critical of attempts to proceed on the basis of content because of the danger of the prejudice of predetermined opinions (p. 99). Because of this danger, he underscores the need to make sure that such abstractions as motifs exist not only in "the head of the researcher" (p. 155). For Richter, *"traditionsgeschichtliche"* research suffers from a methodological weakness—its content beginnings (p. 156). It is doubtful whether Richter's *Traditionsgeschichte* is the exact

It should be noted that such a comment also has some validity for form criticism as well, since that discipline also relies on the criterion of "fixedness" as a guide to its historical conclusions. Nevertheless, because form criticism deals with patterns which exist in a given text and are usually indicated by concrete linguistic markers, it is less open to the danger of a premature identification of the critic with ancient Israel than is Tradition history as exemplified in Huber's fixed meaning complexes. In addition, the use of extra-biblical parallels as controls also contributes to the historical probability of form criticism's "fixedness."[70]

A similar dilemma is raised by Huber's other operative words, "referential" and "independent." When a motif is seen as having the capacity to refer to a larger motif-theme,[71] the question once again arises: "For whom does this capacity exist—for the modern critic or for ancient Israel?" And if the latter is asserted, how can it be proven historically? Similarly, when Huber speaks of the "independence" of a tradition, is he making a "literary" or a socio-historical judgment? That is, does this independence exist in terms of what a modern critic can isolate as a separate idea present "in" the text? Or is one claiming that such an idea actually had an independent socio-historical *traditio*? And, if the latter, by what criterion is this judgment to be made?

It will be evident that this issue is close to that which divided Noth from his critics. For Noth, themes were closely related to traditions in that the isolation of the former was indicative of an actual socio-historical *traditio*. For his critics, such an isolation was merely to "facilitate analysis" as a "rubric of convenience" for the modern scholar and was not an assured step to socio-historical realities.[72] In contrast to Noth, such critics can plainly assert that themes are not a tradition, even though a tradition may contain themes.[73] Rather, a tradition requires the detection of a process of traditioning that is concerned with a discernible content that goes beyond a theme or a set of themes.[74] To the extent that such critics insist on actual evidence of such traditioning, their efforts are on sure ground. However, as they themselves

---

equivalent of the *Traditionsgeschichte* of Steck or Huber, though it would appear to include it as well as certain aspects of *Überlieferungsgeschichte*. The criticism of the above quotes would certainly appear to apply to much of the *traditionsgeschichtliche* work considered in this study.

[70] This is not to say, of course, that form criticism is entirely immune from such speculative dangers, especially when the safeguards mentioned in the text are abandoned completely. The possibility of similar safeguards in doing tradition history will be considered below.

[71] Huber, "Traditionskritik," 102, (*Bildthema* in 2d ed., 102).

[72] Bright, *Early Israel*, 42-43.

[73] Walter Harrelson, "Life, Faith, and the Emergence of Tradition," in Knight, *Tradition*, 17.

[74] Ibid., 18.

sometimes admit, their attempted isolation of "discernible content that goes beyond a theme or a set of themes" is often as hypothetical as Noth's isolation of individual themes.[75] That these difficulties also exist for Steck is indicated by his own use of theme. As may be noted from the above outline of his system, theme is not technically a part of Steck's series of terms. Nevertheless, the term does appear in certain significant places which are instructive because of the underlying methodological issues involved. One may, for example, take note of Steck's definition of a tradition as recognizable in a "thematically centered bond of notions."[76] Similarly, traditions are seen elsewhere as *geprägter Inhalte von geschlossener Thematik*.[77] The connection of the two terms may be further seen in the fact that a "tradition" stream can also be described as an *Überlieferungsström von Themen*.[78]

This relationship of theme and tradition clearly echoes that which was observed in Martin Noth. The methodological issues are much the same as well, with the basic issue again one of the criteria by which one is able to isolate such elements and to determine whether they do indeed reflect accurate sociohistorical circumstances in ancient Israel. As was the case with Huber, the danger lies in confusing the analytic judgments of the modern scholar with the sociohistorical realities of ancient Israel. The mere isolation of "themes" does not prove that those themes had any independent existence in ancient Israel, at least with respect to their ability to point to individual tradition circles.

It must be admitted, however, that Steck is at least partially aware of this problem and has taken certain steps to deal with it. It is in this respect that one may view his concern to include formal elements in his Tradition-historical enterprise. As noted above, forms are less open to subjective speculation, since they are at least to some degree capable of objective isolation and description, even while their significance is open to debate. As such, Steck's inclusion of form, as, for example, in his isolation of a tradition stream, is an attempt to broaden the more conceptually based criterion of "content." Again, Huber also makes allowance for such formal assistance, though its role is emphasized more in Steck's system.

Nevertheless, the role of form in such a content-based discipline remains ambiguous in many ways. This ambiguity may perhaps best be demonstrated by an examination of the ultimate historical fruits which Steck envisions as a result of his method. As noted above, this ultimate historical goal is a clarification of the intellectual (*geistige*) background responsible for the notions and traditions which emerge in various biblical texts. Again, in terms of a specific notion or

---

[75] Ibid., 20.
[76] Barth/Steck, *Exegese*, 74.
[77] Ibid., 70. See Steck, "Problem," 447–448.
[78] Steck, "Problem," 446.

tradition stream, this background is characterized as a stage of mediation of which groups and places are examples.[79]

Along these lines, Steck has isolated various tradition streams with their stages of mediation in the groups and places which bear them.[80] The make-up of these streams and their bearers is instructive. Thus, the streams isolated for the pre-exilic and exilic periods are characterized as Jerusalem cult (especially the temple singers), wisdom, prophetic, priestly, and Deuteronomic.[81] While these streams are open to each other in many ways, they remain distinct over a long period of Israel's history in terms of their essential conceptual design and the historical spheres which are responsible for them.[82]

Once again, one may raise the difficulty outlined above of moving from a conceptual design isolated by a modern scholar to the historical realities of ancient Israel. However, in terms of the streams isolated here by Steck, such reservations may be pushed even further in terms of the use of formal criteria to guard against just such a danger. This is so precisely because it is evident that formal criteria have played a major role in this aspect of Steck's analysis.[83] In almost every case, the streams appear not to have been isolated according to their similar "intellectual" content, but rather according to their functional aspect, as indicated by the forms used by each. That this is the case should not be obscured by Steck's attempt to outline the distinctive theological components of each stream.[84] Almost without exception, these theological components have been based on material already isolated according to function on the basis of form. What Steck has actually done here is to isolate certain functional categories and to highlight the institutional affiliations of those who perform such functions. Descriptions such as cultic, wisdom, prophetic, and priestly all point to the functional-institutional basis of Steck's streams.[85] Even the Deuteronomic tradition stream (which alone bears a seemingly non-functional title) is attributed by Steck to a functional-institutional base — that of the preaching Levites.

---

[79] Barth/Steck, *Exegese*, 72.
[80] See especially, Steck, "Streams."
[81] Ibid., 198-207.
[82] Ibid., 197. See also p. 205, where "more or less close interconnections" are noted, despite the ongoing distinctiveness of the streams.
[83] See ibid., 195, where the spheres of tradition are seen as "above all" having their own special genres in order to express their message in appropriate form.
[84] See, for example, ibid., 201-202, where the prophetic tradition stream is distinguished by a common theology of Yahweh's presence in the prophetic word.
[85] In this respect, it is interesting that Steck denies tradition stream status to the legal "tradition" (*sic*), which "because of its specific function hardly has the character of a theological stream with a conceptual design" (Ibid., 201). The same functional quality is, however, present in the other streams outlined and thus would appear to threaten their designation as tradition streams.

By allowing forms such a prominent place in his analysis, Steck seems to have arrived not at the "stage of mediation" of a distinctive set of ideas, but at the *Sitz im Leben* of a particular set of forms. As such, he has furthered the form-critical enterprise by analyzing the ideas which underlie these forms and settings. However, the larger question of whether one can see all those who utilize a certain form or who belong to a certain institutional setting as a "theological stream"—in terms of a connected socio-historical grouping—is at best unanswered, despite Steck's claims to the contrary.

Thus, while there is little doubt that such functionaries as those which Steck describes were present in ancient Israel, it may be seriously questioned whether these functionaries actually belonged to any existing historical group which may be said to have an overarching unified conceptual design. One has only to remember the bitter conflict between the so-called "true" and "false" prophets and the equally bitter inner-priestly battles to wonder whether such functionally similar elements should be grouped together as adherents of the same conceptual design. What they do share is a common function in society, as indicated by the forms which they use and adapt to their own purposes. However, to the extent that the object of inquiry remains limited to these forms and functions, one has not moved beyond the traditional realm of form criticism with its concern for *Sitz im Leben*. The move to a circle of tradents unified by a comprehensive conceptual design on the basis of *Sitz im Leben* would appear to rest on an unjustified assumption. The fact that similar functionaries may espouse quite different theological ideas clearly shows that a primary emphasis on formal criteria can only lead to a *Sitz im Leben* and not to an ongoing stage of mediation of a theological tradition stream.

This conclusion is indicated in another way as well. Thus, if one follows the primary thrust of Tradition history and isolates a particular set of ideas, one very soon finds oneself crossing the functional lines which Steck has described as his tradition streams. Here again, one need only note the presence of Jerusalemite ideology in both the prophetic and the cultic spheres to assure oneself of this. Admittedly, Steck allows for such an occurrence in his insistence that tradition streams are quite capable of absorbing features from elsewhere while remaining distinct by conforming these features to their own unique conceptual design.[86] Thus, Isaiah could adopt elements of Jerusalemite ideology while distinctly remaining within the prophetic tradition stream. Nevertheless, in historical terms, the question is really one of which element is primary. Does Isaiah as a member of the prophetic tradition stream borrow Jerusalemite ideology to make his point? Or does Isaiah as a member of a Jerusalemite circle express that circle's ideology by means of a prophetic function?

This issue may be seen as especially critical for Steck's analysis of the postexilic period.[87] Here the major divergences are seen as ideological (for example,

---

[86] Ibid., 197.
[87] Ibid., 207-212. See Steck, "Problem."

theocratic vs. eschatological), and the functional elements exist and are grouped within ideological frameworks rather than vice versa. In such a situation, isolating a tradition stream according to function will not lead to an accurate understanding of the comprehensive design which united the groups of that day; nor will isolating a tradition stream in this way present an accurate historical picture of the theological groupings within Israelite society.

All of this suggests that Steck's attempt to use formal criteria as an underpinning for his more conceptual distinctions of content can lead to ambiguous results unless certain historical considerations are kept in mind. In some respects, the problem is the same as that which afflicted the attempt to rely on more conceptual distinctions—namely, the uncertainty as to whether the distinctions made by modern scholars accurately mirror the historical realities of ancient Israel. What has been shown above is that while form can indeed give some historical data concerning ancient Israel, formal distinctions do not necessarily indicate the historical realities of theological transmission and the groups behind such transmissions. As such, the role of formal analysis in isolating "theological streams of tradition" would appear to need some clarification.

A related, though not identical, danger is present when one uses verbal fields to describe the various streams in Israel's intellectual background. As was the case with forms, attention to specific linguistic phenomena[88] would appear to provide a concrete means of underpinning more abstract conceptual similarities. Again, as with forms, such phenomena can be objectively isolated and described even before their significance is debated, thus establishing an undeniable link between otherwise unconnected texts. Nevertheless, as was also the case with forms, one must carefully consider the historical significance of this link. Thus, even in such cases where the phenomena are so distinctive as to be noteworthy, this may not indicate an historical connection in terms of a theological tradition stream. It may, for example, be the case that a distinctive verbal field is indicative of a form rather than a theology. As such, it would once again lead one to a functional or institutional *Sitz im Leben,* but not necessarily to a theologically distinctive group which was active in those functional settings—such a group being the stage of mediation of a specific theology.[89]

CONCLUSIONS

The above analysis has attempted to examine the Tradition-historical method in terms of its potential for illuminating the theological-historical

---

[88] That is, specific words and phrases (and possibly, specific syntactical relationships) as opposed to more broadly defined "semantic" phenomena in terms of "meaning" units.

[89] An alternate use of linguistic data which may lead to information about the *Vermittlungsinstanz* will be noted below. Steck's own use of such data is often quite insightful in this direction. (See especially Steck, *Geschick.*) Nevertheless, there is a real need to be more aware of the possibilities of confusion inherent in such material, as outlined in the text.

background of the biblical text. In this attempt, certain doubts have been raised about the ability to move from the units isolated by that method to historically verifiable tradent groups in ancient Israel. Neither conceptual distinctions of content nor supplementary attention to formal elements was seen to be sufficient to allow historical observations about actually existing streams of tradition to be made with any certainty. The twin dangers of overly modern abstraction in the isolation of conceptual data and overly speculative historical reconstruction based on that data were seen to exist in the absence of any external control.

Despite these reservations concerning the Tradition-historical method as it is now understood, it remains the case that its goal of illuminating the theological-historical background of ancient Israel remains a worthy goal both as an historical task in itself and as an insight into the early development of the biblical text. In such a vein, one may take note of a number of other recent attempts which, while not openly Tradition-historical, nevertheless may be seen to pursue Tradition-historical goals and even to some extent to participate in its methodological assumptions.

Thus, for example, in the last twenty years there have been three independent studies of the post-exilic period which have attempted to describe the theological trends of that time and to isolate the groups which were the bearers of those trends. These are the works of Otto Plöger,[90] Morton Smith,[91] and Paul Hanson.[92] In all of these studies, the literature of the period is examined in terms of its theological tendencies, with special note taken of what appear to be polemical thrusts and counter-tendencies elsewhere in the literature. Each of these studies arrives at a somewhat dialectical opposition of theological trends and their socio-historical advocates.

As noted above, Steck also shares this picture of the post-exilic period to a certain degree. Nevertheless, it is important to note wherein he would dissent from his non-Tradition-historical colleagues. Thus, Steck himself acknowledges his indebtedness to the previous work of Otto Plöger and agrees with it in terms of its isolation of the theocratic and eschatological tendencies in the post-exilic period.[93] Nevertheless, he also sees it as in need of much further refinement in a Tradition-historical direction. Accordingly, in his own analysis, Steck has

---

[90] Otto Plöger, *Theocracy and Eschatology*, trans. by S. Rudman (Richmond: John Knox, 1968).

[91] Morton Smith, *Palestinian Parties and Politics that Shaped the Old Testament* (New York: Columbia University, 1971).

[92] Paul D. Hanson, *The Dawn of Apocalyptic* (Philadelphia: Fortress, 1975). One might also mention here the work of David L. Petersen, *Late Israelite Prophecy: Studies in Deutero-Prophetic Literature and Chronicles* (Missoula: Scholars, 1977) which refers consciously to Tradition-historical studies and methods, but which is somewhat more narrowly focused than the other works noted here. This work will be dealt with in greater detail in the later chapters of the present study.

[93] Steck, "Streams," 208; Steck, "Problem," 456.

fleshed out these abstract theological opposites in terms of his functionally based tradition streams.

This additional step is significant, since it moves the primary historical discussion away from groupings based on theological or ideological grounds to those grouped according to function. As noted above, this disinclination to attribute to theological or ideological criteria a primary historical weight—while somewhat surprising in a content-based method—may be due to Steck's attempts to include formal data in his analysis. Because of this disinclination, he not only moves beyond Plöger but also disagrees with Smith who sees "party" as his basic ideological grouping point.[94]

The difficulties with Steck's attempt to use formal criteria as a control have already been discussed. However, here one should once again underline the difficulties inherent in a purely content-based analysis which led Steck to search for such formal controls—namely, the actual historical uncertainty of any modern abstraction of theological tendencies and the speculative nature of historical reconstructions based on such abstractions. Thus, it is worthy of note that the three modern scholars who have attempted to outline the theological and historical developments of the post-exilic period emerge with three different pictures of those developments according to the different principles by which they group the individual materials.[95]

It may be that these dangers of modern abstraction and speculative reconstruction are inevitable to the historical enterprise, especially in the case of ancient history where the gulf with the modern world is the greatest. Nevertheless, it would appear that arguments which are in their essentials based on content to the exclusion of text or form are especially open to such perils. There is, in this respect, a disconcerting tendency for the neat theoretical divisions of modern scholars to dissolve once some sort of external control is unearthed. One may, for example, note the collapse of Mowinckel's theoretical system concerning Messianic thought in the light of the unexpected combination of ideas found in the single setting of Qumran.[96]

Given these dangers, it may be that the essential task which faces tradition history in the wider sense is the development of certain controls which will contribute to the verifiability of its conclusions so as to render them more than theoretically possible. The ideal, of course, is a situation like Qumran, where

---

[94] Steck, "Streams," 198 n. 15.

[95] Compare especially Smith's dialectic of Yahweh alone/syncretistic parties with the more orthodox dialectic of his colleagues. Plöger and Hanson are closer in their analyses, although the former's theocratic/eschatological elements are by no means identical to Hanson's hierocratic/visionary groups.

[96] Thus, Mowinckel's isolation of "two Messianic types, each belonging to its own circles in later Judaism" (though admittedly, "to some extent allied with each other") breaks down in view of the combinations and complexities of the Messianic theologies found at Qumran. See Sigmund Mowinckel, *He That Cometh*, trans by G. W. Anderson (Nashville: Abingdon, n.d.) 281.

both *traditio* and *traditum* evidence exist together. When such a control of the *traditio* evidence does exist, one may be much more secure in describing the theological and ideological contours of the *traditio* group on the basis of the *traditum*.

It is, nevertheless, impossible to suspend the historical enterprise in the absence of such an ideal situation. Instead, one must continue to search for other means of controlling the speculative nature of the discipline and increasing the verifiability of its conclusions. Such controls may be two-fold, consisting of those internal to the units of the *traditum* themselves, similar to those which exist in form criticism or transmission history, or those external to either the *traditum* or the *traditio*, such as those provided by extra-biblical evidence.[97] Some brief suggestions concerning these controls may be made here.

Given the above analysis, it is perhaps to be expected that internal controls on doing tradition history are the most difficult to come by. Thus, it has been noted that such criteria as "fixedness" and self-sufficiency are themselves speculative and open to the need for historical verification. The same is true of such features as notional contours and typical lines of assertion. The additional criteria of characteristic formulatory structure and genre were seen to be less speculative in terms of the possibility of their discernment, although it was questioned whether such structures lead to a tradition-historical stage of mediation or simply to a form-critical *Sitz im Leben*. A similar problem existed for the criterion of "firm verbal field," since such a verbal field may have form-critical rather than tradition-historical implications and so also lead to a *Sitz im Leben* rather than to the stage of mediation of a tradition element.

Nevertheless, despite these difficulties, the possibility of internal controls on the tradition-historical process should not be ruled out completely. Thus, for example, those elements of the verbal field which do not have formal significance may indeed have the tradition-historical potential that is needed here. This possibility has been explored to some degree in the work of Wolfgang Richter who, as noted above, is also suspicious of any methodology which proceeds from content because of the danger of the prejudice of predetermined opinions.[98] By focusing on those actual word connections and word groups which are repeated in different texts, Richter has outlined an unquestionably objective basis on which to approach the larger pre-textual horizons. These word groups are seen by Richter as *geprägte* elements, but, as was not always the case for Huber who also uses this term, for Richter the actual repetition of specific words and specific syntactical arrangements is vital.[99]

---

[97] Internal controls on the *traditio* are hard to imagine in the case of ancient literature, their being more appropriate to modern anthropological studies where recourse to an ongoing situation is still possible. Comparative evidence gleaned from such modern studies and applied to the situation of ancient Israel would be considered an external, rather than an internal, *traditio* control.
[98] Richter, *Exegese*, 99. See note 69 above.
[99] Ibid., 99-103. Such repeated pre-textual units are known as "formulae." Richter

Especially instructive here are the "horizons" which Richter argues are indicated by these formulae. These are "of a sociological or a *geistesgeschichtliche* nature and they let one gain the intellectual origin or (also?) the *Sitz im Leben* of a work or a fixed ingredient."[100] As noted above, it is possible that a repeated word group or formula would have formal significance and thus lead to a *Sitz im Leben* along form-critical lines (either in itself or as part of a larger whole). Nevertheless, Richter here also seems to be holding out the possibility of such formulas' being indicative of "intellectual origin." This at least suggests the more theological-ideological approach to tradition streams noted above. As such, it would have a specifically tradition-historical integrity and usefulness. Such an internal criterion which has both objectivity and distinctiveness is clearly worthy of attention in any attempt to protect tradition-history from the speculative dangers noted above.

Whereas internal controls are by necessity *traditum*-based, external controls may relate to either the *traditum* or the *traditio*. Thus, for example, in the case of the *traditum*, one might attempt to consider those specific biblical statements which refer to concepts as concepts — that is, which provide some means of verification that such concepts are not simply modern critical abstractions, but that they had some real existence as concepts in the biblical period as well. These concepts could then be investigated as to their socio-historical stage of mediation with more confidence than if their conceptual integrity and existence were simply a matter of modern critical speculation.

As noted above, extra-biblical materials have also been used for such purposes by certain of the forerunners of Tradition history and as such they may also be seen as useful external controls on the biblical *traditum*. Nevertheless, one must admit that the difficulty of isolating and comparing concepts is present here at least as much as it was in inner-biblical comparisons. In addition, there is the need to measure such borrowed concepts against their actual usage in ancient Israel itself. Thus, unlike formal parallels which can plausibly maintain their functional setting across cultural boundaries, the borrowing of a concept — if it is not tied in such a form-related way — is unlikely to have its inner-Israelite socio-historical stage of mediation entirely clarified by any external reference. In other words, while an extra-biblical source may help define the scope of a concept and even the means of its importation into ancient Israel, only inner-Israelite or inner-biblical evidence can verify the continued self-sufficiency of such a concept as well as indicate its place in Israel's theological streams of tradition.

If external controls on the *traditum* may be seen as scarce, the quest for such controls on the *traditio* may seem in certain respects nearly hopeless. One may,

---

distinguishes these from the "fixed phrases" which exist only within the work of a specific author (see p. 101).
[100] Ibid., 117.

of course, gather some information from the Bible itself concerning the mechanical means by which the transmission of information took place within ancient Israel. This in turn can be supplemented by reference to the transmission processes of the surrounding ancient Near Eastern cultures and even to anthropological materials from other structurally similar cultures. In such a way, one may better understand not only the process of transmission but also the function of the material handed down and its setting in Israelite society (its *Sitz im Leben*).

Nevertheless, such information by itself has only limited usefulness in terms of isolating the particular historical groups responsible for the transmission of specific theological materials within ancient Israel (thus, their stages of mediation). Indeed, the Bible is for the most part frustrating in its reticence concerning those groups responsible for the materials which comprise it. Also generally missing are any external indications of which materials shared a common transmission history before their incorporation into the Bible and the individual books thereof. It is the presence of just these types of information that contribute to the importance of Qumran. If there is any possibility of uncovering such evidence for the earlier biblical period, it would be especially helpful in the search for a better understanding of the theological tradition streams ultimately responsible for the Bible.

This first chapter has been an attempt to examine the discipline of Traditionhistory on a theoretical level, to critique it and to suggest certain theoretical possibilities for improving the historical verifiability of the larger discipline. The chapters which follow will continue this three-fold analysis on a more practical level by examining and critiquing a Tradition-historical treatment of a group of biblical texts and by re-examining those texts with a greater emphasis on the possible means of historical verification.

2
Tradition History and the Psalms of Asaph

With this chapter, the methodological analysis shifts from the theoretical discussion of the first chapter to a more practical examination of specific biblical material. To this end, the central focus of the present chapter is a consideration of Karl-Johan Illman's *Thema und Tradition in den Asaf-Psalmen*.[1] As the title itself suggests, this work is an attempt to use such Tradition-historical criteria as theme and tradition in an attempt to isolate a possible tradition circle for the psalms which bear the superscription *lĕ'āsāp*. Both the author's self-consciousness concerning his methodological foundations and his rigor in their application contribute to the value of the work as a test case of the method. Nevertheless, equally important in this respect is the nature of the biblical material in question here. Unlike the subjects of other Tradition-historical studies where new historical possibilities are being expounded whose acceptance is in many ways dependent on an *a priori* acceptance of the method being used, the psalms of Asaph have long been considered suggestive of a distinctive tradition circle responsible for either their origin or transmission. Accordingly, the fact that a study based on a rigorous application of Tradition-historical methods should reach different conclusions would seem to offer the possibility of an instructive contrast in methodology.

ILLMAN AND HIS PREDECESSORS: METHODOLOGICAL CONSIDERATIONS

In his introduction of the problem to be addressed in his work, Illman starts with the fact that Psalms 50, 73-83 are distinguished from the rest of the psalter by virtue of their common superscription, *lĕ'āsāp*. For Illman, this fact motivates the question in what respect these psalms exhibit any common features which go beyond those features common to all the psalms.[2] Because of the readily apparent formal diversity of the psalms in this group, Illman concludes that any such commonality is to be sought among those features of a "content"

---

[1] Karl-Johan Illman, *Thema und Tradition in den Asaf-Psalmen* (Abo: Abo Akademi, 1976).
[2] Ibid., 7.

(*inhaltliche*) rather than of a formal nature.[3] Illman thus poses the question of whether there is in the Asaphite psalms a common property of themes, features, or motifs which makes it possible to describe a common denominator in the psalms. If the answer to this question is in the affirmative, one must further ask whether this commonality could go back to a common "tradition." If this also proves to be the case, one is able to consider the connection between the designation *lĕ'āsāp* in the psalm superscriptions and the bearers of this tradition. For Illman, the last two questions are contingent on the answer to the first.

From these questions, it is evident that Illman's goals and methods are similar to those described in chapter one as Tradition-historical. The ultimate concern for Illman, as for his Tradition-historical predecessors, is historical—the discerning of groups and movements which were theologically active in ancient Israel. These groups are discernible through Tradition-historical means in that their existence is indicated by the presence of common conceptual elements, such as themes, features, and motifs. To be sure, Illman adapts the method to his own needs with respect to the material at hand. Nevertheless, it remains recognizably Tradition-historical throughout.

For Illman, the decisive criterion for determining whether a distinctive common tradition lies behind this group of psalms is the existence of a common property of content elements. Only after such a common property has been isolated does the psalms' common superscription become significant in terms of its connection with a distinctive tradition and the bearers of that tradition. It is important to note that Illman is here specifically concerned with the possibility of the psalms' sharing a "characteristic common content" (*Inhalt*).[4] In keeping with the Tradition-historical method as seen in chapter one, content becomes the critical factor in determining tradition elements or groups.

Before examining both Illman's methods and his results in greater detail, it would be instructive to set forth a contrasting background in terms of some of the previous studies of this group of psalms. Naturally, Illman also offers such a survey at the start of his study.[5] However, his main concern in doing so lies in detailing the various scholars' conclusions concerning any "characteristic common content" in the Asaphite psalms. This concern is, of course, quite in keeping with Illman's Tradition-historical approach to the psalms. Nevertheless, it is significant that even when these scholars discuss such content, they do not always share Illman's view concerning its primacy for the establishment of a distinctive tradition behind the Asaphite psalms. In short, along with their different observations on any similarities in the psalms' content, these scholars also often have methodological priorities which differ from those of Illman's Tradition-historical approach. It is thus instructive not only to compare the various

---

[3] Ibid., 8.
[4] Ibid., 8.
[5] Ibid., 8–14.

scholars' comments concerning the psalms' characteristic common content—as Illman has already done in his survey—but also to pay closer attention to the ways in which they attempt to explain the relationships among the psalms in the first place. It is in this that the most interesting contrasts with Illman emerge. In his survey, Illman has concentrated on those studies which have attempted to consider the Asaphite psalms as related in some way. Studies which ignore the link indicated by the common superscription or those whose main concern lies in the peculiar nature of the individual psalms are passed over, since they contribute only indirectly to the discussion at hand. In such a way, many studies which are primarily philological, strictly form-critical, or interested mostly in dating questions are excluded from Illman's introductory survey.[6] There are, nevertheless, a fairly good number of important scholars who do take note of the link between these psalms and comment on the possible characteristic common content which they share.

The first such work that Illman cites is the classic commentary of Franz Delitzsch.[7] Here, as Illman notes, Delitzsch first offers a consideration of Asaph's place in the Chronicler's material, then moves to the question of the divine names found in the psalms, and finally provides a description of the content (again *Inhalt*) of the collection.[8] In terms of the latter, the Asaphite psalms may be distinguished from other psalms (such as the Korahite) in terms of their "prophetically judicial character." This distinctive character is to be seen in the frequent occurrence of direct divine speech and of God's portrayal as judge, as well as in the future visionary nature of the psalms. There are also repeated references to Israel's *Urgeschichte*[9] as well as to Joseph and the Joseph tribes.[10] It is also noted that in the midst of a delight in frequent variation of the designations for the people of God, there is also a decided preference for describing Yahweh's relationship to Israel in terms of the figure of the shepherd and his flock.

On these grounds, Delitzsch sees in the psalms of Asaph a "peculiar type of psalms,"[11] though this is obviously not meant in any form-critical sense. Accordingly, "the inscription *lĕ'āsāp* has, so to speak, deep-lying internal grounds in its support." Nevertheless, only a few of the psalms can be ascribed to the Asaph of the Davidic period, the rest being composed in the style of Asaph and after Asaphic models, either by later Asaphites who continue the

---

[6] See ibid., 12 n. 26.
[7] Franz Delitzsch, *Biblical Commentary on the Psalms* (3 vols., 2d ed.; Edinburgh: T. & T. Clark, 1871).
[8] Illman, *Thema*, 8; Delitzsch, *Psalms*, II, 122-124.
[9] Ibid., 123, where he cites Ps 74:13-15; 77:15ff.; 80:9-12; 81:5-8; 83:10-12; and Psalm 78 as a whole. Illman notes that Delitzsch's expression, "*die urgeschichtlichen Tatsachen*," includes both *Urgeschichte* and *Geschichte*, which are, in more modern research, kept separate, because of their belonging to two different "traditions" (*Thema*, 9 n. 10).
[10] Delitzsch, *Psalms*, II, 123, where he cites Ps 77:16; 78:9, 61f.; 81:6; 80:2f.
[11] Ibid., 123.

original Asaph's outward marks even into the period after the exile or by "some other person."[12]

Although Illman is especially interested in Delitzsch's observations on the characteristic common content of the collection, it is instructive to examine more carefully Delitzsch's methodological priorities in themselves, since these provide a good contrast to those of other scholars, including Illman. In such a way, one may note that Delitzsch's initial acknowledgment of the psalms as Asaphite is immediately followed by a description of the Asaphite materials in the work of the Chronicler. The historical setting of the psalms is thus felt to be in some way illuminated on the basis of the superscription, even before any reference is made to the content of the psalms. Nevertheless, Delitzsch's movements in the direction of establishing a tradition setting for these psalms in this manner are neither as far reaching or as unambiguous as this immediate foray into the Chronicler's materials would imply. Thus, Delitzsch, noting the later character of some of the psalms, acknowledges that only a few can be attributed to the Asaph of the Davidic period and extends the *lĕ'āsāp* of the superscription to include "sons of Asaph" found in the Chronicler's work.[13] This is, of course, a broadening of the historical setting on the basis of the content of the psalms. Yet, for Delitzsch, even this is too restrictive. He also allows for certain of these later psalms' being psalms of Asaph by virtue of their being composed "in the style of Asaph and after Asaphic models," even if they are composed by "some other person" who is not an Asaphite. Consequently, what originally seemed to be a grouping according to individual or guild authorship has become, in the last resort, a grouping of "a peculiar type of psalms" with a distinctive "style." It is the distinctive "content" of the psalms, as described above, which provides the "deep internal grounds" in support of the superscription *lĕ'āsāp*.

For Delitzsch, the superscription functions in two ways. First of all, it provides, on its own merits and without any support from the psalms' content, an historical referent in the person of the historical Asaph which is nevertheless valid only for the oldest of the psalms. Secondly, it provides a means by which those psalms which imitate these "original" psalms can be grouped with their models. In terms of methodology, the superscription has for Delitzsch both an historical and a literary function.

With the exception of correlating Asaph's designation as a seer with the prophetic character of some of the psalms,[14] Delitzsch is not concerned to theorize as to why the elements which he isolates as peculiar to these psalms are particularly appropriate to their putative composer-ancestor. Nor does he address the question of why it was necessary to ascribe psalms of a similar nature to the same person. Even more importantly, it is never made clear why other

---

[12] Ibid., 124, where he cites Psalms 50 and 78 as such original psalms of Asaph.
[13] Ibid., 124.
[14] Ibid., 123, though Delitzsch is obliged to note that the Chronicler "also applies the same epithet to both the other precentors."

psalms with a similar content are not given the superscription *lĕ'āsāp* nor why some of the Asaphite psalms fit only with difficulty into the Asaphite psalms' supposed "inner ground." As will be seen below, the latter question forms the basis of Illman's critique of the psalms from a Tradition-historical point of view.

The next scholar cited by Illman, Heinrich Graetz, also assigns historical weight to the superscription, though in a much less qualified way than that of Delitzsch. For him, the *lĕ'āsāp* is direct evidence for both the performance and the composition of these psalms by the levitical family of temple singers known by the same name.[15] As Illman notes, there is little effort to characterize the collection on the basis of content or to differentiate it in such a way from other such collections.[16] It should, of course, be noted that without such efforts, the historical significance of the assignment of these psalms to a certain group is only partly realized, since the responsible group remains undefined. Graetz does attempt to move a bit in this direction by noting the frequent expressions of poverty and humility in the psalms of the levitical temple singers and by theorizing that this is indicative of a lower social position.[17] This line of argument, however, is ignorant of the well-known form-critical function of such expressions and so errs in assigning to them a literal interpretation.

In contrast to Graetz, and to some degree also to Delitzsch, Charles A. Briggs appears to have a minimal regard for the authorship information implied by the superscription. Although he mentions the appropriate material of the Chronicler, he denies the possibility that any of the psalms could have been authored by Asaph and also does not advocate their authorship by the related "sons of Asaph."[18] Nevertheless, despite this ambiguity with respect to the significance of the superscription, Briggs does assert that these psalms share certain common elements. These include vivid descriptions of nature, an emphasis on divine providence in the life of the individual, a use of history with a didactic purpose, exalted spiritual conceptions of God, and a sublimity of style. These elements are not, however, sufficient to indicate a common author or even a common guild of authors. Rather, they imply a careful selection by an editor with a plan and purpose to set forth those features. These psalms were originally a collection by themselves, made in the early Greek period, probably in Babylonia![19]

Thus, although Briggs is able to isolate what he feels are common elements shared by these psalms, this does not have any historical significance in terms of the individuals or groups originally responsible for such psalms. Such origins are

---

[15] Heinrich Graetz, *Kritischer Commentar zu den Psalmen* (Breslau: S. Schott Laender, 1882) 16ff.
[16] Illman, *Thema*, 9.
[17] Graetz, *Psalmen*, 20ff.; see Illman, *Thema*, 9.
[18] Charles A. Briggs, *A Critical and Exegetical Commentary on the Book of Psalms* (2 vols., Edinburgh: T. & T. Clark, 1906) lxvi.
[19] Ibid., lxvi-lxvii.

instead left open and the similarity is explained by a later editorial selection. Also left unexplained is why this later selection should have chosen to bind together such similar psalms under the superscription *lĕ'āsāp*. Since Briggs denies Asaphite authorship to all the psalms, Delitzsch's explanation of conformity to original Asaphic models is excluded. The connection of the name Asaph with the common elements which Briggs cites remains unaccounted for.

For Illman's purposes, such critics as Duhm[20] and Kittel[21] are not particularly significant, since he sees neither as attempting to characterize the psalm collection at issue, despite their concern for its individual psalms and for the question of how the psalter as we have it came about.[22] Because of their lack of concern for any common content in the psalms, Illman does not consider how each of these scholars views the collection itself. This is, however, instructive in its own right, since it once again allows for a focus on important methodological issues.

In general, Duhm sees a superscription as a "shabby material" with which to answer questions concerning the origin and organization of the psalter's individual collections.[23] Nevertheless, a collection like the Asaphite or Korahite collection must have had its own particular collector and redactor, and possibly also its "reference points" and a special history as well.[24] Duhm sees these collections as stemming from the singing groups, which are regarded as families descended from a common ancestor. Nevertheless, these psalms were "obviously" not authored by the singers in question but were rather taken up by them into their repertory and worked upon for their musical and liturgical delivery.[25] As such, they should with certainty be regarded as earlier parts of the ritual books of the temple. The superscriptions themselves originally belonged to the booklets and were only transferred to the individual psalms when these were taken up into the larger psalter.[26] The reasons for the superscriptions' adhering to the individual psalms is unknown.

For Duhm, as for Briggs, the individual collection of psalms is the result of an editorial selection process. However, unlike Briggs, Duhm connects this process with the superscriptions by arguing that the psalms were selected by groups of singers for performance in the temple. Still, Duhm does not seem to isolate the reasons behind the selection process[27] nor is he concerned to inquire as to what these particular psalms show about the group which selected them.

---

[20] Bernhard Duhm, *Die Psalmen* (HKAT 14; Freiburg, J. C. B. Mohr, 1899).
[21] Rudolf Kittel, *Die Psalmen* (KAT 13, Leipzig, 1929).
[22] Illman, *Thema*, 10.
[23] Duhm, *Psalmen*, xv.
[24] Ibid., xiii.
[25] Ibid., xvi. For Duhm, psalms such as those found in the Korahite (and presumably the Asaphite) psalter could not have been manufactured in a common setting.
[26] Ibid., xix.
[27] Hence, Illman's complaint about his having no concern for their common content (*Thema*, 10).

It is interesting that, in spite of this, the superscription is seen as bearing witness to a common *traditio* for these psalms, at least at a certain point.[28] In his treatment of this subject, Kittel agrees with Duhm that the Korahite and Asaphite psalms go back to previous individual collections.[29] However, beyond asserting that the establishment of these collections must have taken place in the time of the Chronicler, Kittel is not concerned to characterize either the collecting process or the collections any further. Nevertheless, Kittel still sees the superscription as pointing to a common *traditio* for these psalms, as undefined as this may be for him.

Illman sees Gunkel's treatment of the Asaphite and Korahite collections as similar to those of Duhm and Kittel in that his main interest lies in the individual psalms rather than in the larger collections.[30] Illman, does, however, note that Gunkel sees these psalms as having been brought together for the guilds of temple singers. For Gunkel, the superscriptions indicate that these psalms are of a cultic nature. Still, these collections do contain certain non-cultic or "spiritual" psalms which have been taken up into the collections by virtue of their individuality and beauty.[31]

One may note that Gunkel sees the superscription *lĕ'āsāp* not only as indicative of a *traditio* but also as a reliable historical reference to that group of temple singers for whom these psalms were brought together. The actual authorship of these psalms is not so clearly spelled out, although Gunkel does see most of them as specifically composed for cultic use. Nevertheless, even those which had an originally non-cultic purpose are at home in the *traditio* of the temple guild at some point. The discernment of the ultimate *traditio* is thus based almost entirely on the superscription and not on the content of the psalms themselves—even though the latter may contribute to our understanding of the origins of these psalms. Indeed, the superscription may even be used to trace the historical development and relative importance of the various temple guilds.[32] Still, Gunkel does not attempt to describe the character of these guilds on the basis of the psalms which were attributed to them, nor does he inquire as to why certain "individual and beautiful" spiritual psalms—as opposed to others of a

---

[28] Further, for Duhm, one may note that many psalms which do not have superscriptions may be established as official temple songs on the basis of their content (*Inhalt*). These have no superscriptions since the original collections with superscriptions were at that time already published. The former could then be grafted onto the latter stem without a title, the bare annexation itself marking their character. As such, the psalms which do not have a superscription are to be reckoned as generally younger than those which do. Duhm, *Psalmen*, xvii.

[29] Kittel, *Psalmen*, xviii.

[30] Hermann Gunkel-Joachim Begrich, *Einleitung in die Psalmen* (Göttingen: Vandenhoeck & Ruprecht, 1933); see Illman, *Thema*, 10.

[31] Gunkel, *Einleitung*, 449.

[32] See Gunkel, *Einleitung*, 440–442.

different character—should be absorbed into each of the different guild collections.

For Gunkel's student, Sigmund Mowinckel, the differences in setting and theological attitude among certain of the Asaphite psalms rule out the possibility that the superscriptions provide us with information concerning individual authors of individual psalms.[33] Nevertheless, such superscriptions do contain a real tradition and, in a certain sense, give real names of authors. Thus, although the historical nature of Asaph as set forth in the Chronicler's "legendary and unhistorical" accounts is dubious, he functions as an eponymous ancestor for the guild of the same name.[34] This guild not only collected and used the psalms in question, as Gunkel asserted, but also may be seen as the locus for the composition of these—and other—psalms. These psalms then became a part of the group's spiritual inheritance and were as such copied and transmitted within that locus.[35]

For Mowinckel, the superscription points to an historical *traditio* which can be described on this basis alone. Further, the *traditio* not only seems to encompass the collection and use of the psalms in question but also their original composition as well. All of this notwithstanding, certain of Mowinckel's other remarks tend to complicate his strong affirmation of the guild origins and *traditio* of these psalms. Thus, for example, the same psalms which he uses to disprove the individual authorship of these psalms (by virtue of their different settings and theological attitudes) also raise questions about the theory of such a unified *traditio*. Accordingly, since Mowinckel attributes Psalm 80 to a pre-722 North Israelite setting, Psalm 82 to a provenance in the South sometime after the Assyrian dominance, Psalms 74 and 79 to a time shortly after the fall of Jerusalem, and Psalms 50 and 73 to the post-exilic period, one would either expect him to assert that the guild in question was such as to encompass not only a long period of time but also two distinct kingdoms or to admit that the superscription is not a definitive guide to the composition (as well as the collection and use) of these psalms. Mowinckel's position on this is unclear. Significantly, he is not specific as to the times of the guild's existence[36] or to any further description of its nature. Although he uses the content of the psalms to ascertain their temporal and political setting and to deny their individual authorship, this same content is not used to elaborate further on the nature of the guild to which they can be ascribed on the basis of the superscriptions. Even the "prophetic" content of certain of these psalms does not provide any insight into

---

[33] Sigmund Mowinckel, *The Psalms in Israel's Worship* (2 vols., Nashville: Abingdon, 1962) II. 95.

[34] Ibid., II. 95-97. See also his *Psalmenstudien* (Amsterdam, P. Schippers, 1961) VI, 41-42.

[35] Mowinckel, *Psalms*, II. 93-94.

[36] Though one would think that he leans towards the post-exilic period on the basis of the possible dating of that group's eponymous ancestor.

the particular character of the Asaphite guild, as much as these examples contribute to Mowinckel's discussion of cult prophecy elsewhere.[37]

For Mowinckel's Scandinavian colleague, Ivan Engnell, the superscription also provides real information concerning authorship. As for Mowinckel, the origins and transmission of the psalms are to be sought in the guilds of singers (and groups of temple prophets) which appear in the work of the Chronicler and are reflected in the psalms' superscriptions.[38] Nevertheless, despite this affirmation of the historicity of guild authorship, one cannot simply accept all the details concerning these guilds found in the Chronicler's work, since these are of uncertain historical value in themselves. Still, for Engnell, the originality of the superscription is not only an assumption but is further indicated by the homogeneity of the psalms' language and content.[39] In this way, such indicators as the names of Jacob and Joseph indicate that the origins of psalms are to be sought in Northern Israel, although it is also obvious that they have been reinterpreted in a Jerusalem spirit.[40] Engnell also remarks on the psalms' common conception of God[41] and their prophetic tone, which is emotional and betrays a deep personal involvement. It is also noted that the psalms are predominantly national psalms of lamentation and that the idea of covenant is quite prominent.

For Engnell, the superscription is once again used to set apart this group of psalms as an individual collection with its origins in a certain guild of temple singers. However, although the basic common *traditio* can be established on the basis of the superscriptions, Engnell, unlike the other scholars considered above, does not turn to the Chronicler's material for further information about this *traditio*, since he is skeptical of any details there which go beyond the fact of the guild's existence. Instead, he turns to the content of the psalms themselves and sees in this indications of a *traditio* which includes both Northern Israel and Jerusalem. In this appeal to content for more information about the *traditio*, Engnell takes a decisive step. Nevertheless, he does not attempt to relate the other content features which he has noted to the *traditio* nor does he evaluate the implication of the *traditio* comments he does make in terms of the historical worth of the Chronicler traditions related to the superscription.

In contrast to those who have attempted to distinguish the Asaphite psalms on the basis of literary content, Claus Westermann has argued for a distinction which while described as *sachlich* actually seems to be more closely related to form-critical categories.[42] Westermann sees the Asaphite psalms as consisting of

---

[37] See his *Psalmenstudien* III; also Illman, *Thema*, 10-11.
[38] Ivan Engnell, "The Book of Psalms," in his *A Rigid Scrutiny*, trans. by John T. Willis (Nashville: Vanderbilt University, 1969) 74.
[39] Ibid., 79.
[40] Especially Psalms 50 and 76; see ibid., 79.
[41] Yahweh as the creator and God of fate, though inseparably connected with Israel's history; ibid., 79.
[42] Claus Westermann, "Zur Sammlung des Psalters," *Theologia Viatorum* 8 (1961/1962) 281.

a core of "songs of the community" framed by two psalms of a different type—a pattern echoed in the original Korahite psalms as well. Here, as in the rest of the Psalter, the original *sachlich* organization of the psalms was still known to their tradents.[43]

In the Westermann article cited by Illman (and discussed in the previous paragraph), the former does not spell out the implications of this original *sachlich* organization for the interpretation of the psalms' superscription. In his later book on the subject, however, Westermann goes on to argue that the superscriptions do not belong to the time of the origins of the psalms but rather to the time of their collection, their being the notations supplied by the collector to indicate their origins, type of singing, etc.[44] As such, all psalms may be seen as having lived a long—mostly very long—time in the community without superscriptions, with the result that one can draw conclusions from the latter only about the time of collection and its understanding of the psalms. Thus, the superscriptions of the singers' guilds, such as that of Asaph, point to those groups whose names are met in the Chronicler's work and whose mandate was the handing down (*tradieren*) and development of the temple song. For Westermann, it is probable throughout that certain groups of psalms belong to the tradition of these groups, although it is now impossible to say how far these singers took over some very old songs and altered them.

Westermann's analysis leaves open many questions concerning how the *sachlich* cohesiveness of these psalms relates to their belonging to the tradition of a guild of singers. One especially wonders whether the conjunction of the *traditio* of a particular singers' guild with a specific type of psalms is significant for the further description of that *traditio*. Related to this question is the need to determine more closely the specific types of "communal song" present in these psalms and to inquire as to their significance for the description of the *traditio* to which they belong.

Beyond those listed above, few modern commentaries on the psalms pay much attention to the psalm superscriptions in general and to the *lĕ'āsāp* in particular.[45] At most, they note, with Weiser,[46] that these superscriptions served the purpose of specifying those psalms which originated in the tradition of the singers' guilds and were appointed to be sung by them in the worship of the temple. The tradition-historical implications are not explored beyond noting that these superscriptions are indicative of an earlier subcollection of the psalter.

In contrast to the limited tradition-historical interest of most of the above, an article by Martin Buss is devoted solely to the tradition-historical questions raised by the Asaphite and the Korahite psalms.[47] As such, it assumes an

---

[43] Ibid., 284.
[44] Claus Westermann, *Der Psalter* (Stuttgart: Calwer, 1967) 20–21.
[45] See Illman, *Thema*, 12 n. 26.
[46] Artur Weiser, *The Psalms* (Philadelphia: Westminster, 1962) 97.
[47] Martin Buss, "The Psalms of Asaph and Korah," *JBL* 82 (1963).

important place in Illman's survey of research on this question and continues as an important force throughout the latter's work.[48] However, Buss' article is distinguished by more than a narrowing of concern and its related greater attention to detail. Buss instead is critical of most previous research on these psalms which, despite its long recognition of their relatively homogeneous nature, has neglected the titles.[49] According to Buss, most form-critical analyses in particular have ignored the information yielded by the titles of the psalms and have been more interested in establishing their characterizations of the psalms on the basis of internal evidence alone. To remedy this neglect, Buss has attempted to use form-criticism together with other techniques in order to determine the significance of these groups of psalms which bear the same title.

With respect to both the Asaphite and Korahite psalms, Buss has noted a tendency towards a strong personal element which not infrequently points to the connection of the author with the cult organization. This in turn indicates the Israelite clergy as the tradition behind these psalms, an observation which has been made by many of the scholars considered above. Unlike these scholars, however, Buss bases his argument more on internal criteria, such as the type of psalm, than on any automatic comparisons with the Chronicler's material.[50]

For Buss, such psalm types as communal laments, judgment songs, and songs of Zion point to the religious leadership based in the clergy.[51] Again, unlike the other scholars considered above, Buss does not stop with merely locating these psalms among the cult personnel. He is also concerned with "precisely what kind" of clergy is involved in these psalms. Comparing the Asaphite to the Korahite psalms, for example, he notes in the former a "higher level of cultic poetry" which reveals a closer participation in public life or preaching as well as wisdom of a more religious character. These elements, Buss claims, accord well with the representation in later literature of the respective roles of the sons of Asaph and Korah.

Buss is concerned to go beyond such general observations to the "complex historical development" which lies behind this situation. On the basis of their content and language, he notes the Northern Israelite origins of the Asaphite Psalms 77, 80, 81, and (in a different way) 78.[52] Buss sees the "traditions" contained in these psalms as belonging to a circle of Levites whose original center of activity in Northern Israel moved to Judah with the fall of Samaria. These are described as "a sizable class of religious leaders who were largely engaged in exhortation and in the propagation of the memory of ancient events—in short, the religious education of the people."[53] On the basis of "ideological and verbal

---

[48] Illman, *Thema*, 12-14 and passim.
[49] Buss, "Psalms," 382.
[50] Buss calls this approach "an analysis of their content" (Ibid., 383), though it appears to be more a type of form criticism.
[51] Ibid., 384.
[52] On the basis of their special reference to Joseph and their similarity to Hosea.
[53] Buss, "Psalms," 386.

affinities" to Hosea and the Deuteronomic tradition, Buss describes these as "proto-Deuteronomic levitical traditions."[54] Such traditions continued in the South to the time after the fall of Jerusalem, as may be seen from the content of the psalms.[55]

In contrast to the Northern influenced Asaphite psalms, the Korahite psalms are seen as probably Southern in origin, being centered in Jerusalem.[56] However, alongside this geographical distinction exists a possible functional one as well, since the Korahites may be seen on the basis of content to belong to the "service personnel" of Jerusalem and its temple, while the Asaphites, as members of a Deuteronomic-levitical tradition, are engaged in tasks of religious education. This difference would account for the different types of "wisdom" to be found in each set of psalms.

Buss supports this analysis based on language and content with the form-critical data with which he started. He notes that the heavy Asaphite concentration of collective laments and judgment psalms mirrors a similar use of those forms in the prophetic literature.[57] Since the ancient near eastern parallels to these types of psalms are to be attributed to a definite class of singer-priests, a certain flexibility is mandated between levites, singers, and prophets.

Based on his analysis, Buss sees the titles preserved in the psalter as a relatively reliable guide to the types of psalms.[58] He sees the Davidic psalms as comprising essentially individual laments and related types. The Asaphite and Korahite psalms contain collective laments, Deuteronomic-levitical psalms of judgment, law, and history (among the Asaphite psalms), songs of Zion (among the Korahite psalms), and a few personal psalms involving cult personnel and wisdom reflection. Those psalms with no attribution are primarily hymns. The first group may be called psalms of the laity, and the second, presentations of the clergy, while the third group may well be considered appropriate for both.

When one turns to analyze Buss' treatment of the Asaphite psalms from a methodological point of view, one is immediately struck by certain differences from most of the scholars considered above. Whereas these latter scholars placed great, if not exclusive, weight on the correspondence of the psalm titles with the Chronicler's material as a guide to the group responsible for these psalms, Buss makes relatively little use of such material. For him, the titles function primarily as a means of separating out groups of psalms which have certain similarities of form and content. Further, unlike many of the previous studies which also noted such similarities, Buss argues that these are not the result of a secondary selection process but rather that they stem from the very nature of the historical group responsible for their origin. Because of this, the differences in the nature

---

[54] Ibid., 385–386.
[55] Buss cites Psalms 74 and 79. Ibid., 386.
[56] Ibid., 387–388.
[57] Ibid., 388.
[58] Ibid., 390–391.

of such psalms are indicative of real differences in the nature of the groups responsible for these psalms—which Buss goes on to describe in terms of their temporal, geographical, functional, and ideological setting.

It is again important to note that the description of the groups responsible for these psalms is based almost entirely on the psalms themselves and not on the Chronicler's material which corresponds to the psalms' superscription. Thus, curiously, the ability of the psalm titles to designate a separate *traditio* has been taken very seriously, even while their ability to provide information about that *truditio* has been minimized. At the same time, once the *traditio* has been established by such means, all the internal aspects of the psalms (formal, ideological, verbal) are then seen to contribute to its more complete description and to connect it with other elements of ancient Israel which are seen to possess similar aspects. In such a way, the psalms of Asaph are seen as belonging to the Deuteronomic-levitical "stream of tradition"[59] which stemmed from Northern Israel and survived at least until after the fall of Jerusalem. Further, certain functional aspects of the *traditio* are also illuminated by such means.

By attempting to describe the *traditio* group on the basis of the psalms handed down by that group (their *traditum*), Buss has taken the step before which so many of the scholars considered above stopped short. Nevertheless, certain questions still remain unanswered. So, for example, one wonders about the significance of the name Asaph and its connections with the Asaph material of the Chronicler. While a certain reserve towards this latter material is understandable in Buss' attempt to concentrate on internal evidence, it is only upon consideration of all the evidence available that the true historical significance of these psalms will be discovered. Similarly, while Buss' analysis of the psalms' linguistic relationships is a step in the right direction, there is a need to expand such analysis in a way not possible in his short article.

After his extended consideration of the Buss article, Illman concludes his survey by briefly mentioning a work of F. N. Jasper in which the Asaphite guild is seen as an original group of cultic prophets in Jerusalem who were later relegated to the position of temple singers.[60] While Jasper's primary concern is not the Asaphite psalms as a whole or the distinctive features of the collection, his independent comments on the historical elements of these psalms tend to support much of what Buss has argued, including the Northern Israelite/ Deuteronomic aspects of certain Asaphite psalms.

When one returns from this methodological survey to the work of Illman, one immediately notices the differences in both methodology and results. With respect to the former, one may note first of all Illman's radically different approach to the significance of the superscription. For most of the scholars mentioned above, the superscription was able to indicate the *traditio* of the

---

[59] See ibid., 388, for the term.
[60] F. N. Jasper, "Early Israelite Traditions in the Psalter," *VT* 17 (1967). See Illman, *Thema*, 13-14.

psalms at some stage of their composition, use, or collection process. Further, for most, this *traditio* could be described in at least limited detail on the basis of the related material of the Chronicler, although it is only with the work of Engnell and, especially, Buss that one finds any extended attempt to describe the *traditio* on the basis of the psalms themselves. Both of these approaches, however, share a certain confidence in the ability of the superscription to indicate a group of psalms in some way distinct from other psalms—at least with respect to their *traditio*.

For Illman, on the other hand, the superscription is not assumed to have any such significance in terms of distinguishing a peculiar group of psalms as different from the rest of the psalter. Rather, the distinctiveness of the psalms so specified is seen more as a hypothesis to be tested against the nature of the psalms themselves. Only after a specific common denominator has been established can one inquire whether such a common element goes back to any common "tradition" which lies behind the psalms. And only if such a tradition does exist can one then seek to understand the connection between the Asaph of the superscription and the bearers of the tradition.[61]

Nevertheless, Illman differs from his predecessors even beyond his having made the initial far-reaching methodological decision to place primary emphasis on the psalms themselves and to suspend belief in the superscription's significance with respect to the *traditio*. He differs even from those scholars such as Engnell and Buss who do devote their attention to the internal aspects of the psalms in an attempt to further describe the *traditio*. Thus, whereas Engnell is interested in that material which indicates date and provenance, and Buss is concerned with formal as well as ideological and verbal features, Illman focuses his primary attention on elements of "characteristic common content."

Illman's search for such content as would establish the existence of a distinctive *traditio* for these psalms follows self-consciously Tradition-historical lines. As the reference to a common property of themes, features, and motifs shows, he is indebted to Huber for the basic outline of this methodological system. Nevertheless, he is sufficiently self-conscious with respect to method as to introduce certain modifications in his understanding of these terms. Accordingly, it is necessary briefly to discuss these modifications before presenting a summary of Illman's conclusions concerning the psalms of Asaph.

ILLMAN'S USE OF TRADITION HISTORY

With respect to the term theme, Illman first of all considers Noth's use of the term to designate "content closed narrative unities,"[62] such as the leading out of Egypt. He notes, however, that although these historical "themes"[63] are often to be found in the psalms, their occurrence there is mostly in the form of short

---

[61] Again, see Illman, *Thema*, 8.
[62] "inhaltlich geschlossene Erzählungseinheiten;" ibid., 15.
[63] Quotations Illman's.

allusions, and they are sometimes used for a purpose entirely different from that found in the Pentateuch. Accordingly, Illman considers the term motif to be more appropriate with reference to this sort of phenomenon than is the term theme.

To define motif, Illman quotes the well-known German literary critic, Wolfgang Kayser.[64] According to Kayser, a motif has 1) structural firmness, 2) a presentation of a typical situation which can always be repeated, 3) the function of pointing backwards and forwards in time, and 4) a specific content which is especially suited to certain genres. Illman rejects Huber's attempt to differentiate between a motif and a fixed theme on the basis of Kayser's third characteristic alone, noting that his criterion of referentiality is valid only for a very special application of motif. Instead, the most important difference between motif and theme is seen to be that the former expresses something *concrete*, while the latter expresses something *abstract*.[65] Again quoting Kayser, he argues that "the motif is the schema of a concrete situation; the theme is abstract and designates as a concept the ideal scope to which a work lets itself be ordered."[66] In psalm exegesis, themes are content complexes considered as a kind of abstract framework (for example, "creation"), while motifs are the concrete shapes of such themes (for example, "fight with chaos"). Interestingly, Illman notes that such motifs are still abstractions, even though they designate concretely depicted occurrences. They can also be put together from concrete individualities which are called features, a term which, like motif and theme, is a part of Huber's system.

In defining the final term of his Tradition-historical system, Illman follows Huber fairly closely. A tradition is thus seen to stem from a group of individuals with a certain transmission interest. The latter can be recognized by the various criteria outlined by Huber. A tradition circle also implies a rallying point of some kind (be it geographical, cultural, sociological, or religious), and there must also be a chronological continuity between the origins of a tradition and its literary occurrence in the psalms. For Illman, tradition implies a characteristic content, that is, the occurrence of certain themes, motifs, and features. It must also be at least asked whether or not the "tradition" is recognizable by a certain terminology.

A few comments may be offered here concerning Illman's relationship to the Tradition-historical enterprise as examined in chapter one. First of all, one may note the overall similarity of Illman's task to that of Tradition history in general and the specific relationship of his terminology to that of Huber in

---

[64] Illman, *Thema*, 15. See Kayser, *Kunstwerk*, 60-61.
[65] Illman's italics.
[66] This may mean that motif has more to do with what English and American critics would call a plot or plot element. *Thema* seems to be more similar to the English and American usage of theme.

particular.[67] Nevertheless, while he does use Huber's terms, he has redefined both motif and theme and altered their relationship to each other. Motif is no longer primarily distinguished by its referentiality, as in Huber, but rather by its "concreteness" in relation to the more "abstract" theme. Yet it should be noted that Illman admits the "relativity" of this concreteness in his recognition that motifs may contain within themselves concrete individualities called features. Thus, in place of the varying criteria which distinguished Huber's Tradition-historical elements, Illman has placed a greater emphasis on the single criterion of differing levels of abstraction.

Two other methodological aspects deserve special notice here. First of all, Illman retains Huber's slightly ambiguous attitude towards the necessity of similar language in distinguishing a tradition. For him, it is still only a question whether a tradition can be recognized on the basis of a specific terminology. Secondly, one may note Illman's argument that a tradition implies a characteristic content. What needs further discussion is how wide and diversified a content may be held within a single tradition (in terms of a *traditio* group rather than its *traditum*). Further, one must ask whether the converse of the argument is also true—that is, whether a specific content implies a tradition. These, of course, are the issues which have been discussed on the theoretical level in the first chapter. In what follows they will be discussed in terms of their specific application to the Asaphite psalms.

ILLMAN'S ANALYSIS OF CHARACTERISTIC COMMON CONTENT IN THE PSALMS OF ASAPH

The first theme which Illman has isolated in the psalms of Asaph is that of creation (*Schöpfung*).[68] In defense of his isolation of this theme, Illman notes that while the origins of the various notions of creation (*Schöpfungsvorstellungen*) are to be found in the wider near eastern context, these nonetheless also had an Israelite transmission which can be the object of Tradition-historical research. Further, although he concedes that the ancient psalmists did not distinguish between a mythological *Urzeit* and an historical *Zeit*, Illman still maintains that it is the right of later research to do so. In such a way, he is able to deal with both creation and history (*Geschichte*) as separate objects of Tradition-historical research.

Under creation, Illman is able to distinguish two distinct motifs which occur in these psalms. The first, the fight with chaos (*Chaoskampf*) appears in two of the psalms (74:12ff.; 77:17-19), although it is not a central motif in either. Different chaos phenomena are present in each. The other motif under the theme of creation is that of the "bringing forth of the cosmos" (*Hervorbringung des*

---

[67] Steck does not figure in Illman's bibliography, though, of course, certain terms may be seen to overlap with similar terms in Steck's system.
[68] Illman, *Thema*, 17-19.

Kosmos) which can be found together with the previous motif in 74:12-14 and independently in 75:4. Illman locates the "thematic circle" (*Themenkreis*) of the creation theme in an old Jerusalem tradition stemming from the pre-Israelite epoch of the city. However, since there are only three examples of this theme in the Asaphite psalms, Illman is unwilling to speak of any extraordinary concentration of the creation theme there.

The next theme isolated by Illman is that of history (*Geschichte*),[69] under which he distinguishes four motifs found in the psalms of Asaph. The first of these is entitled "election and covenant" (*Erwählung und Bund*).[70] The election aspect of this motif may be found in the brief but direct statement of 74:2, as well as in the extended election imagery of Psalm 78[71] and the similarly extended allegorical statement of 80:9-12. With respect to the covenant, Illman is once again able to find a brief statement in Psalm 74 (v 20), as well as more extended references in the "prophetic announcement of judgment in the cult" of Psalms 50 and 81, as well as in Psalm 78.[72] In keeping with the grouping of texts on the basis of content rather than specific language, Psalm 81 is included in this group even though it does not specifically mention any *běrît*, on the basis of its citation from the decalogue in vv 10-11.

In terms of the significance of this motif, Illman argues against the existence of a fixed covenant renewal ceremony as has been advocated by Alt, von Rad, and Kraus for Psalms 50 and 81, since there is little independent evidence of such a feast of covenant renewal. Instead he agrees with Kutsch[73] that these references to *běrît* and the decalogue should be seen as ongoing cultic activities by which the worshipper obligated himself to do certain things.

The second motif to be found under the theme of history is that of exodus (*Auszug*),[74] which is not restricted to the flight from Egypt in a narrow sense but which also includes such related events as the plagues. Yet even with this wider definition, it is still necessary for Illman to note the tendency of this motif to be combined with other motifs in the Asaphite psalms. Thus, the description of the fight with chaos in 74:12-14 also includes elements of this motif, and, conversely, the more explicit statement of the exodus in 76:7 may be seen to include elements of the fight with chaos motif,[75] as well as possibly holy war and God as judge motifs. Similarly, in 77:16, the exodus motif comes immediately before a description of the fight with chaos. The reference to the exodus is more extensive in

---

[69] Ibid., 19-29.
[70] Ibid., 19-22.
[71] Which extends beyond the election of the people to that of Zion and David—the latter being for Illman another motif complex in itself.
[72] At the bottom of page 22 in *Thema*, Psalm 81 is apparently a typographical error for Psalm 78.
[73] E. Kutsch, *Verheissung und Gesetz* (BZAW 131, Berlin: A. Töpelmann, 1973) 98ff.
[74] Illman, *Thema*, 23-25.
[75] Here Illman compares this verse's *migga'arāteka* with Ps 18:6; 104:7; Isa 50:2.

Psalm 78, even including a long list of plagues, athough even here it is closely bound up with the motifs of the covenant and the wilderness wandering. This combination is also to be found in Psalm 81 (especially in vv 6-7, 11).

The latter texts have already introduced the next motif to be found under the theme of history, that of the wilderness wandering.[76] This motif is treated extensively in Psalm 78 and in a less expansive, but still specifically detailed, way in Psalm 81. Both of these psalms are seen by Illman as having a "didactic" purpose, and the possibility of Deuteronomistic similarities for each is also raised, though reserved for later discussion.

The final motif to be discussed under the theme of history is that of Zion and David.[77] Reference to the divine dwelling place may be found in the Asaphite psalms at 74:2; 76:3; 79:1; and (at length) in 78:54ff., where it is combined with the divine choice of David.[78] There are, in addition, other "allusions" to the temple as the dwelling place of God which cannot be designated "independent" motifs (cf. 73:17; 74:3, 7, 8; and 79:1, 3). In fact, it is only in Psalm 78 where the motif is expanded in any out of the ordinary way. Since this motif is a common one in the Psalter as a whole[79] and since most psalms have their setting in the temple cult of Jerusalem, one should not be surprised at the presence of this motif here. Similarly, one shoud not speak of any Zion theology in the Asaphite psalms.

In concluding his discussion of these historical motifs, Illman notes that although they occur relatively frequently in the Asaphite psalms, they are concentrated in a few psalms, with only isolated references in others. Thus, Psalm 78 contains many of these motifs, as, to a lesser degree, does Psalm 81, while other psalms such as 50, 77, 80, and 83 exhibit only individual motifs. This model is mirrored by the psalter as a whole where a few *Geschichtspsalmen*[80] exist alongside many psalms with individual historical motifs. As a result, although the Asaphite psalms exhibit a seemingly large number of historical motifs, it does not follow that this is constitutive for the Asapite psalms as a collection.

The next theme which Illman has investigated is that of judgment (*Gericht*).[81] Under this theme, Illman has differentiated three motifs, the first of which being that of God as judge.[82] Usually employing some form of $špṭ$ or $dîn$, this motif appears in 50:6 and 75:8, where God is directly designated as a judge,

---

[76] Illman, *Thema*, 25-27.
[77] Ibid., 27-29.
[78] In the latter case, the Jerusalemite aspects are taken as evidence against Buss' Northern setting for the psalm—though Buss does see a Judean milieu for the transmission of Psalm 78 (Buss, "Psalms," 388).
[79] And especially in the Korahite psalms.
[80] Psalms 105; 106; 114; 135; 136.
[81] Illman, *Thema*, 30-38.
[82] Ibid., 30-31.

and in 50:4, 21b; 75:3; 76:9-10; 82:1, 8; where scenes of divine judgment are presented. These references depict judgment against both Israel and the nations (with their gods). The second motif under the theme of judgment is that of "the opponents" (*die Gegner*).[83] This term may be used to designate the hostile peoples as it is in the references in Psalms 74, 79, 80, 81, and 83, and in the historical allusions of Psalms 76 and 78 as well. The collective laments of this group presuppose a situation where Israel itself has been God's opponent and so is in present need of aid against its national enemies. Israel is also God's opponent throughout Psalm 78, although in the final verses this opposition is narrowed to the Northern kingdom. In addition, other smaller groupings within Israel (such as the wicked or the boastful) may also be seen as opponents in Psalms 75 and 73.[84]

The third motif under this theme is that of "dispute and punishment" (*Streit und Strafe*).[85] As with the other motifs connected with the theme of judgment, this motif contains a number of different aspects in the different psalms. In some (Psalms 50, 73, 74, 77, 79, 80, 81), the punishment is referred to in very vague or general terms, while in others (Psalms 76, 78, 82, 83) it is specific and concrete. The motif is especially prominent in Psalms 76 and 83, although it also is a consistent feature of the so-called prophetic oracles of Psalms 50, 75, 81, and 82.

The fourth theme which Illman has isolated in these psalms is that of trust (*Vertrauen*),[86] under which is distinguished two motifs. The first of these is the shepherd-flock motif[87] which occurs six times in the Asaphite psalms (Ps 74:1; 79:13; 77:21; 80:2; 78:52; and 78:71, where it is applied to David). Although Illman notes that this motif occurs more often in the Asaphite psalms than in the entire psalter, he also argues that it undergoes no extraordinary development there similar to that of Psalm 23 or Jer 23:1ff. Moreover, in these psalms it is found tied to other motifs, such as the wilderness wandering (cf. Ps 77:21; 78:52f.; 80:2), the deity enthroned on Zion (Ps 74:21; 78:52f.; 80:2), and the election of David (78:71f.).

In contrast to the frequently found shepherd-flock motif, that of the nearness of God (*Nähe Gottes*)[88] occurs only in Psalm 73. Since the motif is expressed in phrases which are also the key expressions for the levitical privileges (cf. vv 26-28), Illman sees this psalm as appropriate for a levite in the temple. As Illman notes, this would tend to corroborate Buss' thesis that Psalm 73 was composed for the private use of the Asaphite singers. Nevertheless, it must still be asked whether this conclusion also holds for all of the Asaphite psalms.

---

[83] Ibid., 31-35.
[84] Illman sees Psalm 50 as referring to the whole people, with verse 16a being an interpolation.
[85] Illman, *Thema*, 35-38.
[86] Ibid., 39-41.
[87] Ibid., 39-40.
[88] Ibid., 40-41.

The final theme which Illman isolates is that of "insight" (*Einsicht*)[89] which he sees as a theme of Psalm 73. In isolating this theme, Illman is concerned to distinguish it from the theme of wisdom as put forward by Buss. Contrary to what one would expect from Buss' claim that these psalms are "full of wisdom themes," Illman is able to deny the existence of any wisdom theme there at all.[90] Psalm 73, which might have been seen as wisdom, is in reality not to be accepted as such, since it does not refer to insight in itself (*Einsicht an sich*) but rather to insight in concrete circumstances.[91]

Based on this analysis of themes and motifs in the Asaphite psalms, Illman makes the following observations.[92] First of all, in no psalm are all of these themes represented, although with the exception of the theme insight, all the rest of the themes are represented in Psalm 74. Two themes are missing in Psalm 78 (insight and creation) and in Psalm 76 (insight and trust). A balance of the two important themes, history and judgment, is found above all in Psalms 50, 78, 80, and 81. A concentration of the judgment theme may be found above all in Psalms 82 and 83, but also in Psalm 75. The most individual psalms are Psalm 73 (with its concentration on an individual fate), Psalm 78 (with its broad exposition of historical motifs which are framed in an almost refrain-like way by similar running expressions of judgment, so that the didactic intention of the piece is unmistakable), and Psalm 82 (with its unique scene of judgment in the assembly of the gods).

In assessing these elements of distribution, Illman notes that they do not justify any far-reaching conclusions concerning the Asaphite psalms as a collection. The fact that the theme of judgment can be verified in all the psalms only proves that "conflicts"[93] appear here. These, however, are seen to be of many different kinds—between God and the peoples, God and Israel, God and the godless, and the justified and the godless.

Thus, for Illman, a rigorous search for characteristic common content in the Asaphite psalms has proven unsuccessful. Contrary to the observations of previous scholars, there is no distinctive element of content which would have resulted in the common grouping of these psalms. Consequently, on this basis at least, no direct conclusions can be made about a possible tradition behind the handing down and placing together of this collection.

---

[89] Ibid., 41–42.

[90] This wide divergence of results has prompted Illman to theorize that Buss means something different by either theme or wisdom, a possibility he discusses later in his work. Ibid., 41.

[91] What Illman means by this is not entirely clear—perhaps existential insight of some sort?

[92] Illman, *Thema*, 42–43.

[93] Quotations Illman's.

ILLMAN'S ALTERNATE SEARCH FOR TRADITION IN THE PSALMS OF ASAPH

Despite his failure to locate a tradition on the basis of his analysis of the themes and motifs present in the Asaphite psalms, Illman is concerned that alternate means of isolating a tradition behind these psalms not be overlooked.[94] In particular, the radically different results obtained by Buss have focused his attention on those elements which Buss calls "themes." Since these do not correspond to his own usage of that term, Illman concludes that Buss' references to such entities as "wisdom themes" are actually references to *terminology*[95] and certain formal characteristics which should speak for a kind of wisdom tradition behind the Asaphite psalms as a collection. This, he notes, corresponds with one of the criteria which he himself set up for the existence of a tradition, although he also notes immediately that there is another criterion for a *common* tradition of the entire collection, namely, the presence of certain themes, motifs, and features of a *content* kind which has not been met according to his own analysis (emphasis Illman's). Despite this latter failure, Illman proceeds to test Buss' alternate hypothesis by pursuing the search for a tradition into a number of other areas.

In attempting to determine the existence of this tradition, Illman first turns his attention to the possibility raised by Buss that the Asaphite psalms contain "didactic terminology"[96] which is indicative of a levitical-Deuteronomic tradition. Illman notes that Buss himself supported his attribution of these psalms to such a tradition by citing the links of the word *'ēdût* and the hiphil of *'ûd* with the Deuteronomic tradition.[97] Having determined that Buss' argument for similarity of themes actually is meant to indicate such a shared terminology, Illman undertakes a more intensive search for such linguistic links between the Asaphite psalms and the Deuteronomic tradition.[98] In this analysis, he makes use of Weinfeld's list of Deuteronomic phrases,[99] with which he compares the language of the psalms. Unlike Buss, he is able to conclude that it is only in Psalm 78 that one finds any real concentration of such Deuteronomic terminology. Individual expressions of this sort are also to be found in Psalms 79, 81, 83, and 76 (as well as in 89 and 119). However, for Illman, such individual expressions are not particularly significant, since they also occur in many of the writing prophets, in Daniel, in the wisdom literature, and in the work of the

---

[94] Illman, *Thema*, 45.
[95] Illman's italics.
[96] This is Illman's term for Buss' "wisdom themes." See *Thema*, 46.
[97] It is noteworthy that Buss also sees links with a "broader prophetic stream" here. "Psalms," 389-390.
[98] Illman, *Thema*, 46-50.
[99] Moshe Weinfeld, *Deuteronomy and the Deuteronomic School* (Oxford: Oxford University, 1972) 320ff.

Chronicler. Similarly, the uniquely Deuteronomic nature of Psalm 78 is not felt to be significant for determining the tradition of the Asaphite psalms as a collection.

After denying the possibility of connecting the Asaphite psalms to a levitical-Deuteronomic tradition of instruction on the basis of the presence of Deuteronomic terminology, Illman then goes on to question any correlation on the basis of a common instructional purpose. In such a vein, he concedes that Psalms 73 and 78 share a common didactic nature despite their considerable difference in theme and terminology. Similarly, he admits that a didactic purpose is also possible for those psalms which contain prophetic oracles (Psalms 50, 75, 81, 82). Nevertheless, despite this didactic presence in half of the Asaphite psalms, the other half, containing mostly collective laments, does not share such a direction. Accordingly, it is not possible to admit Buss' claim that the Asaphite palms as a collection are meant to serve the religious instruction of the people. On the basis of the psalms, the Asaphites "not only taught, but also lamented" about national misfortunes![100]

Having disputed the levitical-Deuteronomic provenance of these psalms, Illman goes on to dispute Buss' related claims for their ties to Northern Israel.[101] He notes, first of all, that many of the Asaphite psalms have either explicit or implicit connections to Jerusalem.[102] Of the remaining psalms, three have specific references to Joseph and have been reckoned on this basis as North Israelite psalms. For Illman, however, such references to Joseph do not justify the latter conclusion. Neither does the failure of these psalms to contain positive ties to Zion, which may be dismissed as an argument from silence. Against Buss' attempts to tie these psalms to Hosea, Joshua 24, Deuteronomy 32, and Jeremiah "which all come out of a generally similar tradition," Illman notes both that the Deuteronomic references in such psalms as 81 and 83 are not especially numerous and that the Northern origins of Deuteronomy have not themselves been proven. Given the Jerusalem ties of most of the Asaphite psalms, one would need stronger grounds than these to argue for a North Israelite provenance, especially since a revision in the Jerusalemite spirit is also envisioned.[103] According to Illman, it is best to stay with what we know with certainty—the fact that psalms are written and presented in the temple at Jerusalem.

Having failed to establish the tradition behind the Asaphite psalms on the basis of their linguistic affinities with didactic, levitical-Deuteronomic, and Northern circles, Illman then attempts to determine whether any clues to this tradition may be discovered by analyzing the designations used for God in these

---

[100] Illman, *Thema*, 50.
[101] Ibid., 50-52.
[102] See Ps 50:2, 8; 73:17; 74:2, 3, 7, 8; 75:2, 3ff.; 76 passim; 78:68, 69, 70-72; 79:1, 3.
[103] This is an unusual argument for Illman, since it assumes the very solidarity of the psalms against which he is arguing throughout.

psalms.[104] Since, despite the occasional appearance of Yahweh, these psalms are a part of the so-called Elohistic psalter, little assistance in this respect is afforded by an analysis of the traditional source critical elements, Yahweh and Elohim. Illman goes on, however, to analyze the occurrence of *'ēl, 'elyôn, ṣĕbā'ôt, 'ĕlōhê-ya'ăqōb*, and *'ădōnāy*, as well as the compound designation found in Ps 80:2. On the basis of this analysis, Illman concludes that the designations for God used in these psalms (and in the Korahite psalms as well) are extremely varied, a fact which is not to be explained by postulating a special tradition. Since, however, this variation includes titles of genuine Israelite, common Canaanite, and specifically Jerusalemite origin, one may envision a lengthy process which took place in the Jerusalem cult as a means of accounting for this richness in the possibilities of expression.

With all these attempts at isolating a tradition having proven unsuccessful, Illman finds it difficult to say anything specific about the "Asaphites." If one understands by "Asaphites" the "author" of the Asaphite psalms, at most certain guarded characteristics appear.[105] These include a connection to the temple in Jerusalem for most of the psalms, significant didactic interest manifested in Psalms 78 and 73 (in the latter for internal purposes), and appearance of cult prophecy in four psalms. The function of the lament is also found in the psalms, as is the theme of judgment, though the latter is widely varied. There is also a certain interest in the history of the people, a preference for the shepherd-flock motif in describing the relationship between God and Israel, and an inclination to use designations for God from different places.

Having isolated such characteristics in the Asaphite psalms, Illman then asks how these compare with the descriptions of Asaphites found in the Chronicler's material.[106] Following a brief summary of the significant texts of the latter, Illman concludes that the Asaphites were among those who returned from Bablyon and were as such ultimately traceable to the pre-exilic period.[107] They also were the leading, if not the only, class of singers in the early post-exilic period, at first differentiated from the levites and a step below them, though they were later identified with them. The presence of prophetically gifted singers among the Asaphites can probably be traced back to cult prophecy which was already incorporated into the temple singers before the exile. Finally, one may note from the Chronicler's material that the Asaphites sang hymns, although it is not clear whether they also composed these themselves.

Having listed these characteristics of the Asaphites as seen in the Chronicler's material, Illman then notes two similarities with the conclusions reached through his own work. The first of these is a common anchoring in the

---

[104] Illman, *Thema*, 52-55.
[105] Ibid., 55.
[106] Ibid., 55-59.
[107] Though the connection with David is a tendentious backdating and legitimation of the temple singers. Ibid., 59.

Jerusalem temple. The second, which is even more important, is the presence of cult prophecy in each. In contrast to these similarities, Illman notes the prevalence of laments in the Asaphite psalms, as compared to the Asaphites' singing of hymns in the Chronicler's material. However, here Illman sees no absolute objection, since he theorizes that the Asaphites probably sang other songs than those assigned to Asaph in the psalter, including those ascribed to David. This indeed is where one may see the historical kernel of the Chronicler's account that the Asaphites had led the song according to the commission of David.

Illman also notes that the Chronicler's material contains no indication of any educational work by the Asaphites or the singers in general![108] This, however, was not to be expected (*contra* Buss), since only Psalms 73 and 78 can be considered *Lehrgedichte*. Beyond this, it is only in the aforementioned cult prophecy with its possible didactic interest that there is any meaningful correlation between the sources.

Despite Illman's agreement that the authors of these psalms must be sought in the temple personnel, he nonetheless contends that their relationship to the Asaphites in the Chronicler's material is difficult to ascertain. Although Illman acknowledges that the superscriptions to the psalms could constitute a bridge, the significance of these superscriptions is so disputed that he declines to make use of them. Once again, it is the presence of cultic prophecy in both sources that is seen as the most meaningful line of association. Because of this difficulty, Illman argues that one must content oneself with the understanding that Asaph was the eponymous hero of a singers' guild, in which circle the Asaphite psalms appeared. It is significant that at one point the Asaphites were apparently the only (or at least the leading) group of temple singers. As such, it probably absorbed smaller groups into itself so that the title "sons of Asaph," seems to stand for the singers in general. If indeed the Asaphites were from the beginning a variegated group equivalent to all of the temple singers, it is scarcely to be expected that the psalms which would be ascribed to them should be homogeneous or an expression of one specific tradition.

In conclusion, Illman claims that the theory of Buss concerning a levitical-Deuteronomic tradition as characteristic for the Asaphite psalms is tenable neither on the basis of the psalms themselves[109] nor on that of the Asaphite material of the Chronicler![110] Similarly, the supposed North Israelite origin of many Asaphite psalms is also held not to have been convincingly demonstrated![111] And although a significant concentration of Deuteronomic

---

[108] Ibid., 60.
[109] Since only half can be classified as instruction.
[110] Since they are, at least in the earliest material, differentiated from the levites.
[111] Since the occurrence of the term Joseph is not sufficient for this purpose nor is the comparison with the "real or supposed" North Israelite tradition in Deuteronomy, Joshua, and Hosea.

expressions exists in Psalm 78, individual expressions in such psalms as 81 and 83 are not considered especially significant with respect to indicating a Deuteronomic tradition.

With regard to the evidence of a Tradition-historical nature, Illman notes that the only motif which occurs in all of the psalms is that of dispute and punishment. However, this is so varied in its depiction of conflict that it does not allow one to speak of a special "conflict tradition" in the Asaphite psalms. Similarly, although history has a special place in these psalms, one cannot construct a thesis concerning something like a covenant tradition.

Even cult prophecy, which has a definite and important role in these psalms, resists such generalization, only allowing one to say that cult prophets, or at least the function of cult prophecy, was present under the Asaphites. One also finds in these psalms a tendency to vary the designations of God and a certain inclination to describe the relationship between God and Israel by the motif of a shepherd and a flock. However, neither of the latter allows any further conclusions concerning a tradition behind these psalms.

Thus, according to Illman, one is unable to isolate *one* specific tradition in the Asaphite psalms whose bearers might have been the Asaphites![112] Just as this latter group was a composite of originally different functionaries (temple singers, cult prophets, levites), so many different voices sound from these psalms. Accordingly, since the psalms represent the temple singers in general rather than any one particular tradition, they are not to be seen as specialized, but rather as comprehensive. As such, it is not surprising that they are recognizable more by variation than by concentration.

CRITIQUE OF ILLMAN

Essential to Illman's work is the basic Tradition-historical relationship between content and tradition group which was described in chapter one. For Illman, tradition implies a characteristic common content as defined by the occurrence of certain themes, motifs, and features. Consequently, such a characteristic content is indicative of a distinctive tradition group and its lack indicative of the absence of the same. On the basis of the arguments of the first chapter, one may, of course, question this easy movement from content to tradition group. Certainly, the old issue of separability might arise, since Illman isolates certain elements which are not found by themselves in the psalms at hand![113] Nevertheless, since these issues have been discussed at length above, it seems best to move beyond these general criticisms to examine some of the more specific aspects of Illman's analysis.

Because it is on the basis of characteristic content elements that traditions are to be established, it is especially important to consider what constitutes such

---

[112] Emphasis Illman's.
[113] For example, the wilderness wandering.

elements for Illman. As noted above, Illman's constitutive elements are features, motifs, and themes which he (again, *contra* Huber) distinguishes according to their level of abstraction. Since both motifs and themes appear to be significant for determining a tradition, it is interesting to look more closely at what levels of abstraction are able to do this in Illman's system. In doing so, one finds that these levels are very high indeed. Thus, one may examine Illman's five examples of a theme—creation, history, judgment, trust, and insight. As is readily apparent, most of these fully deserve Kayser's definition of "the ideal scope to which a work lets itself be ordered." Yet one finds it extremely difficult to believe that such abstract entities are actually capable of indicating a specific tradition group. Surely, not every piece of work which deals with "history" or "trust" can be attributed to the same tradition group. Nor conversely, would it be possible to deny that a single tradition group is capable of dealing with more than one of these themes. The very fact that several of these themes are to be found together in a single psalm would seem to be enough to upset such a one-to-one correlation of theme with tradition group.

Given the overly abstract nature of Illman's themes, one may perhaps feel a bit more at ease with the less abstract motif. Here one meets with such familiar elements as the fight with chaos, election and covenant, exodus, Zion, and David, among others. It is, of course, interesting to note that Illman's motif is very often Noth's theme (and sometimes Huber's tradition)![114] Nevertheless, despite this change in terminology and one's possible reservations about Noth, one would hope to be at least on partly solid ground with Illman's motif. This would, however, be to ignore an important difference between the concerns of Noth and Illman. Noth's historical separation of his five Pentateuchal themes is possible only because he envisions the tradition settings of these individual themes as prior to their merging into "G" in the time of the judges. Illman, on the other hand, continues to use these themes as if they maintained their earlier ability to indicate separate tradition settings into a much later (post-G) time. Thus, even if one should accept Noth's thesis concerning these themes, one would not be justified in assuming that they retained their ability to indicate distinct tradition settings or groups in the time with which Illman is concerned here.

There are, however, more difficulties than this in Illman's use of motif. One may, for example, take notice of the continuing high level of abstraction in those motifs which do not represent some sort of "historical" event. This is especially evident in the case of such motifs as God as judge, the opponents, dispute and punishment, and the nearness of God. Once again, one wonders whether it is likely that all the occurrences of these motifs may be traced to the same tradition setting. Indeed, Illman himself adds to one's perplexity on this subject when, after isolating a motif which does occur in all of the Asaphite psalms, he refuses

---

[114] Thus, the exodus is characterized as a theme by Noth, a motif by Illman, and a tradition by Huber.

to use this example of "characteristic common content" to establish a distinct tradition behind these psalms. Thus, although he finds the dispute and punishment motif present throughout (together with the theme of judgment of which it is a part), Illman concludes that such a persistent reference to conflicts does not justify any far reaching conclusions, since the conflicts are different throughout.[115]

The underlying issue is that which was discussed in the first chapter — namely, whether such abstract elements as those cited here have any sociohistorically significant existence as independent entities in Israel or whether they only exist in the mind of the individual critic. In such a vein, it is interesting to recall some comments which Illman offered in distinguishing between mythology and history.[116] Again, for Illman, even if the ancient psalmists had not distinguished between a mythological *Urzeit* and a historical *Zeit*, later research still has the right to make such a distinction. On this basis, he is able to distinguish between the themes of creation and history. In such a way, elements which Illman concedes were never strongly distinguished on a conceptual level in Israel are made the basis for judgments concerning actual socio-historical tradition groupings. Since there is no historical control on the definition and relationship of such concepts, Israel's theological history is dependent on how each individual scholar defines such phenomena.

The difficulties here are only compounded by the abstract level on which such distinctions have been made. As is evident from his refusal to use the comprehensive motif, dispute and punishment, as an indication of an actual tradition behind these psalms, many of Illman's categories are so broad as to make their appearance in a text meaningless in terms of attributing that text to any historically definable tradition. Much more significant for such a purpose would be the way that such themes and motifs are actualized in terms of specific linguistic detail. Thus, for example, the shepherd-flock motif is obviously of a different order than the nearness of God motif, even though both are described by Illman as motifs under the theme of trust. The difference, of course, lies in the specificity of the former image and the specific language that goes along with that image. It is this greater literary specificity which makes the multiple usage of this image in the Asaphite psalms more interesting from a tradition-historical point of view than the more comprehensive usage of the dispute and punishment motif. The common inclusion of such different types of evidence under the term "motif" is, in this respect, quite misleading, since it is not their mere existence as a motif that is significant from a tradition-historical point of view but their being of a sufficient distinctiveness to indicate a specific tradition group.[117]

---

[115] Again, see Illman, *Thema*, 43.
[116] Ibid., 17.
[117] This issue of the tradition-historical use of specific language may also be seen in Illman's perception of the differences between his own and Buss' use of "theme." As Illman is aware, Buss uses theme in a much less technically conceptual way than he does himself.

One may, however, move beyond the issue of the level of abstraction to examine the basic adequacy of Illman's use of the criterion of "characteristic common content" for the determination of tradition-historical realities. It has already been noted how Illman is able to deny that the Asaphite psalms belong to a single tradition because none of the conceptual elements he has isolated may be found in all of the psalms. The attempt of previous critics to see either an historical or a prophetic interest as an aspect of these psalms is not accepted by Illman, because no such interest extends to all of the psalms. There is, therefore, nothing which binds the psalms together but their diversity, since the superscription is of disputed and uncertain meaning.

Although it is certainly the case that there is little "content" shared by all the psalms in question, the significance of this with respect to tradition is open to question. After all, when one looks at either ancient or modern *traditio* groups, one rarely finds them to be distinguished by exclusive concern for one topic![118] Instead, one finds a similar diversity of concerns, though these are, of course, usually—but not always—related to each other. Thus, if Illman's point is that the Asaphite psalms cannot indicate a common historical tradition (that is, an actual *traditio* of some sort) because of their lack of common content, his requirements are not entirely meaningful in terms of his goal.

One wonders, however, whether the presence of such common content in each of these psalms would necessarily point to such a real historical tradition behind them in any case. Once again, even different groups may be concerned with the same content, especially if that content is defined in terms as general as those isolated by Illman. It is rather the specific way in which such content is treated that distinguishes these groups. To be truly indicative of a specific tradition, content must be defined in a sufficiently distinctive manner.

Despite the abstract level of his conceptual elements, Illman would seem to be aware of the need for such distinctiveness, since his "common content" must also be "characteristic." However, it is just those elements which are distinctive enough to be indicative of a tradition that are ruled out by Illman's insistence on commonality. Thus, for example, as noted by previous scholars and confirmed by Illman himself, certain of the Asaphite psalms share a concern for prophecy and history that is distinctive, and therefore potentially useful in a tradition-historical context. Yet because these elements—though distinctive—are not shared by all the psalms, Illman argues that one can not use them to illuminate any tradition which might lie behind these psalms. It is, however,

---

In particular, Buss shows a greater concern for the linguistic evidence, so much so that Illman sees his "theme" as more nearly representative of "terminology." Illman's attempt to complement his own thematic survey with an overview of selected linguistic evidence will be considered further below.

[118] Take as examples the diversity of the texts found at Qumran or those contained in the documents of Vatican II, each of which collection represents a single *traditio* at some point in time.

implausible to restrict any real historical tradition (again, *traditio*) to one distinctive element. If these psalms did belong to a single *traditio*, that *traditio* might well have had a number of distinctive aspects. These elements would then be "characteristic" of the *traditio* yet not of every text which might be traced to that *traditio*. The distinctive elements of each Asaphite psalm would thus be potentially useful in illuminating the *traditio* behind all the psalms, provided that a single *traditio* existed for all the psalms.

It is, of course, the existence of such a *traditio* behind these psalms that Illman has set out to prove or disprove in his study. Nevertheless, even if such characteristic common content as defined by Illman did exist in each of the psalms, it would not prove the existence of such a *traditio*, since such generally defined topics could be shared by many diverse groups. Conversely, even if such content did not exist, it would not disprove the existence of such a *traditio*, since a single *traditio* might have many characteristic aspects which need not show up in all of its textual witnesses. Again, it would seem that the methodology chosen by Illman is not sufficient to accomplish the goals he has set for it.

Although Illman would probably not agree with this assessment of the potential of his chosen method, he does supplement his search for a characteristic common content with an analysis of other aspects of these psalms, including their language. For Illman, language analysis may be described as helpful for the discernment of common content but not as necessary to that process. It is not, however, clear whether Illman also conceives of such language analysis as a possibly independent tool or whether it must correspond to other, more specifically Tradition-historical criteria of common content. This ambiguity is due in part to the fact that Illman's linguistic analysis proves to be as unsuccessful as his Tradition-historical analysis.

One might, however, also question the means which Illman employs in his language analysis. The latter is, in the first place, restricted to designations of God and "didactic terminology" indicative of a Deuteronomic phraseology. The first of these is possibly an extension of the traditional source critical approach, while the latter is an attempt to test Buss' theory of levitical-Deuteronomic ties. Yet while both of these, and especially the latter, considerably enlarges the linguistic evidence considered, it is arguable that even this is too restrictive a linguistic survey.

Even more important, however, is the need for a more judicious handling of those linguistic affinities which are apparent in the psalms. Thus, for example, the presence of similar expressions in "many of the writing prophets, in Daniel, in the wisdom literature, and in the work of the Chronicler" does not in itself add or take away from the tradition-historical significance of such expressions. Rather, one must, among other things, take account of the different tradition-historical connections among the various writing prophets and also be aware of the chronological development in the usage of a particular word or phrase. There is, in general, a need for both a widening of the linguistic analysis and a more subtle handling of that analysis.

The need to tighten up Illman's linguistic analysis is apparent with respect to certain terms which are usually reckoned as tradition-historically significant. Thus, for example, one may consider Illman's treatment of the name Joseph, which occurs a number of times in the Asaphite psalms and which has often been seen as indicative of Northern origins. As noted above, Illman denies that this name is able to indicate such origins, and he points instead to those features which imply that the Jerusalem temple was the setting for these psalms. However, it is striking that Illman leaves unanswered the question of why Joseph occurs so often in these psalms![119] One cannot simply deny the tradition-historical significance of one term because of the presence of other, apparently contradictory, terminology, as Illman seems to do here. Rather, one must attempt to explain the presence of both the former and the latter in the same place. In such a way, the presence of both the Jerusalemite *'elyôn* and the Northern Joseph in the same psalm becomes a vital clue to that psalm's tradition history.

The above comments have challenged Illman's methodology as applied to the psalms of Asaph. A few further comments should be directed to Illman's analysis of the related materials of the Chronicler which he sees as supportive of his conclusions concerning the psalms. Thus, just as Illman sees the psalms of Asaph as a blend of diverse contents and traditions, he also views the Asaphites of the Chronicler's material as equally diverse, containing at one point in time (that of the return) most of the individual groups of singers. Against Buss, he also points out that these singers were at that point separate from the "levites." Although a full discussion of these possibilities must be reserved for a later chapter, it is important to note that these assertions are actually dependent on one's wider picture of the history of the priesthood in ancient Israel. Such questions as who came back in the first return and whether the term "levite" is genealogical or functional in any given text are extremely important for an appreciation of the role of the Asaphite singers.

One may also note Illman's tendency to describe his tradition groups in functional terms,[120] in a way similar to that of Steck. As noted above, the functional character of such tradition groups is itself a matter for historical research and not something to be assumed. In all of these areas, a closer look at the evidence is needed.

Finally, one may note that after all his analysis, Illman has left the common superscription of these psalms essentially unexplained. By arguing that there is no single tradition behind these psalms but only a diversity indicative of the many groups which made up the Asaphites, Illman is in the end unable to explain why this particular group of psalms was singled out of the larger psalter with the superscription *lĕ'āsāp*. This is especially the case if these Asaphites also sang the other psalms of the psalter, as Illman has further contended. It is, of course,

---

[119] Especially since the only occurrences of this term in the psalter are in the Asaphite psalms and in Psalm 105, part of which is attributed to Asaph by the Chronicler.
[120] Illman, *Thema*, 64.

possible that the reasons for the grouping of these particular psalms in such a way have been lost. However, in view of the methodological reservations voiced above, it would seem that the problem is deserving of another attempt at solution beyond that of Illman.

A NEW TRADITION-HISTORICAL STUDY OF THE PSALMS OF ASAPH

If one is to add yet another consideration of the psalms of Asaph to the long and weighty list detailed above, it is important to be quite clear about one's goals from the outset. Accordingly, it needs to be emphasized that the purpose of the chapters which follow is to understand better the tradition-historical significance of the existence of Psalms 50, 73-83 as a group of psalms with the superscription *lĕ'āsāp*. Thus, in contrast to those scholars whose emphasis fell on the form or content of the individual psalms, the following analysis is more interested in the tradition-historical implications of the fact that these psalms exist as a group.

It is clear that to frame the task in this way is explicitly to bring the common superscription of these psalms into the center of the discussion. The reason for doing so lies in the superscription's obvious value as a possible external control from the time of ancient Israel itself. Unfortunately, recognizing this value does not in itself determine how this control is to be understood. The basic question is that of whether the superscription is more indicative of the material of the psalms themselves (the *traditum*) or the group responsible for these psalms (the *traditio*). In other words, the superscription may theoretically act as a means either of linking a particular distinctive type of material or of linking the material of a particular distinctive *traditio* group. If the former is the case, one must further question whether such similar material is indicative of a distinctive *traditio* group responsible for it or whether it is merely the creation of an editor concerned for ordering similar psalter material together. While the latter would not necessarily lead to the discovery of a common *traditio* responsible for the psalms (except possibly at the point of their editorial collection), it would not rule out such a possibility either, depending on the nature of the common elements involved. In any event, the fact that these psalms—and whatever common elements they have—have already been grouped by someone in ancient Israel in itself acts at the very least as a safeguard against the doubtful move from the isolating of such elements by the modern critic to the positing of an ancient *traditio* group.

As has been noted above, however, efforts to find a commonality in such *traditum* elements as form and content have generally been unavailing. Thus, the scholarly attempt to corroborate and explain the grouping of the *traditum* provided by ancient Israel in terms of their own internal controls has usually proven unsuccessful. It is, of course, possible that more detailed study may discover such an internal link. Conversely, however, the lack of such internal similarities in the *traditum* may indicate a need to shift the focus to the *traditio* as the source for the common grouping of these psalms under their superscription.

If, then, there are no reasons internal to the psalms which appear to explain their sharing a common superscription, this must be explained in another way. One possibility is to look away from the psalms themselves to those responsible for them in some way—that is, their *traditio*. Thus, in contrast to the approach of Illman where one needed to determine that the psalms agreed in their content before one could point to a common *traditio* responsible for them, it could instead be argued that it is the very lack of such a common content which leaves no other alternative but that of positing a common *traditio*. To deny this is to deny that the superscription has any meaning in terms of differentiating these psalms from the rest of the psalter—as Illman is forced to do. This, however, leaves the existence of the superscription without any suitable explanation, a move which most of the scholars considered above have rejected as unlikely.

There is, of course, no guarantee against the possibility that the common superscription is simply due to a random attribution of individual psalms to Asaph by a number of unconnected authors, combined with a later grouping together of the already superscripted psalms by an editor concerned for order in the psalter. Although the unwieldy mechanics of such unrelated individual ascriptions would alone argue against this possibility, it is unlikely on other grounds as well. Thus, for example, one may contrast the small number of psalms ascribed to Asaph with the much larger number ascribed to David. David, of course, as a national figure of some importance continued to attract psalms to himself into a much later period. Asaph, on the other hand, inhabits a very specific sphere of interest and the number of psalms ascribed to him remained stable.

Further, even in the unlikely event that the superscriptions may be traced to separate individuals, such individuals are still to be related in some way by their interest in Asaph, an interest which, if not shared by the entire society (as does not appear to be the case), would most likely have been mediated by a source common to all those who made use of such a superscription. Finally, of course, the fact that an Asaphite group of a type appropriate to psalmic activity is known from other sources would seem to place the burden of proof on those who would deny the ability of the superscription to point to a *traditio* of some sort.

In such a way, the superscription would appear to provide a form of external control which groups together otherwise apparently disparate materials under a single *traditio*. As such, it is similar to the external controls of Qumran which, by grouping different scrolls within a single locus, guarantee that those scrolls all are related in some way to a single *traditio*. This fixing of such materials within a single *traditio* is, however, only the first stage of discerning their tradition-historical significance. Once this has been done, one is then able to describe the *traditio* on the basis of the materials which have been connected to it. One is, for example, able to describe the Qumran community on the basis of the scrolls assigned to it without first determining by less controllable literary criteria whether such materials stem from different *traditios*. Similarly, the psalms which make up the Asaphite collection should yield information about the *traditio* responsible for them, whether that responsibility is in the form of composition, preservation, handing down, or collection.

This is, of course, not to deny that either the individual Qumran scrolls or the individual Asaphite psalms might ultimately derive from different sources, either wholly or in part. What the fact of an externally verifiable common *traditio* guarantees is that the disparate materials found within a *traditio* reflect the characteristics of that *traditio* at a certain point of its existence. If they did not, they would not have been preserved. The fact of a unit's existence within a certain *traditio* is potentially important for the description of that *traditio*, whether or not its sources can be determined. To say this is not, however, to say that the discernment of that unit's sources is unimportant. Indeed, such information can be crucial to an understanding of the historical development of the *traditio*. Nevertheless, even without such information, the material illuminates its *traditio* at some stage of its development.

As noted in the first chapter, once such internal elements as form and "content" have been freed from the task of defining a *traditio*, they can provide invaluable insight into the nature of such a *traditio* already defined by other means. To be sure, one must still give consideration to those internal elements which can confirm or call into question the grouping provided by the external control. Such internal controls as language could still cause one to call into question—or at least to refine further—one's theory of a single *traditio* as established by external controls. Similarly, a correspondence in such internal elements would further corroborate the existence of such a *traditio*. However, barring the former wide disparity, the place of such elements is descriptive of the nature of the *traditio* rather than prescriptive of its existence.

How then is one to proceed in the case of the psalms bearing the superscription *lĕ'āsāp*, once one starts with the assumption that this superscription does not derive from either chance or a later recognition of the psalms' common elements but rather is in some way indicative of the *traditio* of these psalms? In keeping with the above, two avenues of investigation then become possible. The first is to turn to the psalms themselves. Here one may initially look for those elements which are able to corroborate the existence of a single definable *traditio*. Among these elements, language may be seen as pre-eminent, since it is least subject to critical manipulation. One must, however, move beyond the task of corroborating the existence of a *traditio* to that of describing that *traditio*. Language plays a central role here as well, since it is also the most secure means for linking these psalms with other already isolated movements in Israel's history. After a consideration of their language, one may look at the form of these psalms as an indication of the *traditio* group's interests and possible functional situation. Finally one may then characterize these interests on the basis of more general "content" categories, though these are the most subject to critical misrepresentation. In all of this, it should again be noted that while form and "content" are in themselves too general to be a real control in the establishment (or questioning) of a *traditio*, they can play a significant role in the description of that *traditio* once it has been established by other means.

The second approach to this material proceeds less from the psalms grouped by the superscription *lĕ'āsāp* than from the connection suggested by the superscription itself. This is, of course, not a new approach, since the significant material concerning Asaph has been considered by many previous scholars. What has generally been lacking, however, is any serious attempt to bring a sufficiently critical understanding of that material into dialogue with such conclusions as can be gleaned from the psalms themselves. It is to be hoped that, if both sides are taken seriously, such a dialogue could to some extent illuminate the *traditio* of the psalms.

The rest of this work will explore these possibilities. The third chapter will be devoted to a consideration of the linuistic evidence offered by the psalms, both in terms of its usefulness as an internal control on the *traditio* possibility suggested by the common superscription and in terms of its further ability to describe that *traditio* once it has been established. The fourth chapter will continue the description of that *traditio* by turning to the form of the psalms and also, in a more general way, to their content. The fifth chapter will move to the external evidence suggested by the superscription and will attempt to relate this to the information gathered from the psalms themselves. The final chapter will then offer some concluding historical and methodological observations.

3
A Linguistic Analysis of the Psalms of Asaph

As noted above, the purpose of the linguistic analysis which characterizes this chapter is two-fold. In the first place, it seeks to corroborate by means of an internal control the existence of the *traditio* suggested for the psalms of Asaph by their common superscription. This purpose is initially served by noting those linguistic elements which bind these psalms to each other as an identifiable entity. One may, however, also help to distinguish the linguistic commonality of these psalms by isolating any distinctive elements which they share as a group with a set linguistic body outside of themselves. This, in turn, serves the second purpose of providing additional information concerning the nature of any *traditio* to which the psalms belong.

In contrast with previous efforts along these lines, the present analysis will proceed on a psalm to psalm basis, analyzing the specific words and phrases as they occur in the psalms.[1] Because the focus here is tradition-historical rather than broadly exegetical, the analysis will comment only on those elements which have been found to have a sufficient tradition-historical distinctiveness. In other words, it will bypass those terms which seem to have an "all-Israel" currency in favor of those which have a more narrow role in Israel's individual tradition streams. To this extent, the emphasis is almost "source-critical" in nature, although the sources in question are not the documents of the older Pentateuchal hypothesis but the *traditum* material connected with those *traditio* groups that can be discerned in ancient Israel. Because of this narrow focus, the more general theological value of most of the terms considered will for the most part be left to the existing psalm commentaries where it is well covered. Only where such theological analysis is important to the making of tradition-historical distinctions will it be considered at any length here.

PSALM 50

Psalm 50 is both the first of the Asaphite psalms in the current ordering of the psalter and the only one to be separated from that group's main concentration in Psalms 73-83. In form it is usually classed as a prophetic liturgy of some

---

[1] One might especially contrast the limited attempt along these lines by Buss and the more extensive, but still restricted, treatment of Illman. See Buss, "Psalms" and Illman, *Thema*.

sort.[2] More specifically, it consists of a theophany (vv 1-4, 6) and a divine speech in the first person (vv 5, 7-23). In the course of this liturgy of divine revelation, the people are taken to task for both their over-reliance on sacrifice and their ethical failings. They are also encouraged to "sacrifice thanksgiving" as a condition for God's future favor. The extent to which some of these formal and theological aspects may be tradition-historically significant will be considered in greater detail in the following chapter.

In terms of specific language, the psalm has several tradition-historically interesting elements. There are, for example, certain examples of language to some degree distinctive of the Asaphite psalms. Perhaps the best example of such inner-Asaphite language is the curious phrase *zîz śāday* (v 11) which appears elsewhere only in Ps 80:14. This link with Psalm 80 is seconded in a less exclusive manner by the divine *hôpîaʿ* of v 2 which also appears in Ps 80:2.[3] One may also point to the *miklē'ōt* of v 9 which is found elsewhere only in the Asaphite Ps 78:70 and in Hab 3:17. Finally, one may also note the close parallel between certain elements of v 7 and the first half of Ps 81:9.[4] It would, of course, be wrong to overemphasize these similarities, especially when they are not exclusive. Nevertheless, such "coincidences" are certainly worthy of note, particularly when they can be coupled with other inner-Asaphite language in the remaining psalms.

Perhaps more tradition-historically significant than such isolated Asaphite cross-references are those linguistic elements which are similar in their common affinity with a distinctive stream of tradition known from outside the psalm. The tradition stream in question is that which has been called Deuteronomic but which should be given a more accurate and comprehensive title, since it includes within itself not only what is usually referred to as either Deuteronomic or Deuteronomistic but also other literature with similar linguistic and theological elements (such as the E strand of the Pentateuch, Hosea, and Jeremiah). In keeping with certain suggestions made by Robert R. Wilson, this stream will be referred to as "Ephraimite" throughout the course of the present study.[5]

There are a number of linguistic elements in Psalm 50 which point to a link with this Ephraimite tradition stream. One may, for example, note the hiphil of *ʿûd* in v 7 which, in addition to its being a part of the already mentioned Asaphite parallel in Ps 81:9, is also suggestive in terms of its wider usage. When used with God as its subject, this word occurs almost exclusively in those sources

---

[2] See Hermann Gunkel, *Die Psalmen* (HKAT II/2, Göttingen: Vandenhoeck & Ruprecht, 1926) 214-218; Weiser, *Psalms*, 392-393; and Hans-Joachim Kraus, *Psalmen* (BK 15, Neukirchen: Neukirchener, 1960) I, 371-372.

[3] As well as in Deut 33:2; Ps 94:1; and four times in Job, though the latter passages are less similar than the first two passages.

[4] Note especially the presence of *šimʿâ/šemaʿ ʿammî* and *weʾāʿîdâ bākkĕ* in each case. The divine self-revelation formula which ends Ps 50:7 is to be found in Ps 81:11.

[5] Robert R. Wilson, *Prophecy and Society in Ancient Israel* (Philadelphia: Fortress, 1980) 17-18 and passim.

connected with the Ephraimite tradition stream.[6] Also worthy of note here is the widespread Ephraimite use of this word with reference to God's warning of the people through the prophets.[7] This is particularly interesting because of the "prophetic" character of both the present psalm and its Asaphite fellow, Psalm 81. The conjunction of Ephraimite language and prophetic form raises tradition-historical possibilities which will need to be considered further in the next chapter.

Another example of a word that is suggestive in terms of its wider associations is the *mûsār* of v 17. Although this word is plentiful in the wisdom literature, even occurring there with the verb *śn'* found in Psalm 50,[8] the usage here is possibly more similar to that of its second major locus, the Ephraimite tradition stream.[9] It is interesting that this is the only psalm reference and that the expression, despite its wisdom currency, is quite rare in non-Ephraimite prophets such as first Isaiah and Ezekiel.[10] Thus, outside of its wisdom base, the word occurs mainly within an Ephraimite locus.

The list of accusations begun by the rejection of discipline continues in the following verse with more suggestive vocabulary. Thus, the series which begins with theft (*gannāb*) and adultery (*měnā'ăpîm*) has clear parallels in the similar lists of Hos 4:2 and Jer 7:9, both of which also begin with these evils. In fact, with the exception of murder,[11] all of the offenses listed in vv 18–20 are paralleled in the lists of Hosea and Jeremiah, though it must be admitted that the vocabulary is not exactly the same in each case.[12] It is, of course, evident that these lists are in some way based on the Decalogue, where much of the same language is used.[13] However, in view of recent suggestions concerning the

---

[6] Exod 19:23 (E); 2 Kgs 17:13; Jer 11:7 (3x); Neh 9:26, 29, 36; (for the "Deuteronomic" nature of the latter prayer, see Steck, *Geschick*, 64–77). The only exception to this is Zech 3:6, which has the warning delivered by the angel of God.

[7] Deut 8:19; 32:46; 1 Sam 8:9; 2 Kgs 17:13; Jer 6:10; 11:7. In contrast, the word is only rarely used in this way by non-Ephraimite prophets, such a usage being missing altogether from Isaiah and Ezekiel. (Isa 8:2 is quite different.) See, however, Amos 3:13 and 2 Chr 24:19.

[8] Prov 5:12; cf. 15:10.

[9] See especially Jeremiah where the refusal of *mûsār* is often a charge against the people: Jer 2:30; 5:3; 7:28; 17:23; 32:33; 34:13. See also Deut 11:2; Jer 10:8; 30:14; Hos 5:2.

[10] The term does not occur in first Isaiah; Isa 26:16 and 53:5 belonging to later redactional levels. It occurs once in Ezekiel (Ezek 5:15) and once in Zephaniah (Zeph 3:2, 7). For the possibly mixed tradition-historical nature of these latter examples, see Wilson, *Prophecy*, 280–281 and 283–284.

[11] It is tempting to attempt various emendations of the awkward *wattireṣ* in v 18 in order to include the missing *rṣḥ*. However, the sense of the text is clear as it stands and there is little justification in the versions for such an emendation.

[12] The language is perhaps more "poetic" in the psalm. Note that Jeremiah adds cultic violations to the list.

[13] See Kraus, *Psalmen*, I, 380.

Northern locus of the Decalogue traditions,[14] it is certainly suggestive that it is precisely within the Ephraimite tradition stream that such Decalogue-based lists appear. It is further suggestive that the prophetic liturgy of Psalm 50 should so closely mirror an element found among the Ephraimite prophets.[15]

The accusatory phrase of the psalm's conclusion, šōkĕhê-ĕlôah, is indicative of a similar tradition-historical affinity. The sin of forgetting things divine — God's law, name, covenant, commandments — is to be found across the broad spectrum of Ephraimite literature. While these sins are to be found elsewhere as well, the forgetting of God as such is almost exclusively to be found in Ephraimite sources, especially the book of Jeremiah.[16] In contrast, this expression only occurs once in first Isaiah (Isa 17:10, in the midst of the oracles against the nations), once in second Isaiah (Isa 51:13), and twice in Ezekiel (Ezek 22:12, 23:35).[17] In view of the overwhelming predominance of this expression in the Ephraimite sources, it would appear that its use in such places as Ezekiel provides an example of how some degree of Ephraimite influence has undoubtedly affected that book and its author(s).[18] The same, of course, could also be the case in the present psalm, although the presence of other Ephraimite elements and the lack of any comparably distinctive elements from another stream would lead one to posit a closer relationship.

One may also note the presence of this expression in Ps 106:21, the only other occurrence in the psalter as an accusation against the people.[19] In this respect, it is significant that parts of Psalm 106 are included in the song to be sung by Asaph in the Chronicler's account of the functioning of the cult (1 Chr 16:34-36). The similarity of many elements of the superscripted Asaphite psalms with those found in the psalms attributed to Asaph by the Chronicler is intriguing from a tradition-historical viewpoint. These latter psalms, which may be conveniently designated deutero-Asaphite, will receive further consideration below.

Another possible link with the Ephraimite stream is to be found in the warning phrase of v 22 which appears to be a shortened, though still verbally exact, parallel of Hos 5:14b. As will be noted below, similar "quotations" of Ephraimite prophets are to be found elsewhere in the psalms of Asaph.

A final term which raises similar tradition-historical possibilities is the tôdâ

---

[14] See for example, Morgan Lee Phillips, *The Significance of the Divine Self-Predication Formula for the Structure and Content of Deutero-Isaiah* (Dissertation completed at Drew University, 1969) 36-39.

[15] One wonders whether such a list is a form in its own right. If so, it is striking that it is to be found precisely within an Ephraimite locus.

[16] Deut 6:12, 14, 19; 32:18; Judg 3:7; 1 Sam 12:9; Jer 2:32; 3:21; 13:25; 18:15; Hos 2:15; 13:6.

[17] One should also note Job 8:13.

[18] See Wilson, *Prophecy*, 283-284. In some ways, second Isaiah is even closer to that stream.

[19] Though see the Korahite Ps 44:18 where the people explicitly reject such a charge.

which appears in vv 14 and 23, and which is in some respects the central focus of the entire psalm. Intriguing in this respect is the connection one finds elsewhere between the tôdâ and both the songs of Asaph and the levitical offering of sacrifice.[20] Since, however, these connections are not strictly linguistic in nature, it may be best to defer their consideration until the chapter which deals with the external evidence concerning the Asaphites.

In view of the above evidence, it is possible to point to a number of linguistic elements which are suggestive for the tradition history of Psalm 50. Some of these elements link Psalm 50 with its fellow Asaphite psalms, while others indicate an affinity with what has been called the Ephraimite tradition stream. The possibilities suggested here are strengthened by the fact that this pattern repeats itself throughout a number of the Asaphite psalms.

PSALM 73

Psalm 73 introduces both the main body of the Asaphite psalms and the third "book" of the psalter. In contrast to the predominantly communal nature of the former, the present psalm is the prayer of an individual. With respect to form, the psalm is usually taken as a Lehrgedicht, though as one which has assumed the shape of a narrative of personal experience and which includes many aspects of the individual lament.[21] It also has a number of cultic aspects which have been taken as signs of a priestly connection.[22]

Linguistically, the psalm is not as distinctive as Psalm 50 and some of the other psalms of Asaph. In other words, it is difficult to make statements of a tradition-historical nature on the basis of language alone. One may, however, briefly note certain elements which Psalm 73 seems to share with other Asaphite psalms. In such a vein, the qal of *hll* in v 3 is of interest, since one may include Ps 75:5 among its comparatively rare occurrences.[23] This similarity between the two Asaphite psalms may be seen as even more exact if one notes that each reference parallels its *hôlēlîm* with a *rěšā'îm* in the second half of the verse.

The *maššû'ôt* of v 18 also provides an example of the parallel usage of a comparatively rare word. This word occurs five times in the Hebrew Bible,[24] but its only plural occurrences are the present case and Ps 74:3. Again this is a possible link between this psalm and others in the Asaphite chorus.

With less certainty, one might also note the *šě'ērî* in v 26. Again, this is a relatively rare word, especially if one is concerned with its literal physical connotation rather than its more abstract extended meaning of kinsman.[25] As

[20] See 2 Chr 29:30-36 and Jer 33:11.
[21] See Gunkel, *Psalmen*, 312. Note further Kraus, *Psalmen* II, 503-504 which also discusses the Scandinavian cultic interpretation of the psalm's form.
[22] Illman, *Thema*, 40-41, 50.
[23] The others being Job 29:3 (though this is possibly derived from a different root) and Ps 5:6.
[24] Job 30:3; 38:27; Zeph 1:15; Ps 73:18; 74:3.
[25] See also Exod 21:10; Mic 3:2, 3; and Jer 51:35. It is interesting that the extended

such, the fact that the former does occur in the Asaphite Ps 78:20, 27 is another possible linguistic link between the psalms under consideration here. It must, however, be admitted that the usage in the psalms is not the same and that a more exact parallel to the present usage may be found in Prov 5:11.

One may finally note the *miqdāš* of v 17. This is a tantalizing word from a tradition-historical point of view, both in terms of its cultic associations and its distribution in the Hebrew Bible. In terms of the latter, its most concentrated usage is to be found in the book of Ezekiel, a fact which, when linked with its further occurrences in Leviticus, Numbers, and Chronicles, would definitely seem to suggest a non-Ephraimite locus for this word. However, it is significant that the word does occur sporadically in the Ephraimite tradition,[26] as well as in the song of Exodus 15 and in other places which have a certain affinity with the Asaphite psalms.[27] In view of this tangled situation, it is all the more striking that such a cultically charged word occurs only five times in the entire psalter: once in the ancient Psalm 68 (v 36), three times in the Asaphite psalms (the present case, Ps 74:7, and Ps 78:69), and once in the deutero-Asaphite Psalm 96 (v 6), part of which is attributed to the Asaphites by the Chronicler. In view of this latter distribution within the psalter, this word would appear to have some significance in terms of linking together the psalms of Asaph, whatever one is to make of its larger tradition-historical connections.

With the exception of some interesting parallels with individual verses elsewhere,[28] Psalm 73 does not appear to lend itself to the type of larger tradition-historical inquiry which was possible for Psalm 50.[29] The expressions used in this psalm either have a general usage throughout the Hebrew Bible or, even more often, are of a sort peculiar to this psalm alone. Either way, the language of this psalm does not seem to be indicative of a place in any larger tradition stream now known.

Having said this, however, one may perhaps point to linguistic elements in the psalm which suggest certain functional ties to the cult, ties which, if a

---

meaning of kinsman is to be found exclusively within the more Southern and priestly "Jerusalemite" tradition stream represented by H and P in the Pentateuch.

[26] Josh 24:26; Jer 17:12, 51:51, among those cases most definitely within its orbit.

[27] Exodus 15 will be seen throughout this chapter to have strong linguistic ties to the Asaphite psalms. Note also certain passages in third Isaiah, such as Isa 60:13, 63:18, for other examples of the use of this term in circles opposite to those represented by Ezekiel, P, and, to some extent, Chronicles.

[28] Compare, for example, the *šēlôm rěšā'îm* of v 3 with Isa 48:22, 51:21, and the *zikkîtî lěbābî* of v 13 with Prov 20:9.

[29] One might perhaps wonder whether the *kābôd* of v 24 is not indicative of a tradition stream which encompasses non-Ephraimite sources as well as many of the psalms. It should be noted, however, that the verse does not refer to the glory of God, as do the latter references. In fact, the Asaphite psalms as a whole are extraordinary by virtue of the absence of this term. Only in Psalm 79 do they even come close to this usage and there, significantly, only with reference to the glory of the divine name.

tradition setting can be established for this psalm on other grounds, might provide interesting information about that setting. Thus, for example, one might note the reference to the pure of heart (bārê lēbāb) in the first verse, a usage which closely mirrors that of Ps 24:4, where such a condition is a prerequisite for "standing in the holy place." Also suggestive are such occurrences of the verb brr as Isa 52:11, 1 Chr 9:22, and 16:41, the last of which refers to the cultic singers.

The washing of the hands found in v 13 raises similar possibilities. Not only is a comparable expression coupled with a pure heart in Ps 24:4 as a cultic prerequisite,[30] but its exact equivalent is to be found in Ps 26:6, tied to going around God's altar and singing a song of thanksgiving.[31] Such elements might not only suggest cultic participation but even a "priestly" role of some sort.

One may, however, inquire further as to whether certain of the psalm's linguistic elements raise even more specific cultic possibilities. One may, for example, note the ḥēleq in v 26. This term is, of course, part of the Deuteronomic expression which both denies the Levites any portion with the rest of Israel and reserves God as such as their inheritance.[32] That such an expression is also used with respect to Aaron alone in Num 18:20 might indicate that the term is at the center of a dispute between the Levites and the priests, a dispute probably concerning sacrifice.[33] One should not, however, fail to notice the similar use of this term in other psalms such as 16:5, 119:57 and 142:6. While Psalm 16 also has a possible priestly situation (cf. v 4), such uses may point instead to a general context for the term.

A similar problem exists for the equally suggestive term tāmîd in v 23. As opposed to its use in connection with the common seeking of the Lord in the psalms, the use of this term to indicate the continual presence of the speaker with his God has interesting ties to the levitical order. One may note the continual presence of the levites before the Lord in 1 Chr 23:31, and, even more interestingly, in 1 Chr 16:6, 37, where it is the Asaphites in particular (along with certain of the priests in 1 Chr 16:6) who are to minister continually before the ark. Such examples, especially in conjunction with the implied setting of the psalm in the sanctuary of God (v 17), argue for an almost literal interpretation of the psalmist's being "continually with God," as well as raising anew the possibility of some levitical connection. The former, at least, is re-enforced by the parallel Ps 16:8, a psalm noted above for its possible cultic connections.[34] Nevertheless, it would perhaps be best not to base too much on this one word, especially with respect to any possible connections with the levites.

[30] nĕqî kappayim (Ps 24:4)/bĕniqqāyon kappāy (Ps 73:13).
[31] This is a suggestive coupling of functions, since in Chronicles those who do the latter are usually prohibited from doing the former.
[32] See Deut 10:9; 12:12; 14:27, 29; 18:1; Josh 14:4.
[33] See Deut 18:1, and also 18:8, which use ḥēleq with reference to the sacrifice.
[34] Ps 16:8 even contains a reference to the right hand, though not in the same usage as v 11 of the present psalm.

While the expressions which have just been considered are suggestive in terms of the psalm's possible cultic connections, they are unfortunately not decisive for determining the tradition stream to which this psalm belongs. Consequently, although the words considered may have had a role in ritual usage and even in the tradition-historically significant inner-priestly disputes, they are not sufficiently distinctive as to allow one to categorize the psalm on the basis of their presence alone. Given the lack of other such tradition-historically significant linguistic indicators, one is left with little linguistic data with which to categorize this psalm beyond that which seems to link it with its fellow Asaphite psalms.

PSALM 74

In many respects, Psalm 74 may be seen as the mirror image of its immediate predecessor. Whereas Psalm 73 was in form an individual lament tinged with wisdom and personal reflections, Psalm 74 is a lament of the community often associated with that ultimate national disaster, the destruction of the temple. Further, while Psalm 73 was almost devoid of any distinctive linguistic elements capable of relating it to a wider tradition stream in Israel's history, Psalm 74 has a number of such elements, in addition to many others which relate this psalm to its fellow Asaphite psalms. This comparative abundance is obviously significant for the purposes of the present chapter.

Looking first at those elements which link this psalm to its Asaphite fellows, one may begin by recalling those terms already considered above. These include the *maššū'ôt* of v 3 which is shared with Ps 73:18, and the *miqdāš* of v 7 which is an almost exclusively Asaphite concern within the psalter.[35] To these, one may add other linguistic elements common to the Asaphite psalms, including those which not only demonstrate this inner-Asaphite connection but also indicate certain wider tradition-historical associations.

One may, for example, note the verbal use of *'šn* in the first verse. There are only three times in the entire Hebrew Bible where God is in some way the subject of *'šn*. Two of these are in the Asaphite psalms (here and in Ps 80:5), while the third occurs in Deut 29:19. The present verse and Deut 29:19 are especially similar in that in both the subject is the anger of God.[36] Elsewhere, the verb is used more with respect to the smoking of mountains.[37] The usage in this verse is thus a possible link both to the rest of the Asaphite psalms and to the Ephraimite tradition stream noted above in connection with Psalm 50.

One may draw a similar conclusion from the expression which describes the object of God's anger, *sō'n mar'îtekā*, the primary locus of which is again that of the Asaphite psalms and those which are possibly related to them.[38] Outside

---

[35] See again Ps 73:17; 78:67; the deutero-Asaphite 96:6; and the ancient 68:36.

[36] And in Deut 29:19 God's jealousy as well. One might also note 2 Sam 22:9 (= Ps 18:9) and Isa 65:5 where the noun is connected with God's *'ap*, though in these cases the latter has more the sense of actual nostrils.

[37] Exod 19:18; Ps 104:32; 144:5.

[38] Thus, it occurs here, in Ps 79:13, 95:7, and 100:3. The last of these is designated

of these psalms this term occurs only in Jer 23:1, part of the Ephraimite tradition stream, and in Ezek 34:31 which, as a secondary redaction,[39] is difficult to place tradition-historically.[40] As has often been noted,[41] even the more general description of Israel in terms of God's flock (*sō'n*) is distinctive for the Asaphite psalms over against the rest of the psalter.[42] Once again, the earliest locus for such imagery outside the psalms is to be found in Jeremiah (especially chap. 23), though it is also to be found in Isa 63:11, in Ezekiel (again chap. 34), and in Zechariah.[43]

The presence of *šēbeṭ* in v 2 is similarly suggestive in terms of both linking the Asaphite psalms together and tying them to a wider tradition stream. While the word occurs relatively frequently in the psalter, its figurative usage to designate a "tribe" is much less common, being in all but one case confined to the Asaphite psalms and those related to them.[44] Even more significant is the fact that the usage of this term as a figurative for tribe outside the psalms lies predominantly (though perhaps not exclusively) in the Ephraimite tradition stream,[45] where it is used in contrast to the *maṭṭeh* common to non-Ephraimite "Jerusalemite" circles.[46] One may in fact further isolate the tradition-historical links of the use of this word in the present psalm by considering the entire phrase *šēbeṭ naḥălāteḵā* which has its most exact parallel in Jer 10:16 (= 51:19; cf. also Isa 63:17).

One may thus point to a series of words which indicate both an inner-Asaphite connection and a link with the same Ephraimite tradition stream which had been noted in the discussion of Psalm 50. In addition to such doubly significant linguistic elements, however, one must further consider those which, while not linking this psalm to its Asaphite fellows, do point beyond to larger streams of tradition. In view of the Ephraimite provenance of those elements common to this psalm and its Asaphite fellows, one would perhaps expect the

---

lětôdâ, a sacrifice which was noted above to have possible Asaphite connections. Psalm 95, while not technically "deutero-Asaphite" like the following Psalm 96, will be seen to have many links to the Asaphite psalms.

[39] Note that it is a second person addition to a third person oracle.

[40] Again see Wilson, *Prophecy*, 283-284, for the place of Ephraimite elements in Ezekiel. As noted before, these elements cannot be restricted to any one redactional level of the book.

[41] See, for example, Delitzsch, *Psalms*, II, 325, 329; and Illman, *Thema*, 39-40.

[42] Ps 74:11; 77:21; 78:52; 79:13; 80:2; 95:7; 100:3. Ps 44:12 uses the term *sō'n* but not in the image of Israel as God's flock.

[43] See especially Zech 9:16, among other places in second Zechariah, a work which certainly does not belong to the central Jerusalemite cult. See Hanson, *Dawn*, 280-401.

[44] In addition to the present verse, see Ps 78:55, 67, 68, and the deutero-Asaphite 105:37. The sole exception is Ps 122:4, a song of ascents.

[45] Note especially the many examples in Deuteronomy and the Deuteronomistic history.

[46] See Wilson, *Prophecy*, 253-295. This Jerusalemite stream is represented by P, Ezekiel, and certain aspects of Chronicles. First Isaiah also has Jerusalemite links.

rest of the psalm to contain other indications of this connection. This is to some degree the case, as will be shown below. However, one should perhaps first consider a number of tradition-historically significant terms which seem to indicate not the Ephraimite tradition stream but the opposite and possibly rival Jerusalemite stream. One example of this has already been seen in the enigmatic *miqdāš* of v 7 which, while belonging almost entirely to the Asaphite and Asaphite-related psalms within the psalter, is also to be seen primarily—though significantly, not exclusively[47]—in the non-Ephraimite locus represented by the P material and certain aspects of Ezekiel. The pattern of a predominantly Jerusalemite locus with a distinctly Ephraimite undercurrent is repeated in several elements of the present psalm.

In this connection, one may note the '*ēdâ* of v 2. This term is used to indicate a gathering of Israel throughout the P material of the Pentateuch. As such, it would appear to point to a "priestly"[48] or Jerusalemite connection for this psalm. Nevertheless, one should also note the presence of this term in certain Deuteronomistic settings such as Judg 20:1; 21:10, 13, 16; and 1 Kgs 8:5; 12:20. 1 Kings 8 is perhaps especially significant, since it is the locus for a number of priestly "loan words" in the Deuteronomistic history.[49] One may also note the presence of this term in such Ephraimite prophets as Hosea and Jeremiah[50] and its absence from such Jerusalemite sources as Isaiah and Ezekiel.

The use in the same verse of the qal of *škn* to refer to the dwelling of God on Mount Zion repeats the pattern just observed. Once again, the main locus of this term is in non-Ephraimite sources.[51] Nevertheless, there is also once again an alternative presence of this term within the Deuteronomistic literature, most notably in 1 Kgs 8:13 but also in 1 Kgs 6:13, where God dwells among the people, as in the many P examples. The latter Kings example is especially interesting since it is part of a typically Deuteronomic conditional promise which is contingent on the observance of the commandments (cf. also 8:27). In considering the Deuteronomic parallels, one should also take note of the frequent piel use of *škn* in conjunction with the divine name to refer to the place where that name should dwell. As has been noted by others,[52] there would appear to be a distinctive Deuteronomic "name theology" which contrasts with a more literal theology of

---

[47] See esecially Jer 51:51 where a foreign intrusion into the *miqdāš* of the Lord's house is being lamented as in the present psalm. See also Josh 24:26; Jer 17:12.

[48] In the technical sense of the term, meaning those circles responsible for the P material of the Pentateuch. Such circles might also be called Jerusalemite, as in the text, so as to distinguish them from other priestly circles with more Ephraimite tendencies.

[49] The tradition-historical status of this chapter is in real need of further study.

[50] See Hos 7:12; Jer 30:20. The term also occurs elsewhere in Psalms and Proverbs.

[51] See especially Isa 8:18; Zech 8:3; Joel 4:17, 21; and Ps 68:19 for specific dwelling on Mount Zion. Also note in this respect, Ezek 43:7, 9 and certain psalms, such as Ps 135:21. For P examples of dwelling "in the midst," see Exod 25:8; 29:45, 46; Num 5:3; 35:34.

[52] Gerhard von Rad, *Old Testament Theology*, I, trans. by D. M. G. Stalker (New York: Harper & Row, 1962) 238.

A LINGUISTIC ANALYSIS OF THE PSALMS OF ASAPH 69

dwelling found elsewhere. While the latter would certainly appear to be what is present here, the former becomes important in the consideration of the *miškan-šĕmekā* in v 7.

Along these lines, one should also note the parallel term *qōdeš* in v 3. Although this term does have an inner-Asaphite parallel in Ps 77:14, its primary locus is non-Ephraimite,[53] as it is used to designate the sanctuary area. Once again, however, there are the same exceptions in the Deuteronomic literature, most especially in 1 Kings 8.[54] Also worth noting here are certain references in the account of the Chronicler which connect the levites with the *qōdeš*.[55] Especially interesting is 2 Chr 35:5 where during the reform of Josiah the levites are to stand in the *qōdeš* and serve the Lord directly (cf. v 2), rather than simply serving the priest as elsewhere.[56] Thus, while the bulk of the material certainly suggests that the *qōdeš* was the concern of Jerusalemite and "priestly" circles, there are suggestions that at certain times, and particularly during the so-called Deuteronomic reforms, the levites also had something to do with the sanctuary. One wonders whether the present psalm bears the marks of just such a mingling of traditions.[57]

Perhaps nowhere in the psalm is the ambivalence of the linguisitic evidence more strongly evident than in the *miškan-šĕmekā* of v 7. Once again, the word *miškān* would appear to have a strong link to those tradition circles responsible for the P strand of the Pentateuch (cf. also Ezek 39:27). In contrast, the word appears only rarely in the Ephraimite tradition stream noted above.[58] Yet, despite this, one can once again point to traces in both the P material and the Chronicler's account which tie the levites—and even more specifically, the Asaphites—to the *miškān*.[59] One even wonders whether the parallel of *qōdeš* and *miškān* is antithetical, the former belonging (normally) to the priests and the latter to the levites. Even more striking than this is the linking of the *miškān* with the divine name, a combination which is without exact parallel in the entire Bible. What does, however, come very close to such a parallel is the same Deuteronomic name theology that was mentioned above, a theology in which God causes the divine name to dwell in Jerusalem.[60] Given the complexity of this term's possible tradition-historical links, it seems best to be guided by more tradition-historically certain elements in the psalm.[61]

[53] Note its very common usage in the P source of the Pentateuch and its presence in Ezek 41:4, 21, 23; 42:14; 44:13, 17.
[54] 1 Kgs 8:6, 8, 10; also cf. 1 Kgs 6:16; 7:50. Also note the deutero-Asaphite Ps 96:9.
[55] 1 Chr 23:32; 24:5. Note the apparent tension with Num 3:32.
[56] These issues will be discussed further in chapter five.
[57] Note that Ps 68:24-25 places the singers in the sanctuary.
[58] See 2 Sam 7:6; Jos 22:19, 29. Also note its inner-Asaphite parallel, Ps 78:60.
[59] See for example, Num 1:50; 3 (vv 7-8 and passim), 16:9; 31:30, 47; 1 Chr 6:17-33.
[60] Using *škn* in the piel. See Deut 12:11; 14:23; 16:2, 6, 11; 26:2; also Jer 7:12 and Neh 1:9.
[61] Also suggestive of a non-Ephraimite locus are the *mô'ēd* of vv 4 and 8 and the *mā'ôr* of v 16. These, however, are less definite than the cases cited in the text, since the usage in the psalm does not correspond to their usage in the Jerusalemite sources.

In contrast to these terms which are unusual, though not impossible, for an Ephraimite setting, one may note other words which return to the Ephraimite pattern first noted above. Perhaps the most important of these is the word *nābî'* in v 9. As has recently been observed,[62] the overwhelmingly dominant locus of this term is to be found within Ephraimite sources, even though, as with such words as *šēbeṭ*, this term does occur in Judean sources. Interestingly, it is a rare word in the psalter, occurring only here, in the narrative title of Psalm 51, and in the deutero-Asaphite Psalm 105 (v 15). The usage here is important, since it indicates that 1) the psalmist considers a *nābî'* at home in a cultic situation, 2) such a presence was a repeated occurrence, and 3) its absence was something to be lamented, at least for the present psalmist. The prophet also appears to be credited with some sort of predictive function here as well, as is indicated by the prophetic language of the rest of the verse. This reference to a prophet is, of course, especially suggestive because of the prophetic nature of so many of the Asaphite psalms.[63]

One may cite other less weighty but still suggestive linguistic affinities in the psalm. Thus, for example, the reference to setting the bounds of the earth in v 17, *'attâ hiṣṣabtā kol-gĕbûlôt 'āreṣ*, recalls the similar *yaṣṣēb gĕbūlōt 'ammîm* in Deut 32:8.[64] One also sees echoes of Deuteronomy 32 in the reference to the *'am nābāl* in v 18, as paralleled in Deut 32:6, though it is used there to refer to Israel. While not verbally exact, the reference to a *gôy nābāl* in Deut 32:21 is even more suggestive, since it refers to the means of Israel's punishment, as in the present verse. One may also note the relatively rare usage of *qn'* with God as a subject to refer to the acquisition of Israel. This is to be found in v 2 of the present psalm, Exod 15:16, and Deut 32:6.[65] A similar affinity with these ancient poems will be noted throughout the Asaphite psalms.

Two other linguistic elements with apparent Ephraimite connections may also be noted here, although how significant they are in tradition-historical terms is difficult to determine. Thus, one may note the syntactical construction *hēra'b* (< *r'*) in v 3 which has its only parallels in Jer 25:29 and the deutero-Asaphite Ps 105:15. Similarly, one might mention the fact that the other occurrences of the rare word *qardōm* in v 5 all occur in Ephraimite sources.[66] Again, it is hard to know whether these parallels are tradition-historically significant or merely a coincidence.

One might also note two theological terms whose tradition-historical connections are difficult to determine. The first of these is the word *g'l* which has

---

[62] Wilson, *Prophecy*, 136. See also David L. Petersen, *The Roles of Israel's Prophets* (JSOT 17; Sheffield: JSOT, 1981), 51–69.

[63] Such as Psalms 50, 75, 81, and 82, all of which contain direct divine speech. See further in the following chapter.

[64] See Ps 82:8 for another Asaphite reference to this verse.

[65] One might also note its use in Ps 78:54, where it refers to the mountain of Zion, and Isa 11:11 where it refers to the remnant.

[66] Judg 9:48; 1 Sam 13:20, 21; Jer 46:22.

a wide (though not universal) usage, but whose main concentration is to be found in second and third Isaiah. This would fit in well with an exilic interpretation of the psalm, and such a juxtaposition between Asaphite terminology and that of the later Isaianic material is not unknown elsewhere. Still, little can really be said concerning its tradition-historical significance until the tradition-historical relationship between the latter material and the various tradition streams of Israel is clarified further. The second term with a tradition-historical significance that is difficult to determine is the běrît of v 20 (cf. 50:16; 78:10, 37). This term, of course, has a prominent place in Deuteronomic and Ephraimite usage, though it cannot be confined to these streams.

Considering the above linguistic evidence, one may, with some degree of probability, link Psalm 74 to both the other Asaphite psalms and to the Ephraimite tradition stream. One may not, however, overlook those indications of familiarity with certain linguistic elements of the rival Jerusalemite stream, even if one acknowledges the ambiguous nature of the evidence and argues for its possible incorporation into Ephraimite usage (as with miškān). Rather, one must accept both of these linguistic clusters as clues to the tradition-historical nature of the psalm and possibly the Asaphite psalter of which it is a part. These issues will be considered further in subsequent chapters.

PSALM 75

The intense national lament of Psalm 74 contrasts sharply with the communal thanksgiving of Psalm 75. With respect to form, it is noteworthy that the latter also announces judgment on the enemies of Israel. Further, it is significant that here, as in Psalm 50, the divine first person is an important part of the psalm.[67] All of these formal traits will be discussed in the next chapter.

Another contrast of Psalm 75 with its immediate predecessor is to be found in the area of linguistic evidence. Unlike Psalm 74, which contained a wide variety of tradition-historically significant linguistic elements, Psalm 75 is more similar to Psalm 73 in its relative lack of any such elements which would illuminate its tradition-historical nature. There are, nevertheless, a few such elements with some possible tradition-historical significance, and these require discussion here.

One may perhaps start with the title of the psalm which, in addition to providing its Asaphite identification, also includes the phrase 'al-tašḥēt. Along with most other features of psalmic nomenclature, this has been subject to a wide-ranging critical debate as to its meaning. However, in terms of its tradition-historical significance, its meaning is perhaps less important than its distribution within the psalter. Thus, in addition to the present case, one finds the phrase 'al-tašḥēt only in the titles of Psalms 57, 58, and 59. The fact that the present psalm is not a part of this series would seem to argue for the former's being handed down in different circles than the latter. The separation of this 'al-tašḥēt

---

[67] One may also note a change in the number of the human speaker in the psalm. Contrast, for example, v 2 with v 10.

psalm from its fellows may provide some supporting evidence for the claim that the *lĕ'āsāp* is indicative of a *traditio* rather than a *traditum* distinction.

Turning from the title to the body of the psalm, one finds several interesting linguistic connections, though only a few of these point to any decisive tradition-historical linkage. In such a vein, one may note a cluster of linguistic elements with an echo in the song of Hannah in 1 Samuel 2. This cluster includes the repeated reference to the horn (Ps 75:5, 6, 11, 11; 1 Sam 2:1, 10), its conjunction with the verb *rûm* (Ps 75:5, 6, 11; 1 Sam 2:1, 10), the further independent use of that verb (Ps 75:7, 8; 1 Sam 2:8), and the rare adjectival use of the root *'tq* (Ps 75:6; 1 Sam 2:3).[68] Perhaps most suggestive is the close similarity between the *zeh yašpîl wĕzeh yārîm* of Ps 75:8 and the *mašpîl 'ap-mĕrômēm* of 1 Sam 2:7.

Even though such parallels are striking, their significance remains unclear for a number of reasons. First of all, most of the individual parallels are not exclusive to these two sources, and their larger distribution does not seem to indicate any tradition-historically significant pattern. Further, it is also possible that these terms are a part of the standard vocabulary of the song of thanksgiving, and, as such, may have a form-critical rather than a tradition-historical significance. Finally, even if the linguistic link were tradition-historically significant, the tradition-historical status of the poem in 1 Samuel 2 would have to be clarified before any conclusions could be drawn about the linguistically similar Psalm 75. Thus, despite the attractiveness of seeing a link with what is now a part of the Deuteronomistic history, it appears best not to place much weight on this parallel.

The reference to the melting of the earth and all its inhabitants in v 4 also has some suggestive parallels that are difficult to evaluate. Thus, one may note that the verb *mûg* is used elsewhere to describe both the physical effects of the divine presence on the natural world and its effects on the human objects of the divine anger.[69] Perhaps the general reference to the melting of the earth in Ps 46:7 (as opposed to the melting of specific peoples elsewhere) is the best parallel to the present case. The fact that both of these psalms are "singer" psalms is interesting in this respect, although this parallel may be best explained on formal rather than tradition-historical grounds.

A more significant link between the so-called "singer" psalms may perhaps be seen in the distribution of the divine title, God of Jacob, as found in v 10 of the present psalm. This title occurs only nine times in the psalms, and of these nine, seven are to be found in the Asaphite and Korahite psalms.[70] Once again, however, because the expression is not exclusive to the singer psalms (or even to

---

[68] One might also note the similar use of the *kî* in 1 Sam 2:3 and Ps 75:7–9. See Gunkel, *Psalmen*, 328; also Delitzsch, *Psalms*, II, 340.

[69] Thus, for example, Exod 15:5; Isa 14:31; Jer 49:23; Josh 2:9, 24.

[70] In the Asaphite psalms: Ps 75:10; 76:7; 81:2, 5. In the Korahite psalms: Ps 46:8, 12; 84:9. The other two examples are Ps 20:2 and 94:7.

the psalms themselves), the tradition-historical implications of this concentration are not clear.

From these ambiguous cases, one may turn to what is undoubtedly the most interesting linguistic element in the psalm from a tradition-historical point of view, namely, the reference to the cup in v 9. The term "cup" is, of course, to be found throughout the Bible, although, significantly, a development in its usage can be traced there. One may first note the use of the term cup as a general image for one's fate or allotment in life, as in Ps 11:6, 66:5, and 23:5. As such, one's cup may be either good (Ps 23:5) or bad (Ps 11:6). More developed than this is the use of the cup as a specific term for a bad fate or a punishment, perhaps because of its association with drunkenness (cf. Ezek 23:31, 32, 33; Hab 2:16; Isa 51:17-23; Jer 25:15, 17, 28; 49:12; Lam 4:21).[71] Finally, in its most developed stage, the cup becomes identified with a specific nation who is the punishment for other nations (Jer 51:7; cf. Zech 12:2). The present example belongs to the middle level of detail. The cup is a clear symbol of punishment, but it has not been more closely identified with a particular nation.

Can this image as used here be more specifically linked to a certain tradition-historical locus? In attempting to answer this question, one may first of all note that those who drink from the cup extend beyond Israel,[72] though this aspect of the psalm does not by itself lead to any tradition-historical definition. The accompanying vocabulary is perhaps a bit more helpful. Thus, the presence of the cup in the hand of the Lord (*běyad-yhwh*) is echoed in certain of the parallels (Isa 51:17-23; Jer 25:15-29; 51:7; Hab 2:16 with *yěmîn*) Further, the specific mention of *yayin* in conjunction with the *kôs* is also paralleled elsewhere (Jer 25:15; 51:7; cf. Isa 51:21). Similarly, the related combination *yimṣû yištû* in the second half of the verse may also be found (Isa 51:17; Ezek 23:34).

These wider linguistic connections point to three prime parallels for the cup oracle in v 9, namely, Isa 51:17-23; Jer 25:15-29; and Ezek 23:31-34. Of these, the Ezekiel parallel is the least exact, since it contains only the *mṣh/šth* as a secondary linguistic support to its use of *kôs* and since it refers to the punishment of Israel rather than the entire earth as in the present psalm. The oracle in Isa 51:17-23 is much closer in terms of its linguistic parallels, since it includes not only the *kôs* and the *mṣh/šth* found in the Ezekiel parallel but also references to *yayin* (v 21) and the divine hand (v 17). The oracle is even ultimately directed to the nations (vv 21-22), although only after Israel's own experience with the cup has been described (vv 17-22). Nevertheless, the extended nature of this oracle would seem to argue for a later stage of development than that to be found in Ps 75:9. Also speaking for this is the fact that when the *yayin* is used

---

[71] It is possible that the imagery stems from the use of the cup in a trial by ordeal—cf. Num 5:11-31 and the work of H. Schmidt, *Die Psalmen* (Tübingen: Mohr, 1934) 144. Such an interpretation is not, however, necessary to account for the image here.

[72] It is, of course, unknown whether Israel had first been compelled to drink of it as in certain of the parallels; cf. Hab 2:15-16; Isa 51:17-23.

in v 21, it is specifically ruled out as the cause of Israel's drunkenness, whereas in the psalm its metaphorical usage is not negated by such a denial.

The remaining full parallel is that of Jer 25:15-29. This lacks the *msh/šth* found in the two preceding examples, but contains the other significant secondary references to the *yayin* and the divine hand. As in the psalm, the wine is here given its full metaphorical dimensions and not negated as in the Isaiah passage. The parallel becomes even more exact if one accepts the LXX reading *akratou* which seems to imply the rare *ḥāmar* found in the psalm.[73] Finally, one may note the fact that the Jeremiah passage is the only unambiguous oracle against the nations among the parallels, and as such it may offer the closest parallel to the present psalm with its apparent supra-Israel reference.

Significantly, there are other oracles against the nations in Jeremiah which also use this kind of cup language (cf. Jer 49:12; 51:7). Jer 51:7 is particularly interesting, since it also contains the secondary features of the divine hand and the *yayin*, noted in both Jeremiah 25 and Psalm 75. Given the central place of the cup oracles in Jeremiah—at the beginning of that book's oracles against the nations and in the critical oracle against Babylon—one might argue for a special affinity for such imagery among the circles responsible for thse oracles. One wonders whether it is significant that this imagery, so promiment here, plays no role in the similar oracles attached to the books of Isaiah and Ezekiel.

Along these lines, one may also note the use of the verb *gd'* to refer to the cutting off of horns in v 11 of the psalm. Once again, this has its closest parallel[74] in the oracles against the nations section of the book of Jeremiah (Jer 48:25), where it also refers to the cutting off of the horn of God's enemies, in this case, Moab. If, as seems likely, the *riš'ê-'āreṣ* of the psalm bear some relation to Israel's—and God's—national enemies, the parellel is almost exact, the only difference being the more specific naming of a single nation in the Jeremiah passage.

These possible links with the Jeremianic oracles against the nations are suggestive in a number of respects. First of all, they provide one of the only tradition-historical clues furnished by the psalm. As such, they point in a direction not unfriendly to the Ephraimite tradition stream noted above for other of the Asaphite psalms—though, of course, it must be said that these oracles against the nations themselves stand in further need of tradition-historical analysis. Secondly, however, the link is suggestive on form-critical and cult-historical grounds, since the present psalm contains prophetic aspects in the shape of first person divine speech. One wonders whether this points to a prophetic role in both the cultic usage of the present psalm and the delivery of the oracles against the nations. The fact that such possibilities correspond to

---

[73] See also Deut 32:14 and the later Isa 27:2.

[74] One might also note the combination of *qeren* and *gd'* in both Lam 2:3 and Amos 3:14, though the context in each of these is quite different from both the psalm and the Jeremiah parallel quoted in the text.

certain descriptions of Asaphite activity found in the work of the Chronicler is even more suggestive.[75] All of these possibilities need to be further examined in the remainder of the present work. Nevertheless, in terms of the present chapter, little more can be said concerning the tradition-historical nature of the present psalm, since its language does not decisively connect it with either its fellow Asaphite psalms or any otherwise known tradition stream.

PSALM 76

On the face of it, Psalm 76 would appear to be a clear exception to the Ephraimite status of certain of its Asaphite predecessors. The reasons for this presumption are, of course, form-critical, since the psalm is accepted by all as a Zion psalm, a genre which would seem to be especially at home among Jerusalemite circles. There are, however, other indications which preclude such an overly easy move from form-critical classification to tradition-historical identity. As might be expected by now, these indications include certain linguistic elements which do not depend on the form and which point in a somewhat different tradition-historical direction.

If one begins the linguistic analysis by looking for distinctive links with the other Asaphite psalms, one unfortunately finds little such evidence throughout this psalm. Nevertheless, one should take note of the reading *pros ton Assyrion* which appears in most of the important Greek texts and which, in a slightly different form, is also to be found in the Greek texts of Psalm 80. One may, of course, debate whether the Greek reflects a primary Hebrew reading which was omitted in the texts which have become the MT[76] or whether the latter is primary and the Greek readings are a later historical specification.[77] Still, it is striking that the only two psalm titles to have this information are also linked by their Asaphite designation. It should also be noted that an Assyrian reference would probably be most apt during the reign of Hezekiah, a king who has certain links with the Ephraimite tradition stream.

In contrast to this lack of inner-Asaphite connections, other significant links are suggested by the psalm's linguistic elements, once again to the Ephraimite tradition stream. One of the most interesting of these is the reference to the *gādôl šēm* in v 2. The reference to the divine name is, of course, a widespread phenomenon in ancient Israel which cannot be restricted to any one tradition stream. Nevertheless, it does seem that the different tradition streams had their own ways of approaching the divine name, as may be seen in the case of the Deuteronomic name theology already mentioned. The present formula *gādôl šēm* may provide another example of such a distinctive approach. In isolating

---

[75] See the holy war oracle by the Asaphite Jahaziel in 2 Chr 20:14–17. This passage will be discussed further in the chapters which follow.
[76] Perhaps for reasons of greater applicability.
[77] As in the titles of such psalms as Psalm 51.

the occurrences of this formula in the Bible, one finds that most of them occur in works with Ephraimite links.[78] On the other hand, when one isolates the occurrences of the formula *šēm qādôš*, one finds a predominantly Southern locus.[79] Accordingly, it is possible that *šēm gādôl* and *šēm qādôš* are parallel terms reflecting different tradition streams. As such, the presence of the former in the present psalm points towards a certain association with the Ephraimite tradition stream.[80]

Another striking link with the Ephraimite stream may be found in the fourfold geographical presentation of vv 2-3. The order of this presentation—Judah, Israel, (Jeru)salem, and Zion—is particularly significant, since exactly the same order is to be found in the judgment oracle of 2 Kgs 23:27.[81] One may even wonder whether the latter is to be taken as a direct negation of the promise implied in the present psalm. It is, of course, possible that this negation is a polemical refutation of a rival stream's promise, though the presence of other Ephraimite elements in the psalm makes it more likely that the present psalm represents an earlier, more hopeful stage in the same tradition.[82]

The list of weapons in v 4 again raises the possibility that a similar order of words may be indicative of larger tradition-historical connections. The language of God's breaking various weapons, especially the bow, is, of course, relatively common throughout the Bible and, therefore, not able to be seen as indicative of specific tradition streams.[83] Nevertheless, the most striking parallel

---

[78] Josh 7:9; 1 Sam 12:22; 1 Kgs 8:42; Jer 10:6; 44:6; also see the later Mal 1:11, 11 which has both Judean and Ephraimite elements (cf. Wilson, *Prophecy*, 290) and which is critical of the priestly elements then in power in Jerusalem. Ps 99:3 is of uncertain tradition status, though one should note the mention of the Ephraimite figure Samuel in v 6. Ezek 36:23 is the only real counter-example, and this shows evidence of typical Ezekiel mixing, especially in its conflation with the next formula to be considered in the text.

[79] Lev 20:3; 22:2, 32; 2 Chr 16:10, 35; 29:16; Ezek 20:39; 36:20, 21, 22; 39:7, 7, 25; 43:7, 8; Amos 2:7. The references in the psalms contain those of uncertain tradition status (Ps 33:21; 103:1; 145:21) along with those which have some links to the Asaphite corpus (Ps 105:3; 106:47). The latter may be an indication of the later nature of these deutero-Asaphite psalms, placing them at a time when some mixing of traditions has taken place.

[80] The more specific question of whether the Deuteronomic "name theology" is present here is difficult to answer, but the parallel of God's making the divine name known in Israel in Ezek 39:7 would make such a presence doubtful at best. One may note in passing that the Ezekiel passage refers to God's "holy" name.

[81] "And the Lord said, 'I will remove Judah also out of my sight, as I have removed Israel, and I will cast off this city which I have chosen, Jerusalem, and the house of which I said, My name shall be there' " (RSV). The Zion of the psalm is, of course, more inclusive than the "house . . ." referred to in this verse, but the parallel is sufficiently exact not to be questioned.

[82] Perhaps from the time of Hezekiah, in accordance with the superscription in the Greek texts.

[83] See Ps 46:9; 1 Sam 2:4; Jer 49:35; Ezek 39:3; Hos 1:5; Zech 9:10; in addition to the Hosea example cited in the text.

to the present verse is undoubtedly that of Hos 2:20 which not only cites most of the same weapons but does so in an identical order.[84] One may also note the weapons list of Hos 1:7 where once again most of the same elements are to be found in the same order, though without their being broken.[85] The tradition-historical implications of these parallels point towards a connection of the present psalm with the Ephraimite tradition stream.

Certain elements of v 9 tend in a similar tradition-historical direction. Among the most interesting of these is God's speaking from heaven. In this connection, von Rad has noted that the presence of God in heaven in itself appears to be a Deuteronomic trait, although he has also admitted that this is not observed so neatly in the cult where God frequently sees or hears from heaven.[86] When, however, one is concerned with those cases of God's speaking from heaven, as in the present psalm, the picture is radically and significantly different. Here there are far fewer examples and those which do exist are tradition-historically noteworthy. Thus, one may find four cases of God's speaking from heaven in what is usually seen as E (Gen 21:17; 22:11, 15: Exod 20:22),[87] one in Deuteronomy (4:36), and one in the "Deuteronomic" prayer of Nehemiah (9:13).[88] Of these references, Deut 4:36 is especially significant since its *minhaššāmayim hišmî'ăkā* is almost exactly parallel to the *miššāmayim hišma'tā* of the present psalm. Together, these parallels point to a consistent Ephraimite usage over a long period of time, as well as to an Ephraimite link for the present psalm.

As may be inferred from the Deut 4:36 reference cited above, the use of the hiphil of *šm'* also has a certain tradition-historical significance. The term, of course, has an independent general usage where it means "proclaim" (cf. 1 Kgs 15:22 among other examples). However, when one looks at those places where God is the subject, the usage becomes much more interesting. In such a vein, one may first note those places in the psalms where God is asked to deliver a favorable proclamation to the petitioner (Ps 51:10; 143:8). How this is to take place is perhaps indicated by the fact that the vast majority of cases where this verb is used also refer to God's talking either to or through a prophet. Significantly, the main loci for such activity are Jeremiah and second Isaiah.[89] Thus, the major

---

[84] One must, of course, note the omission of the *māgēn* in the Hosea passage.

[85] Perhaps even inverting such an action in a positive direction here. Once again the *māgēn* is omitted, while *sûsîm* and *pārāšîm* are added.

[86] von Rad, *Theology*, I, 184, 238. See also Deut 26:15 and Isaiah 63.

[87] See S. R. Driver, *An Introduction to the Literature of the Old Testament* (New York: Scribner's, 1906) 15, 31. Driver does list Gen 22:15 as J, in contrast to the rest of the story which is E. It is possible, however, to see a repetition of the E phrasing of v 11 here, perhaps in the interests of a smooth transition to the second speech.

[88] For the "Deuteronomic" (Ephraimite?) links of this prayer, see again Steck, *Geschick*, 64–77. Deut 26:15 and Isa 55:10-11 might also be seen as implying God's speaking from heaven, but they are too ambiguous to be definitely included here.

[89] Though see Amos 3:9 and 1 Sam 9:27. Isa 30:30 refers to a theophanic storm and not prophetic speech.

pre-exilic reference for such activity belongs to the Ephraimite tradition stream, while its exilic counterpart is one which has often been strongly influenced by that stream.[90]

The prophetic locus for this term is especially interesting in light of its other main usage as a means of expressing human devotion to God. This expression of devotion may be done by the general populace and even by the "peoples" (Ps 106:2; 66:8; cf. Amos 4:5). It is, however, more commonly used in connection with cultic personnel. One may note the explicitly cultic usage in Ps 26:7, where what is caused to be heard is specifically *tôdâ,* which has already been seen to be of some significance for the Asaphites. In the work of the Chronicler, the term is usually used in connection with the singers.[91] Thus, a term which has its pre-exilic and exilic reference in the prophetic material (in the former case, at least, in prophetic material with some connections to the Ephraimite tradition stream) has been appropriated to the singers in the post-exilic work of the Chronicler. The usage in the present psalm is closer to the prophetic model. Still, the fact that the psalm is also linked with the singers by virtue of its superscription raises some interesting tradition-historical possibilities, especially since the psalm is a song of praise, as are many of the seemingly later deutero-Asaphite psalms among which the second usage may be found (cf. Ps 106:2). These possibilities will be considered further in the following chapter.

In contrast to the Ephraimite trend of the linguistic evidence just considered, there is little in this psalm to link it to any other tradition circles.[92] Psalm 76 thus joins with other of the Asaphite psalms that we have seen as exhibiting Ephraimite connections. These connections are especially interesting in the present case because of the form of the psalm. As was noted in the first chapter, once the tradition-historical links of a psalm have been established on other grounds, its form becomes an important datum for further describing the tradition stream of which it is a part. The implications of this for the present psalm will be considered in the following chapter.

PSALM 77

Psalm 77 is in some ways an unusual psalm within the Asaphite corpus. In contrast to the dominant communal spirit of its fellows, Psalm 77 appears to be

---

[90] Other examples of such influence will be noted below.

[91] 1 Chr 15:6, 19; 16:5; 2 Chr 5:13; Neh 12:42.

[92] The term *'anwē* (v 10) is not found in Ephraimite circles and it does occur in Southern prophets such as Isaiah, Amos, and Zephaniah. Still the verbal form is to be found in Deuteronomy, so it is hard to make a firm tradition-historical judgment as to its link here. Similarly, *ybl šay* (v 12) is used elsewhere to refer to a bringing of gifts by the people (Ps 68:30; Isa 18:7), though it is hard to build any tradition-historical conclusions on this fact. Note that Isa 18:7 refers to Mount Zion as "the place of the name of the Lord of hosts" and that it sits loosely in its present context.

an individual lament, a trait which it shares only with Psalm 73. In both of these psalms, however, this appearance of an individual lament seems to be mostly a means for engaging in a more general meditation on a theological problem. Indeed, in Psalm 77 the theological problem so addressed seems to be the contrast between the present fate of the community and God's past actions on their behalf.[93] In such a way, the present psalm has certain communal aspects, even while it retains the voice of the individual throughout.

A more specific structural analysis reveals that the psalm may be divided into two parts. In the first of these (variously seen as either vv 2-10 or 2-11), the "I" of the individual predominates and the appearance of the individual lament is strongest. At the same time, however, the more meditative aspect of this "lament" is underlined by the repeated reference to God in the third person rather than in direct address. In the second part of the psalm, the second person address to God takes over, while the individual recedes into the background. This section of the psalm is usually characterized as hymnic.[94]

These formal and structural aspects of the psalm have been considered at length here because they tend to correspond to the placement of various tradition-historically significant elements throughout the psalm. Thus, it is readily apparent that the language of the first ten verses (vv 2-11) is mostly the stereotypical language proper to the individual lament, with little that can be decisively placed tradition-historically to be found there.[95] In contrast, the remaining verses of the psalm contain several elements that are suggestive from a tradition-historical point of view. Accordingly, it is the second part of the psalm to which this analysis now turns.

Since the form of the first part of this psalm appears to distinguish it from most of its Asaphite fellows, it is especially interesting that some of the most tradition-historically significant linguistic elements to be found in the second part are those which specifically link it to the latter. One may, for example, note the unusual use of the term $ma'ălāl$ in v 12. This word has a heavy, though not exclusive, usage in the Ephraimite tradition,[96] but always with reference to the deeds of mankind. In contrast, both this psalm and its Asaphite successor, Psalm 78 (v 7), contain a rare and possibly exclusive[97] use of this term to designate the deeds of God. This overlapping of Psalms 77 and 78 may also be seen in less

---

[93] See Gunkel, *Psalmen*, 334, and Kraus, *Psalmen*, II, 530. This conclusion is based on v 9.

[94] Again see Gunkel, *Psalmen*, 333, and Kraus, *Psalmen*, II, 530.

[95] Terms like $s'q$ (with a divine object) and $hesed$ have a wide usage in Ephraimite circles but cannot be said to be exclusive there. The best parallel to $m\bar{e}'ănâ\ hinnāhēm$ of v 3 is to be found in Jer 31:15, though little can be made of this.

[96] Especially in Hosea and Jeremiah, though also in Deuteronomic works, in addition to its less frequent usage in non-Ephraimite Southern prophets.

[97] Mic 2:7 is the only other possible place where such a usage may be found, though the answer to the question Micah poses here is a rejection of this term as applied to God.

exclusive fashion in such elements as the divine '*ălîlôt* of v 13[98] and the '*ōśēh pele*' of v 15.[99]

In addition to these links with Psalm 78, one may note other such linguistic elements which have an even wider usage in the Asaphite psalms. One of these which has already been considered is the description of Israel as a *ṣō'n* (v 21). As noted above in the discussion of Psalm 74, this usage provides a good link within the psalter between the Asaphite and Asaphite-related psalms, while its links outside the psalms point fairly strongly to the Ephraimite tradition stream. The use in the present psalm is even more strongly tied to the use in Ps 78:52 and 80:2. In all of these cases the simile *kaṣṣō'n* is used in a specifically exodus setting with a verb of guidance.[100]

Even more significant from a tradition-historical point of view is the presence of *yôsēp* in v 16. Once again, the exclusive locus for this term within the psalter is that of the Asaphite and deutero-Asaphite psalms.[101] As such, this usage seems to argue for some sort of significant connection between these psalms. However, the tradition-historical value of this term goes beyond that of being a connective, since the term Joseph is, on its own, a tradition-historically significant term. More specifically, it is usually seen as indicative of some sort of relationship to the North. Indeed, it was largely on the basis of this term that Gunkel argued for the Northern origins of this psalm and those others which contain the term.[102] While this early "tradition-historical" move on Gunkel's part has not gone unchallenged,[103] the term itself and its Northern associations remain a sigificant tradition-historical datum which needs to be explained.[104]

Although not as impressive as those elements which link this psalm to its Asaphite fellows, there are other linguistic elements in this psalm which may be seen as tradition-historically significant. One may, for example, take note of a cluster of terms which have an affinity with the Song of the Sea in Exodus 15. Exod 15:13, in particular, would seem to have numerous echoes in this psalm, such as in the use of such terms as '*ōz* (v 15),[105] *g'l 'am* (v 16), and *nhh* (v 21). The comparison of God to the gods in v 14 of the psalm also calls to mind Exod 15:11.

---

[98] See 78:11; compare Ps 66:5; 103:7 and the parallel phrase of Ps 9:12 = 105:1 = Isa 12:4 = 1 Chr 16:8. The deutero-Asaphite Ps 105:1 is especially interesting in light of the further similar language contained in v 15.

[99] See 78:12; compare Exod 15:11; Isa 25:1 in the Isaiah apocalypse, and Ps 88:11.

[100] *nhh* in the present psalm. *ns'* in Ps 78:52 and *nhg* in Ps 80:2 (cf. Ps 78:52b).

[101] Ps 77:16; 78:67; 80:2; and 105:17.

[102] Gunkel, *Psalmen*, 325.

[103] See Kraus, *Psalmen*, II, 532-533.

[104] As noted in the previous chapter, Illman's failure to appreciate the tradition-historical value of both the presence of this term in the individual Asaphite psalms and its clustering in them as a whole is certainly puzzling.

[105] '*ōz* is also to be found elsewhere in the Asaphite psalms (Ps 74:13; 78:26, 61; 81:2), though it is not exclusive there.

One final element worthy of note here is the reference to Moses and Aaron in v 21. This is, of course, a common combination in the Pentateuch, where both are central characters. However, while Moses may easily be seen as a prominent figure in the Ephraimite tradition stream, the figure of Aaron would appear to have more Southern links and would at times even seem to be the object of Ephraimite polemic.[106] Because of this, it is noteworthy that the combination of Moses and Aaron as it is found in this psalm is to be found almost exclusively in Ephraimite material, most notably in the Deuteronomic speeches of Josh 24:5 and 1 Sam 12:6, 8.[107] The inclusion of Aaron with Moses here can thus not be taken as an argument against a possible Ephraimite locus for this psalm. On the contrary, it offers a valuable clue as to the more specific location of this psalm within the development of that tradition stream. The question of when such elements would have been found together will have to be deferred until a later chapter.

One should not conclude the discussion of this psalm without some comment on the dual nature of the superscription in which Jeduthun is named as well as Asaph. In view of the fact that the other two psalms in whose titles Jeduthun is named are psalms of the individual,[108] it is tempting to see some connection here with the fact that the present psalm also has certain tendencies in that direction, in contrast to the dominant communal trend of the Asaphite corpus. Further, the fact that most of the distinctively Asaphite and Ephraimite elements occur in the second—less individual—half of the psalm might suggest that what was originally a psalm of the individual from circles connected with the name Jeduthun has been here adapted to a more communal usage in Asaphite circles with the addition of this second half of the psalm.[109]

PSALM 78

Psalm 78 is a monumental work with an historical emphasis. It is also, however, a difficult work to place form-critically. Elements of the hymn[110] and the thanksgiving[111] have been seen in the psalm, as well as elements of

---

[106] See, for example, Exodus 32.

[107] Also note the deutero-Asaphite Ps 105:26; 106:16. Ps 99:6 is a fascinating coupling of Moses and Aaron as priests, which would be most at home during a time of rapprochment between the rival priesthoods, such as the Deuteronomic reforms. (Again note the presence of the Ephraimite Samuel in the same verse.) Mic 6:4 belongs to those chapters of the book which have recently been seen to have Deuteronomic links. See A. S. van der Woude, "Deutero-Micha: Ein Prophet aus Nord-Israel?" *NedTTs* 25 (1971) 365–378.

[108] Psalm 39, a lament of the individual, and Psalm 62, a psalm of trust.

[109] Speaking against this is the apparent structural parallel of vv 2 and 17, though this is far from decisive.

[110] Gunkel, *Psalmen*, 340. Mowinckel similarly considers it to be a hymnic legend, *Psalms*, II, 112.

[111] Kraus, *Psalmen*, II, 539.

paranesis[112] and historical teaching.[113] The most common opinion is that the psalm has a mixed form which was consciously created by the individual psalmist to fit a particular didactic purpose.

In addition to the attempts to describe this psalm form-critically, there have been many attempts to locate it historically. In this respect, however, the variety among the critics has been great, with views ranging from the Davidic[114] to the post-exilic[115] period. This historical endeavor has, moreover, not only been marked by a lack of unanimity but also by an unnecessary tendency towards ascribing to later redactors individual verses which fail to fit the theory![116]

In contrast to these earlier attempts, the present study is not overly concerned with locating this psalm in a specific historical situation. Instead, the emphasis of the present analysis is more strictly tradition-historical in nature. That is to say, the goal is to determine the tradition circles which were responsible for the present psalm. Since these tradition circles span long periods of Israel's history, purely historical analysis is not crucial to the determination of such circles—though, of course, any historical information will be noted. Once again, the primary approach here is a careful study of the linguistic elements of the psalm and an examination of their tradition-historical significance.

A clue to the outcome of this analysis may be found in the fact that most commentators have noted at least some amount of "Deuteronomic" terminology within this psalm. However, by limiting their tradition-historical considerations to those elements which are specifically Deuteronomic, these critics have often been able to confine such linguistic evidence to a few well-marked verses which may then be relegated to the category of later addition. In contrast, when one considers the psalm in the context of the wider Ephraimite tradition stream (of which the Deuteronomic movement is a manifestation at a certain period in time), it is no longer possible to confine the relevant linguistic evidence to a few verses. Instead, one finds a wealth of linguistic similarities to the terminology of that stream, a finding in keeping with that seen in many of the Asaphite psalms considered above. It is to an exposition of this evidence that this work now turns.

[112] Herbert Junker, "Die Entstehungszeit des Psalm 78 und das Deuteronium," *Bib* 34 (1953) 496.

[113] Kraus, *Psalmen*, II, 539.

[114] See Otto Eissfeldt, *Das Lied Moses Deuteronium 32:1-43 und das Lehrgedicht Asaphs Psalm 78 samt einer Analyse der Umgebung des Moses-Liedes* (Berlin: Akademie, 1958), and more recently, Anthony Campbell, "Psalm 78: A Contribution to the Theology of Tenth Century Israel," *CBQ* 41 (1979) 51-79.

[115] Gunkel, *Psalmen*, 341; Kraus, *Psalmen*, II, 539.

[116] See, for example, the analysis of George W. Coats, *Rebellion in the Wilderness* (New York: Abingdon, 1968) 199ff. For a view of the psalm as a mostly unified piece, see Campbell, "Contribution." Campbell still sees evidence of later—Deuteronomic—redaction in vv 5-8, 10, 37, 56b, 58, even though this "does not disturb the structure of the psalm" (p. 52). In a future article on the structure of this psalm, I hope to show that the latter is even more ordered than he has shown here, as one would expect from the uniformity of the following linguistic evidence.

Psalm 78 begins with an eight verse introduction which contains a distinct "generational" emphasis. Because of the many changes in number and person,[117] these verses have often been seen as the composite product of a series of revisions. On the other hand, one may note that the generational interest is to be found throughout these verses, thus suggesting that any such revisions shared a similar purpose and were perhaps carried out by similar theological circles. An examination of the language points to the same conclusion.

One may first of all note the use of the verb *spr* in conjunction with the recital of exodus traditions from one generation to the next, as found in vv 3, 4, and 6 in this psalm. The best parallels to such a usage are to be found in Exod 10:2 and Judg 6:13, both of which are concerned with the fathers' narration of the exodus events to their children![118] Both of these may be seen to have Deuteronomic affinities![119] Judg 6:13 provides a particularly exact parallel to v 4 of the present psalm, where one of the objects being recited to the next generation is God's *niplā'ôt*.

The *'ēdût* of v 5 also exhibits some interesting tradition-historical connections. While the term is common in the Tetrateuch in connection with the ark, the more specifically legal use in which it is separate from the ark is found predominantly in the Deuteronomistic history and the parallel work of the Chronicler![120] The verse's use of *tôrâ* to denote a general body of law instead of individual commands mirrors the usual Deuteronomic use as well![121] Similarly, the combination of the hiphil use of *yd'* with the introduction's pervasive generational intent may also be found in such Deuteronomic passages as Deut 4:9 and Josh 4:22.

Perhaps the most striking tradition-historical clue provided by the introduction may be found in the phrase *sôrēr ûmôreh* in v 8. While the root *mrh* plays an important part in the wilderness narratives of the Pentateuch and the present psalm, its combination with *srr* is rare, occurring only twice elsewhere, with both cases in the Ephraimite tradition stream. Even the usage of this phrase in each of these Ephraimite passages is closely related to the usage in the present psalm. Thus, Deut 21:18 sets forth laws concerning a stubborn and rebellious son, while

---

[117] Note, for example, the first person singular in vv 1-2, as contrasted with the first person plural in vv 3-5. Verses 6-8 are entirely in the third person.

[118] The expression is, of course, used elsewhere with respect to God's actions, especially in the psalms. Ps 44:2, for example, uses it to refer to the conquest, while 48:14 does so with reference to Mount Zion. A previous Asaphite psalm, Ps 75:2, tells the following generations of unspecified divine works, as does Joel 1:3.

[119] For Exod 10:2, see Brevard S. Childs, *The Book of Exodus* (Philadelphia: Westminster, 1974) 142.

[120] 1 Kgs 2:3 (cf. 1 Chr 29:19); 2 Kgs 17:15; 23:3 (cf. 2 Chr 34:31); Neh 9:34; Jer 44:23; also the fellow Asaphite Ps 81:14. One should also note, however, such a usage in Ps 19:7; 119 (often); and 122:4; though the date and tradition status of these are not clear.

[121] See von Rad, *Theology*, I, 199-200. Kraus notes that the correlation of *tôrâ* and history also belongs to this school. *Psalmen*, II, 543.

the present passage is a warning to "sons" not to be stubborn and rebellious (like their "fathers"). Similarly, Jer 5:23 describes the people as having a stubborn and rebellious heart, while the present passage follows the description of the people as stubborn and rebellious with an indictment of their less than steadfast heart.

In addition to these Ephraimite links, one may also note the presence of certain "Asaphite" elements in these introductory verses. Thus, for example, the rare use of the idiom *śîm b* in a legislative context is paralleled in the fellow Asaphite Psalm 81 (v 6). This goes together with the similar Ephraimite use of *'ēdût* in that psalm as well (v 14). The *ma'ălāl* of v 7 has, of course, already been considered in the above analysis of Psalm 77.

The Ephraimite and Asaphite tendencies noted in the introduction continue throughout the rest of the psalm as well. Thus, the description of the people's sin in v 10 continues the series of connections with the Ephraimite stream. Particularly noteworthy here is the use of the verb *m'n* to characterize the refusal of the people, a usage with clear Ephraimite links![122] Particularly striking is its use in the generational passage Jer 11:10, where the iniquity of the people is seen as a return to the sins of their forefathers and a breaking of the covenant that was made with the latter. Once again, the use of the term *tôrâ* to designate a general body of law may be seen to mirror normal Deuteronomic usage.

Verses 12-16 begin the initial recitation of God's mighty acts, again in a generational framework. While these verses contain much that is standard epic language, they also contain certain linguistic elements which give a clue as to the tradition-historical connections of the psalm. One may first of all note the inner-Asaphite links of the phrase *'āśâ pele'* in v 12, as has already been discussed in connection with Ps 77:1. Also significant is the use of the hiphil of *'br* in v 13. Surprisingly, it is only very rarely that either the qal or the hiphil of *'br* is used to describe the exodus crossing![123] On the other hand, the qal is used to describe the crossing of the Jordan in both Deuteronomy and Joshua. The usage of the present verse—the hiphil with God as subject—is also paralleled in the Jordan context of Josh 7:7. Since the latter is probably only meant to be read in the light of the original sea crossing, the use in this psalm may be original, or more likely, may point to a common tradition used in the psalm and developed by the cirles behind Josh 7:7. This would accordingly be a tradition original, or at least familiar, to Ephraimite circles.

This possibility is further supported by the second half of v 13. Whereas the

---

[122] See Jer 3:3; 5:3, 3; 8:5; 9:5; 11:10; Hos 11:15; 1 Sam 8:19; Neh 9:17; also Exod 16:28 which is clearly secondary and which can be attributed to Deuteronomic editing. Isa 1:20 and Zech 7:11 also have a similar usage, though the latter at least is later and possibly derivative from the earlier Ephraimite usage. Prov 1:24 and 21:7 are also in some ways similar, although they do not deal with the response of the people.

[123] See Ps 136:14, a psalm with a refrain similar to that found in levitical circles. Also note the crossing through the hostile peoples in Exod 15:8.

root *ysb* is only used elsewhere for a crossing in the Song of the Sea (Exod 15:8)![124] the *nēd* which follows is found both there and in Josh 3:13, 16, in which latter place it refers once again to the crossing of the Jordan. Although in this case both the present passage and the Joshua passage could be referring back to the usage of the Song of the Sea, the fact that it would be picked up only in these two places once again suggests that this version of the crossing was especially at home in Ephraimite circles![125]

Verse 15 repeats the *bq'* of v 13, though changing it to a piel usage and switching its reference from the sea to the rocks in the wilderness. The combination with the following *ṣūrîm* is paralleled by Isa 48:21, where it occurs in the context of the new exodus and wilderness guidance envisioned by second Isaiah. Again, the question of the priority of traditions would seem to be resolved in favor of the originality of those traditions represented by the psalm, since the Isaiah passage seems to be referring to an already established exodus tradition. That this tradition is one at least familiar to Ephraimite circles is suggested by the use of *ṣûr* in a similar context in Deut 8:15![126]

Verse 17 begins a long section concerned with Israel's sinful response to God's gracious acts. The section contains many linguistic elements which offer clues to the tradition-historical locus of the psalm. One may begin by noting the verb *mrh*, the hiphil of which is often (though not exclusively) found in Deuteronomy, the Deuteronomistic history, and other Ephraimite works![127] Similarly, the phrase *wayyôsîpû 'ôd laḥăṭō'-lô* has its closest parallel in the Ephraimite Hos 13:2, though one cannot rule out a coincidence here.

The verb *nsh* of the following verse is also noteworthy in terms of its tradition-historical connections. The testing of God is specifically forbidden in Deut 6:16. It is connected with the testing in the desert both there and in the Asaphite-related Psalms 95 (v 9) and 106 (v 14). The two Tetrateuchal references

---

[124] And even there in the niphal, unlike in the present verse.

[125] The "guidance" of the following verse is present in most of the epic sources. Perhaps its closest parallel may be found in Exod 13:21-22, probably a J passage, which contains the unusual *'ôr*, though not in exactly the same usage. Deut 1:33 is, however, similar to both the psalm and the J passage, lacking only the *'ôr*.

[126] The *tĕhôm* in the second half of the verse also mirrors epic language, again as found in the Song of the Sea (Exod 15:5, 8), as well as in the deutero-Asaphite Ps 106:9. Nevertheless, the term's use in each of these cases refers not to the rock, as it does here, but to the sea. The same is true of the rock's *nôzĕlîm* in v 16, which refers to the sea in Exod 15:8. The same term is nevertheless picked up again in Isa 48:21 where it refers to water from the rock in a context similar to the present verse. This may be indicative of a certain flexibility of epic language.

[127] Deut 1:26, 43; 9:7, 23, 24; Josh 1:18; 1 Sam 12:14; Neh 9:26; also the deutero-Asaphite Ps 106:7, 33, 43. For non-Ephraimite uses, note Ezek 20:8, 13, 21, though this may once again be due to Ephraimite influence. See also Job 17:2; Isa 3:8; and Ps 107:11. It is interesting to note that the use of this verb in P is always in the qal (Num 20:10, 24, 27; 27:14), although the qal is also to be found in Ephraimite sources.

to testing are suspected of Deuteronomic influence,[128] while Judg 6:37 provides a Deuteronomistic example of the dangerous nature of such testing. The only non-Ephraimite occurrence of the testing of God is that of Isa 7:12, where the reluctance to do so on the part of Ahaz the king is condemned by the prophet Isaiah. This different evaluation of "testing" God may be an indication of a difference between the Ephraimite and Jerusalemite schools of prophecy.

God's reaction to the people's rebellion begins in v 21 with a similar Ephraimite echo. Thus, while the rare hithpael of ʿbr is also to be found in Proverbs and Ps 89:38, its only use in an exodus context occurs in Deut 3:26. Similarly, while the verb ʾmn has a wide distribution throughout the Bible, the charge of refusal to believe in God has a much smaller distribution, and the application of such a refusal to an exodus context a smaller one still. In fact, the latter belongs almost entirely to the Ephraimite tradition stream.[129]

Although vv 23-29 appear to diverge from the punishment introduced in v 21, vv 30-31 show that what appeared to be God's graciousness was in reality a punishment similar to that connected with the quails in Numbers 11. Of particular interest here is the fact that the manna has become a part of the people's punishment. This usage may be closer to the view of Deut 8:3, 16 than to the Tetrateuchal passages, since in the former the manna is seen as a means of "humbling" and "testing" the people. Admittedly, this does not necessarily entail punishment, though it does mean that in Deuteronomic circles the manna signified something in addition to God's gracious care for the people. Similarly, while the term itself is also found in the manna account of Exod 16:8, 12, the sense of *wayyiśbě'û* here may instead be closer to its use in Hos 13:6, where there is a similar tradition of a wilderness feeding followed by an ungrateful "forgetting" on the part of the people.[130]

The account of the people's continued sinfulness and their false repentence (vv 32-37) contains many terms which have a wide usage in Ephraimite circles, such as *drš*, *šûb*, *běrît*, and *g'l*. However, while these words are quite at home

---

[128] Exod 17:7 and Num 14:22. For the former, see Deut 6:16 and Childs, *Exodus*, 306-307. For the latter, cf. even Martin Noth, *Numbers*, trans. by James D. Martin, (Philadelphia: Westminster, 1968) 108.

[129] Deut 1:32; 9:23; Num 14:11b (again cf. Noth, *Numbers*, 108); also the deutero-Asaphite Ps 106:24. One should also possibly note 2 Kgs 17:14 in this context, since the downfall of the Northern kingdom is here seen as a result of being like their fathers with whom God made a covenant and who would not believe.

[130] The *ta'ăwātām* in verses 29-30 appears to be a closer reference to the "Tetrateuchal" account in Numbers 11, where the people's craving (11:4) is later of aetiological significance (11:34). Nevertheless, it is noteworthy that the tradition is already known to the circles behind Deuteronomy (cf. Deut 9:22) and in such a form that it is possible merely to allude to it by its aetiology. It is also interesting that the object of the craving is represented by the general term *'oklām* (v 30), perhaps in order to include both the quails and the manna, both of which are seen here as objects of the people's sinful demands.

in an Ephraimite setting, the fact that they are not exclusive to such a setting prevents them from being of decisive tradition-historical significance in their own right. The use of the verb *kpr* in v 38 is possibly more instructive tradition-historically. Although this term does have a more general secular usage, the cultic usage which concerns expiation for sins is overwhelmingly dominant. The locus of this latter usage is the priestly material of the Pentateuch, the Holiness Code, and the book of Ezekiel. Significantly, however, this priestly usage is distinguished by the presence of a human subject, usually a priest. In the present passage, on the other hand, God is the subject. The use of this verb with a divine subject is much less common in the Bible and its distribution is tradition-historically interesting, if not entirely decisive. One thus finds this usage in the old poetry of Deut 32:43 and in the prayer of Deut 21:8. It is also to be found in Jer 18:23 and in the Asaphite Ps 79:9. The cases cited so far would, of course, all be at home in the Ephraimite tradition stream. The use in 2 Chr 30:8 would also fit with such a tradition connection in certain ways, since Hezekiah was certainly influenced by that stream and is often portrayed in such terms in the Chronicler's account. The fact that it occurs in a body of literature that is not part of that stream proper makes such an identification problematical, though again by no means impossible![131] The presence of such usage in Ezek 16:63 (in contrast to the dominant usage of that book) is perhaps more telling, though once again not decisive, since Ephraimite language has certainly influenced Ezekiel[132] and is especially to be found at the end of his extended units, as in the present case. Finally, one may note the presence of such usage in Ps 65:4, the only other psalm reference besides the two Asaphite occurrences. In keeping with this evidence, then, one may perhaps point to a primary, though not exclusive, Ephraimite locus for the use of *kpr* with a divine subject. In view of the dominant cultic usage of the term with a human subject, one might even suggest the presence of an opposite theological pair, such as was seen with *šēm gādôl* and *šēm qādôs* in Psalm 76![133] It would, of course, be premature to characterize the different theological systems on the basis of these oppositions alone.

Verse 40 begins the second half of the psalm's main body with what appears to be a summary of that which has gone before, while v 41 continues this summary in a way parallel to the first half. In these verses certain important terms are used, one of which is the designation of God as *qĕdôš yiśrā'ēl*. The main reference of this term is to be found in the book of Isaiah where it occurs throughout all of its literary and historical layers. It does occur sporadically

---

[131] Was the Chronicler trying to approximate Ephraimite usage here in keeping with his subject matter? It would certainly seem that he was interested in making certain allowances in this direction because of either his tradition or the contemporary situation (cf. 29:34).
[132] Again see Wilson, *Prophecy*, 282-286.
[133] And on a seemingly non-theological level, the opposition of *šēbet* and *maṭṭeh*.

within the books associated with the Ephraimite stream,[134] as well as elsewhere in the Bible.[135] Nevertheless, the primary reference is undoubtedly to be found in Isaiah, and, as such, is an indication that the psalmist—and possibly the tradition circles behind him— was familiar with, and capable of an occasional reference to, other theological terminology. This crossover, for the most part isolated here, is a precursor of the more extensive mixing of traditions which occurs in the exilic writings of second Isaiah and Ezekiel, as well as in the Pentateuch itself.

Despite this unusual shift into another tradition, the following verse returns once again to the psalm's more normal Ephraimite tendency. The reference to the hand of God recalls the presence of that image in the usual Deuteronomic exodus formula.[136] Furthermore, the connection of this image with the *pdh* in the second half of the verse is even more indicative of Deuteronomic usage as seen in Deut 7:8 and 9:26.[137]

Verse 43 contains two terms which, while not appearing to be significant in their individual manifestations, have interesting tradition-historical connections when used together. Thus, while both *'ôt* and *môpēt* may be found throughout the Bible, their combined use seems to have a formulaic integrity of its own. As such, there appears to be two areas in which the combination is found. It may, on the one hand have its reference to prophetic activity.[138] It is, however, the second usage of this combination in the description of God's activity in the exodus that is especially significant for the present case, since the dominant locus of this usage is to be found within the Ephaimite tradition stream.[139]

The verses which follow the structurally important location *śĕdēh-ṣō'an* once again specify the mighty acts of God whose general mention formed the last part of the indictment of the people. The first part of this detailed enumeration, vv 44-51, is a description of the various plagues inflicted upon the

---

[134] See Jer 50:29; 51:5; Hos 11:9. 2 Kgs 19:22 is part of an oracle by Isaiah.

[135] Job 6:10; Ps 71:22; 89:19; Ezek 39:7; Hab 1:12; 3:3.

[136] See Brevard S. Childs, "A Traditio-Historical Study of the Reed Sea Formula," *VT* 20 (1970), which deals with this formula.

[137] For *pdh* see also Deut 13:5; 15:15; 21:8; 24:18, in a more general context, Hos 7:13; 13:14; also Neh 1:10. In Isaiah it is connected with Zion and in 2 Sam 7:23 with the conquest. The psalms again have a general usage.

[138] See Isa 8:18; 20:3; Deut 13:2, 3. With respect to these cases, one wonders whether there is a difference in the evaluation of these signs and wonders which might reflect a difference between Jerusalemite and Ephraimite prophetic streams. One might also note the use of these terms in connection with blessings and curses in Deut 28:46.

[139] Deut 4:34; 6:22; 7:19; 26:8; 29:2; 34:11; Jer 32:20, 21; Neh 9:10; also the deutero-Asaphite Ps 105:27 and the later Ps 135:9 which may have other Asaphite elements as well. The only use of the combination in an Exodus context which does not appear to have Ephraimite connections is to be found in Exod 7:3. An Ephraimite locus is even more strongly indicated when one looks at the combination of these terms with the divine hand in Deut 4:34; 7:19; 26:8; Jer 32:21.

Egyptians. Critical attention has often focused on these verses in an attempt to determine the extent of the psalm's dependence on the different sources of the Pentateuch. Gunkel, for example, sees in this plague list evidence that the psalmist was acquainted with that work's final form.[140] A. Lauha, on the other hand, sees in these verses an awareness only of those plagues which are normally thought to belong to the J source.[141] It may, however, be questioned whether the parallels are as exact as Lauha's analysis would seem to suggest. Certainly, the order of the plagues as presented in the psalm does not match the order of any of the sources. Further, the parallels in vocabulary are as undependable as those in order. In part, the absence in the sources of such terms as $ḥāsîl$ (v 46), $ḥănāmal$ (v 47), and $rĕšāpîm$ (v 48), as well as their supplementary expressions $wîgî'ām$ and $bĕ'îrām$, seems to indicate a certain independence with respect to the epic tradition. Moreover, while this independence is probably not to be attributed to ignorance of that tradition, it may indicate knowledge of it in another form, as might also be suggested by the different order in this version. Alternately, it may demonstrate a knowledge of supplementary traditions or at least of a high degree of artistic creativity and flexibility, as is suggested by the development of the tradition of the final plague.

Considering these various possibilities, it seems unlikely that a strong case can be made for dependence on any known source. It must be said, however, that these verses which deal with the plagues contain only an occasional presence of the Ephraimite elements which may be found in the rest of the psalm.[142] This does suggest that an earlier source, or at least an earlier set of traditions, is being used. At the same time, however, it is clear that this section is part of the author's original composition and not something added by a later redactor, since its additional length helps to compensate for the extended character of the first half of the main body of the psalm.

Verse 52 moves from the plagues to the further divine acts on behalf of the people. It also returns to the use of terms with significant tradition-historical links. The first example of the latter may be seen in the hiphil use of ns'. This usage is relatively rare and its connection with the exodus rarer still. Significantly, its only other exodus use with a divine subject is to be found in a fellow Asaphite psalm (Ps 80:9). It is also found in the hiphil with Moses as the subject in Exod 15:22. This verse's deviation from the usual priestly itinerary formula has often been noted,[143] as has the Deuteronomic nature of certain additions to the account which follows.[144] If these elements are in some way related, this passage might

---

[140] Gunkel, *Psalmen*, 341.

[141] A. Lauha, *Die Geschichtsmotive in den alttestamentlichen Psalmen* (Helsinki: Druckerei der finnishchen Literaturgesellschaft, 1945) 50–51. Cf. also J. Schildenberger, "Psalm 78 (77) und die Pentateuchquellen," *Lex Tua Veritas. Festschrift für Herbert Junker* (ed. H. Gross und F. Müssner; Trier: Paulinus, 1961) 243-250.

[142] Though note the expression $rē'šît 'ônîm$ (v 51) which is echoed in Deut 21:17 and the deutero-Asaphite Ps 105:36.

[143] Childs, *Exodus*, 266. Coats, *Rebellion*, 47.

[144] See Childs, *Exodus*, 266-267.

further substantiate the Ephraimite nature of this usage. At the very least, however, one may see the overlap of the usage in this passage with that of Ps 80:9 as providing yet another indication of the "Asaphite" links of the present psalm. The latter is especially the case when one considers the *kassō 'n* in the same verse. As has already been noted in the discussion of Psalms 74 and 77, this description of the people is an indication of both inner-Asaphite links and a larger Ephraimite connection![145]

As has been seen elsewhere, many of the elements found in vv 53–54 are also to be found in the Song of the Sea in Exodus 15. Among such elements, one may note the use of verb *ksh* (Exod 15:5, 10), the hiphil use of *bô'*, especially in connection with a mountain (Exod 15:17), and the similar, though not exactly congruent, use of *qnh* (Exod 15:16). Many of these elements are also to be found in contexts which have been seen to have Ephraimite links. Thus, the "credo" of Joshua 24 contains both the *ksh*[146] and the hiphil of *bô'*. The former may also be seen in Ps 106:11, while the latter may be found in Neh 9:23. These and further similarities with other epic poetry[147] provide additional support for the idea of an epic vocabulary which is both pervasive and flexible![148] It is, of course, impossible to base any conclusive tradition-historical connections on such elements. Perhaps the most that one can say is that such vocabulary was both familiar and acceptable to those active in the Ephraimite tradition stream.

The verb *grš* of v 55 is perhaps a bit more conclusive in terms of its tradition-historical connections. One may once again begin by noting the overlap with the Asaphite Ps 80:9![149] Further, one may again turn to the Joshua "credo," where the term is found twice in its description of the driving out of the nations (Josh 24:12, 18). Judg 2:3 and 6:7 also reflect this usage, both passages sharing the "credo" context as well. The Pentateuchal occurrences of the word may be divided into two categories. One is represented by Exod 6:1; 10:11; 11:1; 12:39 and Num 22:6, 11, where Israel is the object of the verb. The other has a usage more similar to that found in the present verse, where other peoples are the object. Significantly, this second usage is found exactly in those sections where

---

[145] One may also note the similar presence of *nhg* in both the present verse and Ps 80:2, though the latter is now found in the qal. A similar exodus usage of this term may be found in Isa 63:14, while Isa 49:10 is an application to the second exodus. Deut 4:27 and 28:37 are possibly ironic reversals of the previous gracious shepherding of the exodus. The use of *nhm* in the following verse (and in v 14) is also similar to its usage in Ps 77:20, though here there are other parallels, some of which are not exclusively Ephraimite (Exod 13:17, 21; 15:13; Deut 32:12; Neh 9:12, 19).

[146] The only other use of *ksh* is in Exod 14:28 (P).

[147] Such as Deuteronomy 32 (as noted by Eissfeldt, *Lied*) which also uses such words as the *qnh* found here.

[148] See especially Dennis J. McCarthy, "What Was Israel's Historical Creed?" *Lexington Theological Quarterly* IV (1969) 46–53.

[149] The only other occurrence to be found in the psalms, Ps 34:1, is not similar.

Deuteronomic influence can be seen![150] The only non-Ephraimite use of this word to describe the driving out of the nations is to be found in the later Davidic "credo" of 1 Chr 17:21.

The combination of *ḥebel* and *naḥălâ* later in v 55 is also worthy of tradition-historical scrutiny. Although the individual terms are common throughout the Bible, their combination in a construct chain is much more unusual. Indeed, such a combination is only to be found in Deut 32:9 and the deutero-Asaphite Ps 105:11 (= 1 Chr 16:18), a fact which is once again suggestive for the tradition-historical links of this psalm.

A final element of v 55 which is of some tradition-historical significance is the *šēbeṭ* of the concluding phrase. As was seen above in the comments on Ps 74:2, this word has a predominantly Ephraimite locus, in contrast to the largely Jerusalemite locus of the parallel word *maṭṭeh*. Accordingly, its use here is yet another indication of this psalm's connection to the Ephraimite tradition stream.

Verse 56 begins the description of the people's new sinfulness in the land to which God has brought them. The section is especially interesting from a tradition-historical point of view, since the specific sins of the people have certain affinities to those offenses condemned elsewhere. However, even the general statements of v 56 are of tradition-historical interest, since they repeat such significant terms as *'ēdût* and *nsh*, terms which have already been discussed in connection with this psalm's introduction![151]

Verse 58 opens with the verb *k's*, a word which occurs in almost every source connected with the Ephraimite tradition stream![152] In fact, its piel usage is almost exclusively connected with that stream![153] and, as such, its presence here may be taken as a positive indication of Ephraimite connections for the present psalm. Significantly, the deutero-Asaphite Ps 106:29 provides the only other occurrence of this term in the psalter![154] The causes of the provocation, the *bāmôt* and the

---

[150] See Exod 23:28, 29, 31 in a section which may be compared to Deuteronomy 7 (Childs, *Exodus*, 486, though Childs makes no claim for Deuteronomic editing here), and Exod 34:11 (in the qal) which is even more Deuteronomic in style (see Childs, 613). Exod 33:2 is more difficult to place, though a Deuteronomic setting is not inconceivable here either. One might also note Deut 33:27.

[151] Verse 57, while not allowing any such tradition-historical statements, is structurally significant within the psalm, containing both the pervasive generational design and a reference to the deceitful bow of v 9.

[152] Hos 12:15; Deut 4:25; 9:18; 31:29; Judg 2:12, along with many examples in the Deuteronomistic history (and its Chronicles parallels), Jer 7:18 and passim. One might also note its use in Deut 32:16, 21.

[153] Out of over 40 occurrences, there are only four possibly opposite cases, none of which is decisive. These are found in Ezekiel (8:17; 16:26; 32:9) and third Isaiah (Isa 65:3). As noted above, each of these may be seen to be open to a certain amount of Ephraimite influence.

[154] The word parallel to *k's* in 78:58, the hiphil of *qn'*, is also noteworthy, since it is to be found only here and in Deut 32:16, 21, where it is also connected with the *k's*.

pĕsîlîm, are, of course, prime objects of Ephraimite and Deuteronomic scorn,[155] though they are not exclusive to this tradition stream.[156]

Verse 59 parallels the similar v 21 as an introduction to God's anger, and the former also includes the tradition-historically interesting *wayyit'abbār* which occurred in the latter. The *wayyim'as* of the second part of the verse is also interesting, since the construction *m's b* with a divine subject is found exclusively within the Ephraimite tradition stream.[157]

God's punishment is initiated in v 60 with the forsaking of the divine *miškan* at Shiloh. As seen above in connection with Psalm 74, the word *miškan* appears elsewhere in the Asaphite psalms, even though its larger tradition-historical connections are more complex. Like *miškan*, *'ōhel* has a predominantly non-Ephraimite reference,[158] though it does occur in some of that stream's sources.[159] The parallel of *miškan* and *'ōhel* may also be found in 2 Sam 7:6, where it refers to the pre-Davidic dwelling place of God, and in 1 Chr 5:17, where it is connected with the arrangement of levites—including Asaph—before the ark.

The following verses continue the account of God's rejection of Ephraim through specific imagery which, despite some problems, inevitably calls to mind the events surrounding the Philistines' capture of the ark, as recounted in 1 Sam 4:5. Thus, the *'ōz* has been seen as a designation for the ark which never again returned to Shiloh after its capture.[160] Similarly, v 62 may be seen as referring to the defeat of the army connected with the ark's capture, while the death of the priests in v 64 seems to be a reference to the deaths of Hophni and Phinehas, as related in 1 Sam 4:11.

It is, however, doubtful whether this reference is sufficient to account for all the aspects of this psalm. The list of offenses in particular would seem to point beyond the time of the Philistine crisis, as would the presence of such a developed Ephraimite vocabulary. It is likely that the rejection of Ephraim here is symbolic of the more radical rejection of the Northern kingdom in 721, while the choice of Judah and David is symbolic of the continued existence of that tribe under a Davidic monarch. In view of the Ephraimite nature of the psalm, it is likely that this monarch is to be seen as either Hezekiah or Josiah, the two great reforming kings of post-721 Judah.

---

[155] For *bāmôt*, see Hos 10:8; 1 Kgs 15:14 and often; Jer 7:31 and often. For *pĕsîlîm*, see Deut 7:5, 25; 12:3; 2 Kgs 17:41; Jer 8:19, and other references under *pesel*. Curiously, there is no such negative reference to *bāmôt* in Deuteronomy itself.

[156] It is nevertheless intriguing that the pre-exilic references to *bāmôt* in non-Ephraimite sources seem to be neutral at worst.

[157] 2 Kgs 17:20; Jer 6:30; 31:37; see also v 67 of the present psalm and Jer 2:37.

[158] Note its overwhelmingly dominant usage in the P source of the Pentateuch.

[159] See especially 1 Kgs 8:4. Also note Josh 18:1 and 1 Sam 2:22, both of which refer to Shiloh.

[160] G. Henton Davies, "The Ark in the Psalms" in F. F. Bruce, ed., *Promise and Fulfillment* (Edinburgh: T. & T. Clark, 1963) 51–60.

The rejection of Ephraim and choice of Judah is described in language similar to that employed elsewhere in the Ephraimite literature. Thus, in discussing v 67, one may not only recall the seemingly Ephraimite idiom *m's b* but also take note of the particular use of this phrase in 1 Sam 15:2 and 2 Kgs 17:18-20. In both of these cases, the context is one of rejection of the North in favor of the South.

The opposite to this rejection is the important verb *bḥr*, which is repeated three times in the climactic last six verses. While this word is used with a divine subject in certain psalms whose date and provenance are uncertain, it is clear that the main pre-exilic locus for this usage of *bḥr* is firmly within Deuteronomic circles.[161] In addition to this general Deuteronomic locus, one may point to a number of specific contexts which closely mirror the present divine choice of Jerusalem and David.[162] The verb *bḥr* is not, however, the only indication of Deuteronomic and Ephraimite connections. One may again point to the use of the more Ephraimite *šēbeṭ* rather than the alternate *maṭṭeh*.[163]

One may conclude this lengthy linguistic analysis with some fairly straightforward conclusions. First of all, Psalm 78 shows many positive links to both the rest of the Asaphite psalms and the larger Ephraimite tradition stream. Secondly, the linguistic evidence which indicates these links is to be found throughout the psalm and cannot be confined to either one section or one level of a redaction process. In such a way, the above analysis both supports those arguments for the essential unity of the psalm and argues for a tradition setting firmly within Ephraimite circles. It should be noted that the latter conclusion is based solely on linguistic grounds without reference to the more conceptual aspects of the psalm's theological argument. The place of such an argument within the proposed tradition setting will be further discussed in the chapters which follow.

---

[161] It is, for example, striking that there is no use of this word with a divine subject in any of the pre-exilic non-Ephraimite prophets. Isa 14:11, the only possible exception, is clearly a later addition. The word is used in this way in post-exilic non-Ephraimite sources.

[162] In the case of Jerusalem, see especially the Deuteronomic phrase, "the place which the Lord shall choose" (Deut 12:5, 11, 14, 18, 21, 26; 14:23, 24, 25, etc.), which is later explicitly identified with Jerusalem in the Deuteronomistic history (1 Kgs 11:13, 32, 36; 14:21; 2 Kgs 21:7; 23:27). For the choice of David, see 2 Sam 6:21 (in which David defends himself against his Benjaminite wife with the statement that he was chosen over all of her father's house) and 1 Kgs 8:15 (where the choice of the Davidic line is connected with the usual Deuteronomic exodus formula). Even more significant than these cases are those passages where both the choice of Jerusalem and the choice of the Davidic monarch are to be found together (1 Kgs 11:13, 32; also cf. 34:36; 1 Chr 38:4; Jer 37:24).

[163] As seen above in connection with Ps 73 and 74, the *miqdāš* (v 69) has an inner-Asaphite reference even though its larger tradition-historical links are more complex.

PSALM 79

Like Psalm 74, Psalm 79 is a clear example of a collective lament. In a similar way, this psalm has been related to the ultimate national catastrophe of 587, although it has also been acknowledged that the language is sufficiently stereotypical as to preclude any really definitive conclusions in this respect.[164] The present analysis will again not be as concerned to locate this psalm historically as to establish its larger tradition-historical connections. Once again, an analysis of the language of the psalm will be seen to be helpful in such an endeavor.

One may begin this linguistic analysis with an examination of the distinctive word '*iyyîm* in the first verse. Although this word may be found in the place name of Num 21:11; 33:44, 45, the primary locus for its independent use is in the book of Micah. In Mic 1:6, as in the present verse, one finds the construction *śîm lĕ'î / lĕ'iyyîm*. The plural '*iyyîn* is to be found in Mic 3:12, where it refers to the predicted destruction of Jerusalem, a destruction apparently being lamented in the present psalm. If these were the only other occurrences of this word, one would have a case for assuming a tradition-historical link with this Southern (though non-Jerusalemite) prophet. However, one also finds this word used one other time, in Jer 26:18, where the words of Mic 3:12 are quoted as a precedent for the destruction prophecies of Jeremiah. This passage is not only interesting in terms of the tradition-historical links of the word in question here; it also provides an insight into how the tradition-historical process (that is, the *traditio*) works. Thus, one may see how the Micah prophecy has been kept alive and passed down by certain circles actually active in Jerusalem a century later. Further, one can see how the prophecy is not only remembered but also used in a new situation. Finally, with respect to isolating the tradition-historical links of the present passage, one may note the significant fact that the circles which have provided the *traditio* for this prophecy are those "elders of the land" which are friendly to the Ephraimite prophet Jeremiah. It is also significant that these circles speak favorably of the Deuteronomic reformer king Hezekiah (Jer 26:19), and that they apparently include Ahikam, son of Shaphan, (26:24), whose family is involved in the Deuteronomic reform of Josiah. From this, it appears that at least one *traditio* of the Micah prophecy was among certain pro-Deuteronomic circles who were friendly to the Ephraimite prophet Jeremiah. Such a *traditio* would also be appropriate for the "actualized prophecy" of the present psalm.

The tradition-historical affinities of the language of the second verse point even more strongly in this direction. The word *nĕbēlâ* is a good indication of such affinities. This word may be used for either an animal carcass or a human corpse. Significantly, such usage appears to be largely determined along tradition-historical lines. While one finds the word used to describe an animal carcass in

---

[164] See Kraus, *Psalmen*, II, 550–551; also Weiser, *Psalms*, 544. The Scandinavian cult-historical interpretation of both this psalm and Psalm 74 will be considered at length in the following form-critical chapter.

such sources as Leviticus and Ezekiel,[165] these works never use it to describe a human corpse. It is mostly the latter use, on the other hand, which is found within the Ephraimite corpus![166] The more normal Southern word for a human corpse is *peger*.[167] Accordingly, the simple presence of *nĕbēlâ* in this psalm is a probable indication of links with an Ephraimite, rather than a Jerusalemite, tradition stream.

The tradition-historical links of this word are, if anything, made even clearer when the rest of the verse is considered. Thus, the description of such corpses as *ma'ăkāl lĕ'ôp haššāmāyim* is in line with what appears to be a set Ephraimite formula.[168] The fact that this formula is always used to describe the horrible fate of the sinful people is quite consistent with its role in the present psalm of lament.[169]

The description of the fate of the people is continued in v 3, where the final phrase *wĕ'ên qôbēr* is of particular interest from a tradition-historical point of view. Once again, this threat seems to be particularly at home in the Ephraimite tradition stream.[170] A similar combination with the threat just considered may be seen in Jer 16:4.

Verse 4 has a tie of a different sort—to Ps 44:14, which is almost a verbatim parallel.[171] The question in this case, however, is one of what significance this parallel has. In such a vein, one may note Ps 31:12 which mirrors the opening half of the verse and Jer 20:8 which combines language from each half.[172] Since

---

[165] Lev 5:2; 7:24; 11:8 and passim; 17:15; 22:8; Ezek 4:14; 44:31.

[166] Deut 21:23; 28:26; Josh 8:29; 1 Kgs 13:22 and passim; 2 Kgs 9:37; Jer 7:33; 9:21; 16:4; 19:7; 26:23; 34:20; 36:30. Deut 14:8, 21 does use *nĕbēlâ* to refer to an animal carcass.

[167] Lev 26:30; Num 14:29, 32, 33; Ezek 6:5; 43:7, 9; cf. also Isa 14:19; 34:3; 37:36; 66:24; Amos 8:3; Nah 3:3; 2 Chr 20:24, 25. Isa 5:25 and Isa 26:19 of the Isaiah apocalypse provide the only Southern examples of the use of *nĕbēlâ* for a human corpse. *Peger*, on the other hand, refers to an animal carcass in Gen 15:11 (J) and to a human corpse in the Ephraimite 1 Sam 17:46 and 2 Kgs 19:35.

[168] Deut 28:26; Jer 7:33; 16:4; 19:7; 34:20, the last two cases also mirroring the present passage's use of *ntn*. Also note the case of 1 Sam 17:46, where the same idiom uses the term *peger* instead of *nĕbēlâ*. The same formula also speaks of such corpses being food for the beasts of the earth, a clear parallel to the present usage despite the fact that the usual word in the parallels is *bĕhēmâ* as opposed to the *ḥayyâ* present in the psalm.

[169] The present passage further specifies the owners of the corpses as *'ăbādekā* and *ḥăsîdekā* (in addition to adding *'āres* to the latter to fill out the parallelism). Such complimentary terminology would, of course, be quite out of place in the judgment nature of most of the parallels, though it is natural to its use in the lament.

[170] For the exact phrase, see 2 Kgs 9:10, where it is used in a prophecy against Jezebel. For a similar threat against the people, see Jer 8:2; 16:4; 25:33; cf. 22:19. For a similar phrase with the verb in the piel, see Jer 14:16. One wonders whether this threat is in some way related to the law in Deut 21:23.

[171] Only the opening verb is different.

[172] Ps 31:12: *hāyîtî ḥerpâ wĕlišăkēnay mĕ'ōd*

both of these latter cases, along with Ps 44:14 and the present verse, occur in the midst of laments of various sorts.[173] there is at least the possibility that the language used here belongs to the form and, as such, is not necessarily tradition-historically significant. Nevertheless, the fact that the parallel with Ps 44:14 is so close may mean that some sort of tradition-historical link should not be entirely ruled out. The fact that both of these psalms are singer psalms may be a further indication of such a link.

Much of the language in v 5 poses the same dilemma. While the verb '*np* has certain links with the Ephraimite tradition stream,[174] its usage here appears to have more in common with the lament form *per se*, as seen in the close parallel Ps 85:6.[175] The same, of course, is to be said for the introductory '*ad-mâ*.

In contrast, vv 6–7 offer a much more significant clue to the tradition-historical links of this psalm, in spite of the fact that none of their individual linguistic units appear to be of much tradition-historical interest. This is the case because these verses are an almost verbatim parallel to Jer 10:25.[176] For the purpose of this paper it is not necessary to attempt to resolve the matter of priority (or common tradition) between these parallels. Rather, the mere fact that they are undeniably related would seem to indicate that the tradition-circles behind each passage were at least in some form of contact with each other, if not directly related.

Like the language of vv 4–5, the petition of v 8 is in some ways common to the form of the lament.[177] On the other hand, certain linguistic combinations may have tradition-historical significance here. One of these is the combination of the verb *zkr* with '*āwōn* which appears to have its primary locus in the Ephraimite tradition stream.[178] As was noted in connection with Ps 78:38, the use of *kpr* with a divine subject (v 9) also seems to be connected with this stream.[179]

Jer 20:8: *lĕherpâ ûlqeles kol-hayyôm*
Jer 20:8; Ps 44:14; and Ps 79:4 are the only examples of the noun *qeles*.
[173] Ps 31:12 and Jer 20:8 in laments of the individual; Ps 44:14 and the present verse in laments of the community.
[174] Though more exclusively in the hithpael than in the qal.
[175] Notably, another singer psalm.
[176] Minor differences include the use of '*al* in Jeremiah for '*el* in the first half of v 6, *mišpāhôt* for *mamlākôt* in the second half of that verse (though cf. the versions), the plural of '*ākal* for the singular in v 7, and the Jeremianic addition of *wa'ăkāluhû* between the two halves of that verse in the psalm.
[177] Compare, for example, the initial phrase with Ps 25:7.
[178] Note its use in the judgment oracles of Hos 8:13; 9:9; Jer 14:10; a similar use in a collective lament may be found in Isa 64:8, a later work which has been seen to be influenced by the tradition stream in question here.
[179] For its use with '*al*, see Jer 18:23; Isa 6:7 combines *kpr* with *ht'*, but the verb is in the passive and so the tradition-historically crucial question of agent cannot be precisely determined.

A number of the more striking elements of vv 9-10—such as the references to the divine name and the question about God's presence—are common to widely varying sources and, as such, cannot be isolated tradition-historically. Such elements of v 11 as the *'enqat 'āsîr,* on the other hand, appear to have some parallels with Ps 102:19, though the significance of this may be form-critical rather than tradition-historical.

One final piece of linguistic evidence to be noted in this psalm is the *sō'n mar'îtekā* of the last verse. This phrase is, of course, also to be found in Ps 74:1, and as such has been discussed earlier in this chapter. Here it may simply be noted that in addition to suggesting yet another link to the Ephraimite tradition stream, this phrase also positions the present psalm firmly within an Asaphite sphere.

In light of the evidence outlined above, Psalm 79 may be said to provide a clear example of a correlation between an Asaphite psalm and elements proper to the larger Ephraimite tradition stream.

PSALM 80

Like Psalm 79, Psalm 80 is widely accepted as an example of a communal lament. Of all the Asaphite psalms, however, the history of research on this psalm is perhaps one of the most interesting for the present work, because of the concern of certain scholars with issues that are in some way tradition-historical in nature. As with the more tentative moves in this direction with Psalm 77, the impetus behind this development may be traced to Gunkel's assertion that the psalm has certain elements which point to a home in the Northern kingdom.[180] In the present case, Gunkel was followed by some scholars, such as Eissfeldt, who elaborated on his theory;[181] while others, such as Kraus, pointed to those elements of the psalm which seemed to indicate a Southern home.[182]

Although this concern for the geographical location of the psalm is undeniably important in its own right, its ultimate fruitfulness lies in the use to which such a determination is put. Most of the scholars who concerned themselves with the geographical question did so in order to determine the historical situation to which the psalm "refers."[183] As has been argued above, this does not seem to be a productive approach in view of the stereotypical nature of most psalms and their apparently repeated use within the cult. However, such attempts at geographical determination can indeed be valuable as an element of tradition-historical—rather than purely historical—research. That is to say, the ultimate concern of such research should not be focused on an individual

[180] Gunkel, *Psalmen,* 353.
[181] Otto Eissfeldt, "Psalm 80" in *Geschichte und Altes Testament* (Tübingen: Mohr, 1953); also see his "Psalm 80 and Psalm 89," *WO* III (1964-1966) 27-31.
[182] Kraus, *Psalmen,* II, 557.
[183] See especially Eissfeldt, "Psalm 80."

historical situation as much as on those circles who were active in the theological definition and subsequent transmission of the present psalm. Such is, of course, the concern of the present study.

One may begin the tradition-historical research on the present psalm by noting the many links with its fellows within the Asaphite corpus. Many of these have already been noted above and so only need to be mentioned here. One may, for example, note the use of $sō'n$ to designate the people, a use distinctive to the Asaphite psalms and those related to them over against the rest of the Psalter![184] Even more important is the designation $yōsēp$ which is again unique to the Asaphite family of psalms![185] As noted above, this term is tradition-historically significant in its own right, and as such it figured largely in Gunkel's placing of this psalm in the North.[186] Also noted above as both a link between the Asaphite psalms and a possible indication of their larger tradition affinities are the '$šn$ of v 5[187] and the hiphil of ns' in v 9![188] Finally, one should again note the unusual $zîz šāday$ of v 14 with its exclusive parallel in Ps 50:11![189]

Some of these elements already suggest a link between this psalm and the Ephraimite tradition stream which has been characteristic for many of these psalms. Other elements individual to this psalm also point in the same direction. One of the most striking of these is the mention of Ephraim, Benjamin, and Manassah in v 3. The listing of these three Rachel tribes, especially in conjunction with the Joseph of v 2, has been seen as primary evidence for the Northern provenance of this psalm.[190] Such a provenance would, of course, fit in well with the proposed Ephraimite locus. Nevertheless, one should not underestimate the difficulties with such a view. First of all, one should note that the combination of the three tribes listed is itself problematical for any actual situation in the history of the Northern kingdom. Thus, while a pre-Davidic setting[191] would appear to be ruled out by the Davidic overtones of v 12, a setting in the period of the divided monarchy is rendered difficult by the historical inclusion of Benjamin with the South. This difficulty is compounded by certain more Southern linguistic elements still to be considered. The tradition setting of this psalm would thus appear to require a closer analysis.

A similar mixing of tradition elements may be seen in the psalm's central image of Israel the vine (*gepen*) in vv 9-17. Once again, the tradition-historical

---

[184] See the discussion of Ps 74:11 above. The term is to be found in Ps 74:11; 77:21; 78:52; 79:13; 95:7; and 100:3, in addition to the present occurrence.

[185] Ps 77:16; 78:67; 80:2; 105:17; in addition to the present case.

[186] Gunkel, *Psalmen*, 352.

[187] See Ps 74:1 and Deut 29:19, as well as the above consideration of the former passage.

[188] See Ps 78:52 above.

[189] Among other less exclusive parallels, one may include the $hôpîa'$ of Ps 80:2 and 50:2 and the nhg of Ps 80:2 and Ps 78:52.

[190] See Gunkel, *Psalmen*, 352, followed by Eissfeldt, "Psalm 80."

[191] As suggested by H. Heinemann, "The Date of Psalm 80," *JQR* 40 (1949/1950), 297-302, and Alexander Roifer, "The End of Psalm 80," *Tarbiz* 29 (1959) 113-124.

links suggested by this evidence are Northern, since one first meets this image in the book of Hosea (Hos 10:1; cf. also 14:7). However, this term is also applied to Israel in Jeremiah, especially in 2:21 where it is used with the *nṭ'* also found in v 9 of the present psalm.[192] The presence of the same usage in Hosea and Jeremiah would thus suggest a home in the Ephraimite tradition stream of which both are a part. This would also suggest a link with that stream for the present psalm. The fact that this terminology also appears in Ezekiel[193] is not in itself damaging to such an Ephraimite hypothesis, since its use there is clearly a later allegorical elaboration of the simpler image and since such Ephraimite influence is not unknown in Ezekiel.[194]

There is, however, one element of the vine imagery of this psalm which is foreign to its usage in the Ephraimite tradition and which may point to at least some links with a different—and Southern—tradition stream. In v 13, the image apparently shifts from that of a vine to that of a walled vineyard. This shift naturally brings to mind Isaiah 5 where Israel is seen as God's vineyard. This possibility is further strengthened by the similarity of the language used to describe the destruction both here and in Isa 5:5.[195] Such language is found elsewhere,[196] though the Isaiah passage most clearly parallels the usage of the present case.

The listing of tribes in v 2 and the image of the vine are two cases whose dominant locus is clearly either Northern or Ephaimite, but which upon closer analysis betray some links to the South. Such Southern links are in themselves, however, no real obstacle to locating this psalm within the Ephraimite tradition stream, since that stream clearly had a Southern locus throughout most of its history.[197] In fact, it can be plausibly argued that such elements as the grouping of Ephraim, Benjamin, and Manassah would be most at home in such times of Ephraimite ascendency as the reign of either Hezekiah or Josiah, since during both periods attempts were made to reclaim parts of the Northern kingdom. The possible link with Isaiah is a bit more problematic since this would represent an opening not just to Southern elements *per se* but to another tradition stream.

[192] Also Jer 6:9 and 8:13.
[193] Especially Ezekiel 17 but also see Ezekiel 15 and 19:10-14.
[194] The vine in Ezekiel 17 appears to signify not so much Israel as its king; cf. also 19:11. The added details of the shade and the branches are striking, although the usage of these terms is very different from their use in the present psalm. If there is a relationship here, it would certainly be easier to imagine the traditions represented by the psalm as having influenced Ezekiel rather than vice versa, especially in view of the already mentioned Ephraimite influence on Ezekiel.
[195] Ps 80:13: *pārastā gĕdērêhā*; Isa 5:5: *pārōs gĕdērô*; each following God's past favorable activity on behalf of the people.
[196] See Ps 89:41.
[197] Note its Southern manifestations in Deuteronomy, the Deuteronomistic history and Jeremiah. Also see Wilson, *Prophecy*, 298-299.

If such an Isaiah link does exist in v 13, it is both alone in the psalm[198] and subordinate to the dominant Ephraimite image of the vine. Even so, such extensions beyond the expected Ephraimite language have been seen elsewhere in the psalms considered above and may indicate a certain limited openness to prophetic elements in the South, even when these are not Ephraimite in nature.[199] The crucial question is, of course, that of whether such an openness has become so great that one cannot speak of a distinctive tradition stream. At least with respect to the present psalm, this does not appear to have happened.

In addition to these two major elements which appear to indicate a connection to the Ephraimite tradition stream, one may note other linguistic elements which point in the same direction. One may, for example, note the *grš gôyim* in v 9, a combination also to be found in Ps 78:55. As was seen in the comments on the latter passage, the use of this verb with a divine subject to describe the driving out of the nations is to be found almost exclusively within the Ephraimite tradition stream.

The use of the verb *nṭ'* with a divine subject also points in the same direction. As has already been noted, the most exact parallel to the use in v 7 is to be found in Jer 2:21 where it occurs in the context of the vine metaphor. However, even the general use of *nṭ'* with a divine subject has a special place in Jeremiah, occurring some nine times there.[200] It also occurs elsewhere in the material of Ephraimite tradition stream.[201] The only other occurrences of such usage are to be found in the Song of the Sea (Exod 15:17), Ps 44:3,[202] and Ezek 36:36. Its occurrence in the Song of the Sea should not be unexpected by now, considering the many cross references between that piece and the Asaphite psalms. Similarly, its occurrence at the end of an oracle in Ezek 36:36 also does little to damage its Ephraimite credentials, in view of the Ephraimite influence on that book. The very similar usage in Ps 44:3 is a more important occurrence, since it might indicate that the term was originally at home within the genre of collective lament—thus making it of formal rather than tradition-historical significance. However, in view of the heavy concentration of this usage within the book of Jeremiah, it is more probably the case that the links are to be sought in this direction. This is, of course, certainly the case for the term's use in the vine metaphor.

Another possible link with the Jeremiah tradition is to be found in the complaint of v 6, where the hiphil use of both *'kl* and *šqh* to designate a divine

---

[198] The *sûḥâ* of v 17 and Isa 5:25 may offer another parallel between this psalm and Isaiah, though most modern scholars emend the former. See Kraus, *Psalmen*, II, 555.
[199] Also see the *qĕdōš* of Ps 78:41, as noted above.
[200] Jer 2:21; 11:17; 12:2; 18:9; 24:6; 31:28; 32:41; 42:10; 45:4.
[201] Note its occurrence in the Balaam oracle of Num 24:6, passed down in the Ephraimite E tradition; in the crucial oracle of 2 Sam 7:10 (= 1 Chr 17:9); and in the possibly Deuteronomic ending of the book of Amos (Amos 9:15).
[202] A very close parallel in view of its inclusion of the similar, though not identical, *gôyim hôraštā*.

punishment is closely paralleled by Jer 9:14 and 23:15.[203] Such usage may in both cases, however, simply be an ironic reversal of the usual use of these terms to denote God's feeding of the people in the wilderness. One should also note the similar image of tears as bread in Ps 42:4.[204]

Two descriptive titles of God also deserve some attention here. The first, the *yōšēb hakkĕrûbîm*, as found in v 2, would certainly appear to be a Southern and even a priestly term, in view of the frequent mention of cherubim in P and Ezekiel.[205] However, it is significant that the actual term in question here with its participial use of *yšb* has a much more restricted distribution, most of it surprisingly within Ephraimite works.[206] In contrast, such a phrase is not to be found in either P or Ezekiel.

The second descriptive element is the familiar *ṣĕbā'ôt*, as seen in v 5. While this term is obviously too widespread to be assigned to any one tradition stream, its distribution does allow one significant tradition-historical conclusion. When one compares the wider use of this term in such Southern prophets as Isaiah and Jeremiah with its almost complete absence from the book of Hosea,[207] it is possible to see its presence here as an argument against a strictly "Northern" provenance for the psalm.[208]

One final aspect of the present psalm which may have some tradition-historical significance is the superscription in the Greek manuscripts, *hyper tou Assyriou*. As noted above, in the discussion of the similar superscription in Psalm 76, this would fit quite well with a tradition setting in the time of Hezekiah and, as such, would suggest certain Ephraimite connections. It is, of course, impossible to determine the status of this phrase, though it is striking that such a phrase appears only among the Asaphite psalms.

In conclusion, then, one may see that the above linguistic analysis has provided a significant clarification of Gunkel's early tradition-historical assignment of this psalm to the North. By noting the many links between Psalm 80 and both its fellow Asaphite psalms and the larger Ephraimite tradition stream, this analysis has moved beyond a strictly geographical classification to an identification with definable groups within Israel's history. The result of this

---

[203] Such unfavorable uses of these terms also occur singly in Jer 19:9 (*'kl*) and 2:14; 25:15, 17 (*šqh*).

[204] As has often been noted, this phrase also has Ugaritic parallels. See Mitchell Dahood, *Psalms* (Garden City: Doubleday, 1968) II, 257; John Hastings Patton, *Canaanite Parallels in the Book of Psalms* (Baltimore: Johns Hopkins, 1944) 37.

[205] Also note 1 Kgs 6:7, 8.

[206] 1 Sam 4:4; 2 Sam 6:2 (= 1 Chr 13:6); 2 Kgs 19:15 (= Isa 37:16); also see Ps 99:1.

[207] It does occur in Hos 12:6. In contrast, the shorter, yet Southern, book of Amos uses the term six times.

[208] *Contra* Eissfeldt who argues that much of the psalm's language was connected with the ark and remained traditional in the North even after the ark went south. The distribution of the term *ṣĕbā'ôt* supports the more likely thesis that such ark language moved South with the ark, where it manifested itself in such pieces as the present psalm.

analysis is quite in keeping with the conclusions found for many of the psalms already considered.

PSALM 81

Psalm 81 is similar to Psalm 50 in that each has usually received the form-critical designation of prophetic liturgy.[209] However, although both psalms contain an extended section of first person divine speech, the material which precedes this speech is different in each. Whereas the introductory vv 1-6 in Psalm 50 are third person confessional statements specifically related to the theophany which follows, vv 2-6 in Psalm 81 also contain second person hymnic injunctions to the community. In this respect, Psalm 81 is even closer form-critically to Psalm 95 which also has both hymnic injunctions and direct divine speech. This comparison is especially interesting since Psalm 95 has already been seen to have a number of ties to the Asaphite psalms. These form-critical connections will be considered further in the following chapters.

Like Psalms 77 and 80, Psalm 81 is another Asaphite psalm for which Gunkel claimed links to Northern Israel, again largely on the basis of the reference to Joseph in v 6.[210] As with those other psalms, this attempt to determine the provenance of the psalm has been disputed by subsequent scholars who have pointed to the psalm's Southern features.[211] As noted above, this discussion as to geographical location is a significant but ultimately insufficient tradition-historical move. Attention must again be focused on the possible tradition circles that lie behind the psalm, the identification of which is assisted but not determined by the psalm's geographical links. In the attempt at such identification of tradition circles for the present psalm, other linguistic elements again offer valuable clues.

The opening verses of Psalm 81 constitute a hymnic call to worship. As such, a number of linguistic elements are determined by the form. Both the opening verbs and the divine titles employed in the first verse appear to be more distinctive of the form than of the theological and literary tendencies of any tradition stream. Interestingly, the parallel of *rnn* and *rû'* is also to be found in Ps 95:1, though not in the imperative, while the same parallel may be found in the imperative in Ps 98:4. Still, given the formal nature of these terms, little can be said about the tradition history of the psalm on this basis.

The musical terminology found in the next verse continues the list of linguistic elements which appear to have a formal rather than a tradition-historical significance. Although one may again note a number of parallels with Psalm 98,[212] these would still appear to be a part of the form.

[209] Gunkel, *Psalmen*, 356; Kraus, *Psalmen*, II, 562.
[210] Gunkel, *Psalmen*, 357, 359.
[211] See Kraus, *Psalmen*, II, 564. In contrast, Weiser is more inclined to agree with Gunkel on the Northern significance of *yĕhôsēp*; *Psalms*, 553.
[212] Especially the relatively rare nominal form *zimrâ* (v 5) in addition to the *kinnôr* and the *šôpār* (v 6).

The three-fold *tōp, kinnôr,* and *nābel* of this verse is a bit more suggestive in view of its connections elsewhere with both the ark and prophecy,[213] though again little definitive may be said, since these elements also appear to have both a secular usage[214] and a place in the larger form.[215] The connection of certain of these instruments with the Asaphites and other singers is also interesting, especially in view of a similar connection with the ark and with prophecy.[216] Once again, however, no definite tradition-historical statements can be made.

The blowing (*tq'*) of the *šôpār* in v 4 is a bit less form-critically pervasive and so at least potentially more tradition-historically informative.[217] The use of the verb *tq'* calls to mind the statutes concerning trumpets in Num 10:1-10, especially in light of the provisions made for the sounding of such trumpets at the beginning of the month (Num 10:10). If this parallel were to hold, it would have considerable tradition-historical significance, considering the restriction of the blowing of these trumpets to the priests (the sons of Aaron) in v 8. This mirrors the usage in the work of the Chronicler which also restricts the trumpets to the priests, as distinguished from the singers and the levites. Nevertheless, it is doubtful whether such a parallel will indeed hold, since in none of these cases are the trumpets mentioned the *šôpār* of the psalm. Indeed, the term *šôpār* has little place in either P or the work of the Chronicler.[218] One may, of course, recall the priestly blowing of the *šôpār* in the battle of Jericho. This is not, however, a feast day, nor is the identity of the priests clear here, given the fact that this is a part of the Deuteronomistic history. Considering the wide range of reference to the *šôpār* elsewhere—especially in psalms which are form-critically similar to this one[219]—it once again seems best to take this as a formal element rather than as a clue to the tradition-historical nature of the psalm.

Like the references to musical instruments, the festival references in v 4 are suggestive in terms of their possible tradition-historical connections. Most critics accept this verse as a reference to the fall festival, the feast of tabernacles, usually on the basis of Lev 23:24 and Numbers 29.[220] Whether one can also on this basis

[213] 2 Sam 6:5 (= 1 Chr 13:8—note the substitution of trumpets for castanets); 1 Sam 10:5.
[214] See for example, Isa 5:12.
[215] See Ps 150:3-4.
[216] See especially 1 Chr 15:16-24 where the singers (although not the Asaphites) are to use their instruments before the ark, and 1 Chr 25:1, where all the singers, including the Asaphites, are to *prophesy* with such instruments. Also note 2 Chr 5:12; 9:11; 20:28; 29:25; Neh 12:27.
[217] While the *šôpār* does appear in Ps 47:6; 98:6; and 150:3, the present case is the only reference to its actual blowing in the psalter.
[218] In P it is only connected with the Jubilee year (Lev 25:9). Its only independent use in Chronicles is 2 Chr 15:14; 1 Chr 15:28 being dependent on 2 Sam 6:15. Neh 4:12, 14 belong to the Nehemiah memoirs.
[219] Again note its use in Ps 47:6; 98:6 and 150:3.
[220] See Kraus, *Psalmen,* II, 563–565; Weiser, *Psalms,* 553. Gunkel sees the possibility of a North Israelite feast here; see his *Psalmen,* 357.

accept a priestly setting for the present verse is more difficult. Certainly, passages such as 1 Chr 23:30-31 indicate that the priests were not the only participants in the festivities mentioned here. Further, as noted above, one should also not take the references to the trumpets too far, since Lev 23:24 lacks the term šôpār.

Equally interesting for these attempts to define the feast in question are the activities which are at home at the new moon. One such activity which may be significant here is the common near eastern practice of seeking oracles at that time.[221] That this practice was also to be found in Israel (at least among Ephraimite circles) is indicated by 2 Kgs 4:23. It is, of course, tempting to see a connection here in view of the prophetic nature of the second half of the psalm. Whether one is justified in doing so will be discussed further below.

Verses 5-6a provide a grounding of what has gone before in the divine legislation. Such a grounding is not unknown to the psalms (cf. Ps 122:4), though the emphatic nature of the grounding here has prompted some scholars to suspect that the cultic action so specified was in some way threatened.[222] Unfortunately, little definite can be said on this issue. However, these verses are significant in another respect in that they mark a shift in the linguistic specificity of the psalm. It is noteworthy that up until this point the psalm's language seemed to provide little information about its tradition-historical nature, since most of the terms were form-critically rather than tradition-historically specific. With these verses, however, this pattern reverses itself, so that much more can be said about the psalm's tradition-history.

Such tradition-historical evidence would not appear to be found in v 5, since the terms found there are common to most of the Bible. Once again, however, one must consider not only the individual terms but also their combined usage. Thus, the triplet $ḥōq$, $mišpāṭ$, and $'ēdût$ (v 6) finds a close parallel in both Deut 4:45 and 6:20 which also combine these three elements.[223] Even more striking is the similar exodus connection of both these passages, the former of which even uses the phrase $bĕṣē'tām$ $mimmiṣrāyim$.[224] The presence of the same three elements in the Deuteronomistic 1 Kgs 2:3 is also possibly significant, although this passage adds $miṣwāh$ to the given triplet.

Verse 6 adds other tradition-historically significant phrases as well. One may again note the Ephraimite use of $'ēdût$, as discussed in connection with Ps 78:5. Also of possible significance is the use of the phrase $śîm$ b as a legislative idiom, a usage which has its closest parallel with the same Ps 78:5.[225] Finally,

---

[221] See Kraus, *Psalmen*, II, 564.
[222] Ibid., 565.
[223] Though in the plural and in a different order.
[224] An especially close parallel to the LXX of 81:6 (*ek gēs*) which is possibly more original than MT *'al-'ereṣ*. The former is also possibly an Ephraimite phrase in itself, though it is used in the Priestly dating formula.
[225] Only here and in Ps 78:5 is this idiom used with a divine subject, though Exod 15:25 is ambiguous and of uncertain tradition-historical status with possible Deuteronomic ties.

one may again note the mention of Joseph here, since this is a term which has both a distinct inner-Asaphite connection and further tradition-historical significance in its ties to the North. Although the latter ties are not sufficient to mandate a Northern setting for the psalm, they at least introduce a Northern element which must be accounted for in some way—perhaps by once again pointing to the Ephraimite tradition stream.

Although the prophetic introduction in verse 6c does not seem to allow any tradition-historical conclusions, this is fortunately not the case for the oracle itself. However, the opening phrase of v 7 appears to have its tradition-historical connections not with the Ephraimite stream which characterizes much of what precedes and follows but rather with the Jerusalemite prophet Isaiah. Thus, the best parallels to v 7a are to be found in the promise oracles of Isa 9:3 and (especially) 10:27, and the oracle against Assyria of 14:25.[226] While it is debatable whether these stem from Isaiah of Jerusalem himself, their occurrence in the Isaianic corpus is yet another example of minor ties in that direction in a group of texts whose dominant tradition-historical dimensions are quite different.[227]

Although the opening phrase of v 8 is paralleled closely by the Asaphite Ps 50:15, the language is common to the psalms and thus unable to be categorized tradition-historically. The language of the verse's final phrase is, however, a bit more significant in that respect. The phrase is, of course, dominated by the reference to the waters of Meribah, a place with an interesting tradition-history of its own. It is, for example, noteworthy that most of the references to Meribah in the Bible recount how either Israel or its leaders put God to the proof there.[228] The present reference is, however, quite different in that it is now God who tests Israel there. Only in Deut 33:8 does one find a parallel to such a testing,[229] in the context of the special consecration of Levi to the priesthood. That the present passage may be referring to this or a similar tradition is perhaps indicated by its place in a list of positive acts done on behalf of Israel by God, beginning with the exodus (vv 6–7).

Exod 15:25 and Josh 24:25 use the preposition *l* rather than *b* to designate those for whom the laws were made. See also Prov 8:29 and Isa 42:4.

[226] There are certain differences between these and the present case—thus the latter has the use of the hiphil rather than the qal, *šikmô* as the direct object rather than the object of *mē'al*, and *sēbel* as the object of *mn* rather than the direct object—though the parallel is unquestionable.

[227] Also note the *qĕdôš* of Ps 78:41, the possible vineyard imagery of Ps 80:13, and the use of Micah terminology in Ps 79:1.

[228] Exod 17:7; Num 20:13, 24; 27:14; Deut 32:51; Ps 95:8; 106:22. Ezek 47:19 and 48:28 are "neutral" references to Israel's ideal boundary. Also note the testing of the people at Marah in Exod 15:25.

[229] Even there the word for "test" is different; *nsh* rather than the *bḥn* of the present verse.

With v 9 the focus shifts from God's past gracious actions to a present warning of Israel. The opening phrase of this divine admonition is of some tradition-historical interest. One may first of all note the particularly close parallel of Ps 50:7 which contains both the imperative of *šm'* with "my people" as addressee and the first person divine warning followed by a self-revelation formula (see 81:11).[230] The Ephraimite possibilities of the hiphil of *'ôd* with a divine subject have already been noted in connection with this parallel, as has its appropriateness for such prophetic psalms as Psalms 50 and 81.

One should also underline the particularly close similarities between the present passage and Jer 11:7. The latter not only has both a similar (and even more emphatic) use of *'ûd* but also an exodus reference and an indictment for not obeying the divine voice (Jer 11:7; see Ps 81:12) and for walking in the stubborness of their heart (Jer 11:8; see Ps 81:13). The function of solemn warning was apparently seen to be especially appropriate to Ephraimite prophets such as Moses, Samuel, and Jeremiah.[231] This is, of course, suggestive for both the tradition-historical and formal description of the present psalm.

Verse 10 follows this warning with an apodictic rejection of other gods. The language of this apodictic injunction is once again tradition-historically significant, particularly in the second half of the verse.[232] There one finds the phrase *'ēl nēkār* whose primary locus is the Ephraimite tradition stream.[233] The *lō' tištaḥāweh* is also interesting in this respect, since it is connected with the worship of other or foreign gods (as opposed to either idols or the host of heaven) almost exclusively in the Ephraimite tradition stream.[234] The parallel with Deut 8:19 is particularly interesting in this respect since it is part of a divine warning (using *'ûd*) and an accusation of not listening to the voice of God, both of which also occur in the present psalm.

---

[230] The *šĕma' 'ammî* is perhaps worthy of note in its own right, since it calls to mind the important vocative of Deut 4:1; 5:1; 6:4; 9:1; etc. However, this usage is much too wide to make any definite tradition-historical statements on its basis alone.

[231] See Exod 19:21 for a warning by Moses which is the same warning as that of God in Exod 19:23. Deut 4:26; 8:17; 31:17, 28; 32:46 contain similar Mosaic warnings. 1 Sam 8:9 shows a similar warning by Samuel, as Jer 11:7 does for Jeremiah. Also note 2 Kgs 17:13 and Neh 9:26, 27, 30 for general statements of warning by (Ephraimite) prophets. On the other hand, Amos 3:13 is non-Ephraimite, though it does take place in the North.

[232] The closing phrase of the first part of the verse, *'ēl zār*, is suggestive, though not distinctive enough to indicate a tradition-historical link of its own. See Deut 31:16; Ps 44:21; Isa 43:12; Jer 2:25; 3:13; (5:19); Ezek 16:32.

[233] Gen 35:2, 4 (E); Deut 31:16; 32:12; Josh 24:20, 23; Judg 10:16; 1 Sam 7:3; Jer 5:19. Also note the later Mal 2:11; Dan 11:39; and 2 Chr 33:15.

[234] For its use with the worship of other gods, see Exod 23:24; 34:14; Deut 8:19; 11:16; 17:3; 29:25; 30:17; Josh 23:7, 16; Judg 2:12, 17, 19; 1 Kgs 9:6, 9 (= 2 Chr 7:19, 22); 11:33; 16:31; 22:54; 2 Kgs 5:18 and passim; 17:35; Jer 13:10; 16:11; 22:9; 25:6. For its use with idols, see Exod 20:5; 32:8; Lev 26:1; Deut 5:9; 2 Kgs 21:21; Isa 2:8, 20; 44:15, 17; Jer 1:16; Ps 106:19. 2 Chr 24:18 has both idols and Asherim. For its use with the host of heaven and the like, see Deut 4:17; 2 Kgs 17:6; 21:3; Jer 8:2; Ezek 28:16; Zeph 1:5; 2 Chr 33:3.

The phrases of v 11 also deserve some comment despite the fact that they are for the most part common throughout the Bible. Perhaps the key to any tradition-historical distinctiveness in this verse is the phrase *hamma'alkā mē'ereṣ miṣrāyim*. Like the introductory self-revelation formula, this phrase has a wide usage. However, when one looks at how this language is used in oracles of judgment or warning such as in the present psalm, an interesting pattern begins to emerge. One can isolate in certain places a two part sequence of divine deliverance (using this formula) followed by the people's ungrateful response. While this pattern is too varied to be a form or even a formula, it does seem to restrict itself to a certain tradition stream, namely the Ephraimite.[235] In several of these parallels, language similar to that of the present psalm is used.[236] The fact that this pattern often occurs in prophetic oracles is, of course, quite appropriate for its usage in the present psalm.

Israel's ingratitude to God's divine acts shows itself first of all in the refusal to obey the voice of God. It is instructive to note where else such concern for obedience to the divine voice (*qôl*) occurs in the Bible. After a few occurrences in the Tetrateuch, the expression is found almost exclusively in Ephraimite sources, especially in the books of Deuteronomy and Jeremiah. In contrast, it is rarely found in first Isaiah[237] or in Ezekiel. In fact, the only occurrences of this phrase in strictly Jerusalemite circles are Hag 1:12 and Zech 6:15, spoken by two prophets who appear to have self-consciously taken over certain speech forms of their rivals.[238] Significantly, it is almost exclusively with the Asaphite and deutero-Asaphite psalms that such usage is to be found in the psalter.[239]

Verse 13 continues the divine indictment of the people once again in Ephraimite terms. One should especially note the phrase *bišrîrût libbām*, since this is an exclusive Ephraimite reference,[240] admitted even by those who are reluctant to categorize the psalm tradition-historically.[241] The combination of this phrase with the second half of the verse makes the parallel with Jer 7:24 a particularly close one.

In contrast to the language used to describe the divine activity and the people's ungrateful response, the language of promise in the final four verses is not very tradition-historically specific. One may point to a few similarities

---

[235] See Judg 2:1; 6:8; 1 Sam 10:18 (cf. 8:8; 12:6); 2 Kgs 17:36-40; Jer 11:7; Hos 12:14; Amos 2:10 is possibly part of the Deuteronomic redaction of that book.

[236] Note, for example, the already mentioned Jer 11:7, as well as Judg 2:1; 6:8; 2 Kgs 17:40 among others.

[237] It is not common in the entire book of Isaiah either, though it does appear in Isa 28:23 and the later Isa 66:8.

[238] See Hanson, *Dawn*, 245.

[239] It appears here, in Ps 95:7, and in Ps 106:25, though in Ps 103:20 the "angels" do obey.

[240] Deut 29:18; Jer 3:17; 7:24; 9:13; 11:8; 13:10; 16:12; 18:12; 23:17. Also note that it is usually used with *hlk*, a word to be found in the parallel half of the present verse.

[241] Illman, *Thema*, 47.

between v 17 and both Deut 32:13-14 and Ps 147:14,[242] but such language may be proper to blessing language *per se* rather than to any tradition-historical link. The same may also be true of the rest of the promise here.

In conclusion, then, Psalm 81 may be seen to have definite linguistic links to both its fellow Asaphite psalms and to the larger Ephraimite tradition stream. Such language is not sporadic or occasional, as is claimed by some critics.[243] Rather, it is remarkably plentiful and definitive. Significantly, it is to be found in both the introductory and the oracular sections of the psalm, although in places language more specific to the form has left little room for tradition-historically specific language. The evidence is such, however, to make Psalm 81 one of the clearest examples of Ephraimite linkage among the Asaphite psalms.

PSALM 82

Psalm 82 is similar to a number of the Asaphite psalms considered so far in that it can be categorized as a "prophetic" psalm distinguished by a section of first person divine speech. In contrast to these other psalms, however, the divine speech section of Psalm 82 is not addressed to the people of Israel (Psalm 81) or to various elements therein (Psalm 50). Neither is it in the first instance addressed to Israel's national enemies or to the overall "wicked of the earth" (Psalm 75). Instead it is addressed to the *'ĕlōhîm* in the midst of the divine council (*baʻădat-'ēl*), a situation almost unknown elsewhere in the Bible.[244]

Given the distinctive theological stance of this psalm, it is both notable and unfortunate that its language does not appear to provide any clue as to the tradition circles in which it was at home. Indeed, the language used throughout is language common to almost all the streams present in the Bible. The comparative brevity of the psalm is perhaps a contributing factor to the lack of tradition-historically specific elements.

One must, of course, still note certain linguistic parallels which are tradition-historically suggestive, even though in almost every case, little can be seen that is in such a way decisive. Thus, for example, the *niṣṣāb* of the first verse has its best parallel in Isa 3:13, where God judges those who have despoiled the

---

[242] Thus, both the present verse and Ps 147:14 mention the *ḥēleb ḥittâ/ḥittîm*, and the latter also has the verb *šbʻ*, though not in exactly the same connection. Deut 32:13-14, on the other hand, mentions both honey and wheat, though the latter occurs in the more elaborate phrase *ḥēleb kilyôt ḥittâ*.

[243] Illman, *Thema*, 48, 63.

[244] Though Ps 58:2 may be a possible parallel, depending on how one understands (and points) the *'lm* there. On the divine council in Israel and its world, see E. Theodore Mullen, *The Divine Council in Canaanite and Early Hebrew Literature* (HSM 24; Chico, CA: Scholars, 1980. Cf. esp. pp. 226-44 for issues related to Psalm 82. One might also mention the earlier study of Julian Morgenstern, "The Mythological Background of Psalm 82," *HUCA* 14 (1939) 29-126, though its conclusions are too speculative to be accepted generally. On this see Roger T. O'Callaghan, "A Note on the Canaanite Background of Psalm 82," *CBQ* 15 (1953) 311-14.

poor of Israel. Although this verb is used of God elsewhere,[245] the Isaiah passage is the only example of such an overtly judicial setting. The object of God's judgment there is not, however, the gods, as in the present psalm, but rather "peoples" (MT) or God's people (versions). Thus, while the parallel is by no means tradition-historically worthless, it does not appear to be a sufficient basis on which to assert a decisive tradition-historical link.

The *'ādat* in the same verse is similar. The usage of this term to denote Israel has already been discussed in connection with Ps 74:2. The present usage for the assembly of the gods is, on the other hand, unique.[246] Suggestive, however, is its use elsewhere in connection with the assembly of the peoples.[247] Together with the MT of Isa 3:13 and certain elements to be considered later in the psalm, this usage raises certain possibilities for the function of this psalm within ancient Israel. Unfortunately, however, this usage does not appear to be distributed along any clear tradition-historical lines.

With respect to the *'āwel* in v 2, it is even uncertain as to what exactly is the best parallel. In view of the general accusation of the present psalm, one must certainly take notice of the use of this term in the legal and "judicial" settings of Lev 19:15, 34 and the similar, though less exact, Deut 25:16.[248] On the other hand, it is striking that most of the attributes which the gods are found not to possess are, in fact, seen elsewhere to be attributes of Israel's God. One may perhaps point to those cases where God is asserted to be without *'āwel* as an implicit parallel to the present usage.[249] Given such ambiguity, it is even more difficult to determine the exact tradition-historical locus for the first half of v 2.

Similar difficulties are to be found in the second half of this verse as well. The expression *nś' pĕnê* is also to be found in Lev 19:15, thus seemingly providing a strong connection between these examples. However, the forbidden object of partiality in Lev 19:15 is the poor (*dal*), in striking contrast to the concerns of the present psalm (vv 3-4). Prov 18:5, on the other hand, is a much more exact parallel, since it too condemns partiality towards the wicked (*rāšā'*). In view of the implicit contrast in the present psalm between God and the gods, one must also mention Deut 10:17 as a strong parallel, since in it the Lord is both God of gods and one who does not show such partiality.[250] Once again, it is difficult to affirm a decisive tradition-historical locus here.

Similarly, the terms in vv 3-4 have little tradition-historical specificity. The concern for the poor (*dal*) is a common element of the wisdom books (especially Proverbs and Job). Perhaps not coincidentally, the Southern prophets Amos and

---

[245] Gen 28:13; Num 22:23, 31, 34; Amos 7:7; 9:1.
[246] Though, of course, not in the ancient near east.
[247] Ps 7:8; 68:31; Jer 6:18.
[248] Lev 19:15, 35 also have the term *mišpāṭ* which is lacking in Deut 25:16. None of these cases have *'āwel* as the object of the verb *špṭ*.
[249] See for *'āwel*, Deut 32:4; Jer 2:5. If one also considers the similar *'awĕlâ*, one may find other parallels as well, such as 2 Chr 19:7; Ps 92:16; Zeph 3:5.
[250] Job 34:19 is a similar denial of such partiality for God.

Isaiah are especially critical of the the oppression of the poor.[251] Such a usage is also found in the psalms (Ps 41:2; 72:13), as is the confession of God as the protector of the poor (Ps 113:7). The latter is also to be found in such places as 1 Sam 2:8 and Job 34:19 and may once again form the basis for the implicit comparison of the present psalm. Finally, one must again mention the use of *dal* in Lev 19:15, though the emphasis is very different from that of the present psalm and the other cases listed here.[252] Considering all of this, it would seem difficult to isolate concern for the poor as a distinguishing feature of any one tradition circle.

The attempt at tradition-historical distinctiveness is even more difficult with respect to the other terms used in these verses. All are common in Psalms and Proverbs, as well as being spread throughout the rest of the Bible. Similarly, all seem to be at home both with judical language on the one hand and in confessions of God's attributes on other.[253] In any event, little tradition-historical weight can be placed on such terms and their usage here.

The final phrase of v 5 is a bit more distinctive than those found in the preceding verse. Still, this distinctiveness does not appear to lead to tradition-historical conclusions as much as to conclusions of a form-critical nature. Thus, one may note that the verb *môṭ* is often used in connection with direct divine speech to describe the effects of that speech on the world.[254] Yet, in other places God is the guarantee that the earth shall not be so moved.[255] The term *môsād* has a similar double usage.[256] The fact that the present use of these terms is similar to their use in connection with direct divine speech may be seen as indicative of language common to a particular form.

The language of vv 6-7 is obviously too common to have any tradition-historical significance on its own, even though the thoughts expressed there are almost unique to this psalm. The last half of v 8 is, however, a bit more intriguing in this respect. The most interesting aspect of this verse is the use of the verb *nḥl* with God as a subject and the nations as some form of object (after *b*). The only real parallel to this usage is to be found in Deut 32:8, where what is undoubtedly the original reading is concerned with the division of the nations according

---

[251] See especially Isa 10:2; Amos 2:7; 4:1; 5:11; 8:6; also cf. Isa 11:4.

[252] See Exod 23:3.

[253] The best parallel to the use of *yātôm* here is possibly Isa 1:17 (cf. v 23), where it is the object of the imperative of *špṭ*. One may also note, however, the similar use in Jer 5:28 (with the imperative *dîn*) as well as such cases as Deut 10:18, where it is God who *'ōśeh mišpāṭ yātôm* (cf. 24:17; 23:19). Many other parallels could be cited here (cf. for example Ps 10:14, 18). Similarly, the judicial use of *haṣdîqû* may be seen to have its best parallels in Deut 25:1 and 1 Kgs 8:32, in the latter of which it is applied to God. Nevertheless, one can also note such similar cases as Exod 23:7; Prov 17:15, and Isa 5:23 which make any tradition-historical conclusions difficult.

[254] Ps 46:3, 7; 60:4; cf. Isa 24:19.

[255] Ps 93:1; 96:10 (= 1 Chr 16:30); 104:5.

[256] Compare such cases as Deut 32:22; 2 Sam 22:8, 16 (= Ps 18:8, 16); Isa 24:18; with the usage of Prov 8:29 (Isa 40:21); Jer 31:37; Mic 6:2.

to the "sons of God" (see LXX and Deut 4:19). What makes this parallel so intriguing here are those previous hints which suggest that the nations are also involved in the judgment of the present psalm. In such a vein, this psalm may not be a purely theological polemic but may also be to some degree an oracle against the nations in which the fate of the nations' protective deities mirrors their own fate once God arises to "judge the earth."[257] However, even if this suggestion has some validity, one has again not described the tradition-historical nature of the psalm as much as its formal status, since the reference to Deut 32:8 is not strong enough a basis by itself on which to make any decisive tradition-historical comments.

In conclusion, then, it may be said that the theological and poetic distinctiveness of Psalm 82 is not matched by a similar linguistic distinctiveness which might lead to any decisive tradition-historical conclusions. In terms of the larger task of determining the tradition-history of the Asaphite psalms as a whole, Psalm 82 is, in effect, a neutral datum. With respect to the already observed Ephraimite tendencies of these psalms, Psalm 82 furnishes neither supportive nor contradictory evidence. Its theology may, of course, be seen to be similar to that expressed in certain Ephraimite sources,[258] but it is part of the methodological caution of this study not to base its tradition-historical judgments on a criterion so open to diverse interpretation. Accordingly, in the present case, the tie to the Asaphite psalms (and possibly to the Ephraimite tradition stream of which some of these are a part) rests on the superscription alone.

PSALM 83

With Psalm 83, one returns to the genre of collective lament, a genre which has been seen to have a prominent place in the Asaphite psalms. The present psalm does, however, present some striking differences from the previous Asaphite examples of this form, most notably in the specificity with which the national enemies are named in vv 7-9. It is this specificity which has been at the root of most of the critical discussion of this psalm, with older critics attempting to determine the historical situation which would accommodate the enemies listed in these verses[259] and more recent critics advocating a "cultic" or poetic solution to the problem.[260] In this, the latter are certainly closer to the truth, since the combination of opposing forces in vv 7-9 better fits a poetic attempt at comprehensiveness than any hypothetical historical situation. As has often been noted, the threat here is similar to the semi-mythological *Völkersturm* in

---

[257] See Amos' cataloguing of the offenses of the nations as the grounds for their judgment by God (Amos 1-2). Also note the similar views of M. Tsevat, "God and Gods in Assembly: An Interpretation of Psalm 82" *HUCA* XL-XLI (1969-1970) 123-137.

[258] Note especially the view of other gods as the minor deities of the nations in Deut 4:19 and 32:8 (LXX).

[259] So even Gunkel, *Psalmen*, 364-365.

[260] See Kraus, *Psalmen*, II, 577.

which a wide array of national enemies threaten either Israel or Zion but are then thoroughly defeated by Israel's God.[261] This is not to say, however, that the list of specific enemies is devoid of historical—or tradition-historical—interest. Rather, the names of the enemies which comprise the *Völkersturm* in this case may give real clues as to the historical—or tradition-historical—standing of the "author." In such a vein, the presence of a number of Southern enemies has usually been taken to indicate a Judean setting, although the presence of elements such as Tyre keeps the picture from being completely uniform.[262] In terms of temporal implications, the presence of Assyria in this list—together with the omission of Babylon—has been taken as an indication of a pre-exilic setting.[263]

Both of these historical assessments may well be correct, although one can never rule out the presence of consciously archaic elements which would make difficult any definitive temporal placement. In any event, in tradition-historical terms such an historical location is not sufficient in itself. Rather, it must be viewed as only the first step towards a more comprehensive tradition-historical definition of the piece. In this, one must consider not only vv 7–9 but also the evidence provided by the rest of the psalm. Once again, the language of the psalm may be seen as one of the most significant of these tradition-historical elements.

Having said this, however, it must be noted that much of the language of the call to attention (v 2) and the general complaint (vv 3–9) is more indicative of the form of lament than of any specific tradition-historical significance. Where such formal influence does not dominate, the language is either common to the entire Bible or unique to the present psalm. One possible exception to this pattern is the second half of v 5. The best parallels to this half verse are Jer 11:19; Hos 2:19; and Zech 13:2, all of which combine the elements, *šēm, lōʾ, ʿôd,* and the niphal of *zkr.* The closest of these parallels is Jer 11:19 which has a very similar phrase (*ûšmô lōʾ-yizzākēr ʿôd*) in a quotation by adversaries in the midst of a lament. Also striking in conjunction with this is the similarity of the immediately preceding section of this threat with the preceding section of the threat in Ps 83:5: *wĕnikrĕtennû mē ʿereṣ hayyîm* (Jer 11:19); *wĕnakhîdēm miggôy* (Ps 83:5). Each imply a separation of the lamenter from his existence. Both Hos 2:19 and Zech 13:2 have certain structural similarities with this usage,[264] though the subject matter is quite different—these being not laments but oracles against idols.

If only the Jeremiah parallel were to be considered here, one might argue that the similar usage was proper to the genre of lament. Even so, it would be striking that the only real parallel would occur in the Ephraimite tradition

---

[261] Ibid., 577.
[262] Ibid., 577, though compare Gunkel, *Psalmen,* 364–365.
[263] Kraus, *Psalmen,* II, 577; Weiser, *Psalms,* 563. Again compare Gunkel, *Psalmen,* 365.
[264] Notably the *min* and the verb of separation.

stream. However, the link to Hosea in a completely different literary setting would appear to both downplay the merely formal nature of this link and upgrade its tradition-historical significance. Zech 13:2 is, of course, a later work, although it is by no means antithetical to the Ephraimite tradition stream.[265]

The specific complaint detailing Israel's enemies in vv 7-9 is unfortunately difficult to pin down tradition-historically. Again, most of the enemies are common both to many periods of Israel's history and many parts of the Bible. While a few, such as the Hagrites, are less common, these still provide little decisive historical evidence.[266] One might, however, take notice of the phrase *bĕnê-lôṭ* in v 9, since its only occurrence outside the etiological story in Gen 19:30-38 is to be found in the Ephraimite tradition stream (Deut 2:9, 19). Nevertheless, since the latter's positive usage contrasts sharply with the negative tone of both the original etiology and the present psalm, it would perhaps be best not to place much weight on this.

Verse 10 begins the petition section of the psalm with a series of names as specific as those in the verses which have just been considered. There is, however, an interesting and possibly tradition-historically significant difference between these two lists. Whereas the national enemies detailed in vv 7-9 may be seen as having a predominantly Southern locus, those named in vv 10-13 belong to the North. Even more significantly, most of the latter are only known because of their preservation in the Ephraimite Deuteronomistic history. Thus, the events surrounding Sisera, Jabin, and the Wadi Kishon are recounted in Judges 4-5, while those involving Oreb, Zeeb, Zebah, and Zalmunna are to be found in Judges 6-8. The reference to Midian also probably pertains to the latter chapters of Judges as well.[267]

Since all of the events connected with these names concern both specific Northern tribes and only Northern tribes, it would appear likely that their tradition-history at least originates in the North. The presence of such stories in the Deuteronomistic history would indicate that these events continued to be remembered within the Ephraimite tradition stream. Their continued life in this stream is also attested to by the mention of Jabin and Sisera (as well as Jerubaal) in the Deuteronomic "credo" of 1 Samuel 12.

That these terms were at home in the Ephraimite tradition stream is then both natural and unquestionable. Whether they belonged exclusively to that

---

[265] See Hanson, *Dawn*, 281; also see Ezek 21:37; 25:10, for less exact parallels with no *šēm* or *'ôd*, though they do refer to the nations rather than Israel.

[266] Thus, while it is interesting to note that the Hagrites are the opponents of Northern tribes in 1 Chr 5:10, 19, 20, there are certainly grounds to link them to the South as well (cf. Genesis 16).

[267] Although it is just possible that it could refer to conflicts with that country in the Mosaic period (cf. Num 22:4, 7; 31:3, 7, 8; Josh 13:21). The argument for the Midian conflict in Judges is its compatability with the other events mentioned here. The argument for the Numbers tie is the presentation of Midian before the events of Judg 4-5, rather than afterwards, as one would expect in a strictly chronological recounting.

stream is a bit more difficult to determine. Most of the terms have no reference outside that stream. However, for Midian and Oreb one must also consider two references in Isaiah (Isa 9:3 and 10:26). These passages are both in promise oracles which depict the return of God's favor to Israel. The presence of a Northern element in a Southern setting is not the only interesting thing about these oracles. Also striking is the fact that both of these passages use similar language about the removal of the burdensome yoke from Israel's shoulders — language that has already been noted in connection with the close parallel in Ps 81:7. Such a double connection to the Asaphite psalms would seem to argue for a tradition-historical link of some sort here.[268]

The implications for the tradition-historical significance of these terms in this psalm are less clear. It is, of course, possible that, given the Isaianic references, such elements were common throughout all of Israel and thus not indicative of any one tradition stream. However, since in at least the first of these passages it is the situation of the Northern kingdom that is being referred to, it is possible that Northern traditions are being consciously taken up as especially appropriate to the subject matter. On the other hand, one must also consider the fact that most of the other elements of these verses have their sole locus outside this psalm within the literature of the Ephraimite tradition stream. The closeness of the parallel with the Ephraimite book of Judges would seem to argue for some sort of tradition-historical link with that tradition stream here.

The plausibility of such an Ephraimite link for this psalm is considerably strengthened by the language of the second half of v 11. There the word *dōmen* may be seen to be an exclusively Ephraimite word.[269] The parallels in Jer 8:2; 16:4; and 25:33 are particularly close since they also refer to the *'ădāmâ*.[270]

The language of the rest of the psalm is, however, not so decisively categorized tradition-historically. Thus, while verbs like *šmd* and *yrš* are quite common in Ephraimite sources, the fact that they are not exclusive to these sources considerably reduces their value as tradition-historical indicators. More interesting perhaps is the parallel of the burning of the mountains in v 15 with the similar passage in Deut 32:22: *tĕlahēṭ hārîm* (Ps 83:15); *wattĕlahēṭ môsĕdê hārîm* (Deut 32:22). One may also note the similar use of *galgal* in v 14 and in the *Völkersturm* of Isa 17:13,[271] and the combination of *saʿar* and *sûpâ* in v 16 and the *Völkersturm* of Isa 29:6.[272] On the basis of such parallels, it would be

---

[268] Since the Midian tradition at least is certain to have originated in the North, it appears likely that the Isaiah passages have drawn upon elements of the Northern tradition.

[269] Outside of this psalm, it occurs only in 2 Kgs 9:37; Jer 8:2; 9:21; 16:4; 25:33.

[270] Though with *'al-pĕnê* rather than the simple *l* found here.

[271] Isa 5:24 has both the *qaš* of v 14 and the *lehābâ* of v 15, but the usage is different and there are better parallels elsewhere for at least the first image (see Jer 13:24 where the wind is a factor; also Isa 40:24; 41:2).

[272] Note the same combination in Amos 1:14. These words are, of course, common elsewhere. See, for example, Jer 23:19; 25:32; 30:23 etc.

possible to argue that much of the language of the last section of this psalm is drawn from the genre of the *Völkersturm.* Nevertheless, given the similar use of much of this language elsewhere, it is hard to draw any conclusions, whether of a formal or a tradition-historical nature. Any attempt to describe the tradition-historical links of this psalm must thus be based on four elements: the Ephraimite structural parallels of v 5, the predominantly Southern list of enemies in vv 7-9, the Northern (Ephraimite?) list of divine victories in vv 10-12, and the Ephraimite language of the last half of v 11. As noted above, a Judean location is no objection to an Ephraimite tradition setting, since that stream was active in the South throughout monarchical times and at least into the exile. Accordingly, even though the evidence is not as abundant as one would like, what evidence there is would seem to indicate a link between this psalm and the Ephraimite tradition stream. Such a result is, of course, not completely unexpected, given the similar links for so many of the other Asaphite psalms.

CONCLUSIONS

This chapter has attempted a detailed linguistic analysis of the psalms of Asaph with a view towards using the linguistic evidence as an aid in the tradition-historical definition of those psalms. This analysis has resulted in the discernment of a significant block of linguistic links both among the individual Asaphite psalms themselves and between those psalms and the larger tradition stream designated as "Ephraimite." These linguistic links may thus be seen to function first of all as a form of internal control on the assigning of these psalms to a single *traditio,* as suggested by the external control of the superscription. Secondly, these links appear to make it possible to describe the nature of this *traditio* in terms of its relationship to the different theological movements within ancient Israel. The evidence may be briefly summarized as follows.

Of the twelve Asaphite psalms, eight contain language which has its dominant and often exclusive reference within the Asaphite corpus.[273] Nine contain language which has its dominant and often exclusive reference within what has been described as the Ephraimite tradition stream.[274] It is significant that these two sets do not coincide. Thus, of the three psalms that do not have any decisive links to the Ephraimite tradition stream, one (Psalm 73) contains language which links it fairly strongly to its fellow Asaphite psalms. Similarly, of the four psalms that do not have any significant links to their fellow Asaphite psalms, two (Psalms 76 and 83) contain language which links them to the Ephraimite tradition stream.

Only two psalms lack any decisive links to either their fellow Asaphite psalms or the Ephraimite tradition stream. Of these, Psalm 75 may perhaps be seen as a borderline case, since it contains a number of possible Ephraimite links,

[273] Psalms 50; 73; 74; 77; 78; 79; 80; 81.
[274] Psalms 50; 74; 76; 77; 78; 79; 80; 81; 83.

though none which could be accepted as determinative. Psalm 82, on the other hand, furnishes little tradition-historically significant linguistic evidence, and as such more closely approaches the status of a tradition-historically neutral datum. It is significant that neither of these psalms contain linguistic evidence which would decisively link it to a *traditio* outside the Asaphite psalms or to a tradition stream other than the Ephraimite.

Along these lines, there was found to be relatively little linguistic evidence within the entire Asaphite corpus which was decisively out of place within the dominant Ephraimite tradition stream. In the rare cases where language was found which was seemingly more at home in another tradition stream, it was usually also found either to be not entirely absent from the Ephraimite tradition stream or to be used in such a way as to make it more at home in that stream. Significantly, such language invariably existed alongside other language in the same psalm which had clear Asaphite and Ephraimite links.[275]

Since appropriate linguistic evidence does not exist in all the psalms and is of varying strength and persuasiveness in those psalms where it does exist, the above analysis cannot be said to have "proven" either the existence of a distinctive Asaphite *traditio* or the setting of all of these psalms within a single larger stream. However, when one considers the internal evidence discussed in this chapter in conjunction with the external evidence of the common superscription, the two combine to suggest that both of these hypotheses are (*contra* Illman) not only possibilities but even strong probabilities. The next two chapters will continue to analyze these tradition-historical possibilities on the basis of both the internal and external evidence.

---

[275] Thus, see Psalm 74 where some possibly Jerusalemite language exists alongside clear Asaphite and Ephraimite links, and Psalms 78, 80, 81, and possibly 83 where some minor links with Isaiah were to be found alongside the latter as well.

4
A Form-Critical Analysis of the Psalms of Asaph

In most studies of the psalms, a form-critical analysis precedes any consideration of non-formal details. Indeed, the determination of the form is usually seen to be a necessary pre-requisite for the interpretation of a psalm's more individual aspects. This is undoubtedly the correct procedure both for the sociohistorical task of determining a psalm's setting in life and for any subsequent literary and theological exegesis. However, as has been argued in the first chapter, form-critical analysis does not retain its priority when the concern is not to determine the institutional situation of its use but rather to distinguish the specific tradition groups responsible for its existence. To give formal data the priority in the latter inquiry is to prejudge the question of whether similar functionaries all belonged to the same tradition group — a possibility which was seen above to be doubtful at best. It is the desire to avoid such dubious assumptions that has mandated the placement of the present form-critical chapter *after* the attempt to corroborate the tradition-historical implications of the common superscription by means of a detailed analysis of the internal linguistic evidence.

It might be well to begin by recalling the function of form criticism within a larger analysis with tradition-historical goals. First of all, one should again emphasize that form criticism should not be expected to provide any real corroboration of the existence of a distinct *traditio*. This is quite clear in the present case, since the forms which make up the Asaphite collection are for the most part shared by the rest of the psalter. Rather, it is only after a *traditio* has been established on other grounds that form criticism can be expected to provide any reliable data concerning that *traditio*. In such a case, one may use the formal aspects of the *traditum* to further describe the functional character of the *traditio* group and the institutional settings in which that group was at some point active. In addition, one may use any significant deviations from the common form as a clue towards any distinctive functional or theological aspects which that group may have.

In keeping with these methodological considerations, the present chapter will use the form-critical data supplied by the Asaphite psalms as a means of further describing the distinctive *traditio* which was suggested by the common superscription and rendered plausible by the linguistic analysis of the preceding chapter. Since the latter analysis has not only reinforced the possibility of a common *traditio* for these psalms but also implied that that *traditio* was part of the larger *traditio* of the Ephraimite tradition stream, any description made possible by the form-critical analysis of these psalms has implications not only for the former *traditio* but for the latter as well. Conversely, the presence of such a point of comparison outside the psalms makes it possible to corroborate the socio-historical possibilities suggested by the formal aspects of the psalms themselves.

In analyzing the tradition-historical significance of the forms present in the Asaphite psalms, the following approach will be used. First of all, the psalms will be classified form-critically and the settings indicated by the forms will be discussed. Secondly, the presence of any formal characteristics which set the Asaphite form apart from the same form as known from elsewhere will be commented upon, along with the implications of this for the description of the *traditio*. Finally, an attempt will be made to correlate the possibilities suggested by the above analysis with similar socio-historical possibilities present in the Ephraimite tradition stream. In the following chapter, an attempt will be made to correlate this evidence with that which is available for the Asaphites themselves.

Because the analysis which follows is not form-critical in the strict sense, little attention will be given to the classification of individual parts of the form for its own sake. Such classification is readily available in any form-critically informed commentary[1] Accordingly, once the initial form-critical identification has been made, only those details which are of potential tradition-historical significance will be noted. In most cases, this means that such individual formal elements will be noted only where there are divergences from the established form. On the other hand, the question of the life setting of the forms is of particular importance, since this necessarily figures large in the description of the psalm's *traditio*. Whenever appropriate, comparative material—both from the ancient near east and from modern anthropological works—will be used to clarify the various social and formal possibilities.

THE COLLECTIVE LAMENTS

The collective or communal lament is perhaps the most easily ascertainable genre present in the Asaphite psalms. Four of the psalms (74, 79, 80, 83) are clear examples of the form and are accepted as such by most form-critical commentators. Indeed, these four psalms make up the accepted core of most critical collections of this genre,[2] though individual elements are present elsewhere in the

---

[1] Such as Gunkel, *Psalmen;* Weiser, *Psalms,* or Kraus, *Psalmen.*

[2] See Gunkel-Begrich, *Einleitung,* 120; Kraus, *Psalmen,* I, li; Claus Westermann, "Struktur und Geschichte der Klage im Altern Testament," *ZAW* 66 (1954) 50; (also see his *The Psalms* [Minneapolis: Augsburg, 1980] 29); all of these include the four Asaphite

psalter[3] and other more complete examples are to be found elsewhere in the Bible.[4] It is, however, potentially significant from a tradition-historical point of view that most of the unambiguous examples of this genre are to be found within the Asaphite psalms. To appreciate this more fully, one must first look at both the genre of the communal lament and the Asaphite manifestations of this genre.

According to the classical definition of Gunkel which is accepted by most scholars, the collective lament has two main sections.[5] These are the lament proper, which gives the cause of the distress, and the petition or *Bitte*, which requests its relief and the restoration of God's good favor. Other elements include some form of invocation of God, motives of various sorts, and possibly an expression of certainty of hearing. The use of the first person plural is characteristic of most of the communal laments, though the more usual ancient near eastern first person singular is also to be found among the Israelite communal laments. This difference may indicate a difference in the means of performance, a possibility which will be further considered below.

As with the form, scholars have displayed a great degree of unanimity concerning the setting of the communal laments.[6] They have generally seen this setting in the various ceremonies of national lamentation described throughout the Bible. Unlike those psalms which had their place in the regular festivals of Israel's cult, the communal laments and the ceremonies which encompassed them appear to have been occasioned by military or natural disasters which could occur at any time. Along with the communal lament, fasting and other expressions of mourning, as well as sacrfices of various sorts, are often seen to have been a prominent part of these ceremonies.

In addition to those just named, there is one other aspect which has been accepted by most scholars as an integral part of such ceremonies of national lamentation — namely, some form of divine answer.[7] This appears to be called for by the psalms themselves and is also indicated by a number of passages in the prophetic books where a communal lament is followed by just such a response on the part of God. Such a response may even be found within certain of the collective laments themselves, though this will need further discussion below.[8] In

---

laments in their list of communal laments. Psalms 44, 60, 85, and 90 are also included with some regularity in these lists, though not always and sometimes with reservations.

[3] See Gunkel-Begrich, *Einleitung*, 120ff., for the most complete list of such elements.
[4] See, for example, Isa 63:7-64:12; Jeremiah 14; Lamentations 5; Hos 6:1-3; for examples in the first person plural form.
[5] Gunkel-Begrich, *Einleitung*, 121ff.
[6] Again see the authors cited in n. 2.
[7] See Gunkel-Begrich, *Einleitung*, 136; Kraus, *Psalmen*, I, lii; Westermann, *Psalms*, 42-43.
[8] Several of the prophetic examples will also be discussed below. For others, see Westermann, *Psalms*, 43. Psalms 60 and 85 are often seen as communal laments which preserve such a response, though the nature of this response is not exactly clear. These psalms will be discussed further in the following section on prophetic psalms.

any event, the evidence does seem to favor the presence of some kind of divine response in the ceremonies of national lamentation.

In accord with the above, the presence of communal laments among the Asaphite psalms would seem to indicate for the *traditio* group behind these psalms a role in, or at least some connection with, the ceremonies of communal lamentation. Further, since this *traditio* was seen to be related in some way to the larger Ephraimite tradition stream, such a connection might also be indicated for the latter as well. These in themselves are significant tradition-historical observations. One may, however, go even further by re-examining the above data with a more critical — and tradition-historical — eye.

One especially needs to reconsider the question of setting. There is little question that the placement of these psalms in ceremonies of national lamentation is correct. However, more attention needs to be paid to the actual mechanics of these ceremonies and, in particular, to the tradition-historically crucial question of the personnel involved. One must ask the question of who actually does the lamenting in these ceremonies, and further, how—that is, through whom—the expected divine answer is to be received.[9] Since the laments themselves can provide only indirect answers to these questions, narrative descriptions of lament ceremonies become particularly important in this regard.

One such narrative description may be found in 2 Chronicles 20. In this passage, a complete ceremony of national lamentation is described, including its situation and its consequences.[10] Particularly interesting is the question of who does what here. While the people are present throughout the ceremony, they are not portrayed as active participants. Instead, the lament proper[11] is verbalized by the king, though it is done in the people's name, as indicated by the use of the first person plural throughout. The response to the king's prayer is delivered by "a levite, of the sons of Asaph," upon whom "the Spirit of the Lord came." The answer is not delivered to the king alone but to all those assembled. After this response, the people and the king bow down to worship, while the levites of the Kohathites and the Korahites stand up to give praise.

It is important to note that, at least in this idealized portrait of the functioning of a national lamentation ceremony, the verbalizing of the lament prayer is to be distinguished from the generalized activity of the people. Instead, it is a specific cultic act performed by a specific cultic official. The fact that it is here verbalized by the king is in line with common ancient near eastern practice where

---

[9] As the evidence will show, it is too simple an answer to say merely "singers."

[10] This is quite possibly a hypothetical, rather than a purely historical, situation. Even as such, however, it probably reflects the cultic usage of Israel at some point in its history. The tradition-history of this passage will be discussed further in the following chapter.

[11] The prayer in vv 6–12 is certainly not a pure lament, though lament elements are clearly present. Of note is the specificity of the complaint which is here tied to the narrative situation.

the king had such a role.[12] Such a royal role is also reflected by the fact that most ancient near eastern national laments are in the first person singular, as are many of their Israelite counterparts.[13] It is striking in this respect that the king's prayer is here in the plural.

Also noteworthy here are the mechanics of the divine answer which is delivered in at least a quasi-prophetic manner.[14] It is, of course, significant for the purpose of this study that an Asaphite is portrayed as the means of communication. This will receive further consideration below.

Similar to 2 Chronicles 20 is the earlier passage, 2 Kgs 19:8-37, though there is no indication that the latter was set in the context of a national ceremony of lamentation. Here, once again, it is the king who verbalizes the lament proper, which is again in the first person plural. In response, he receives an oracle against the nations only secondarily directed to himself. The means of this response is even more explicitly prophetic, namely, the prophet Isaiah.

Variations on this pattern may be seen elsewhere. One may, for example, note certain passages in the book of Joel where priests seem to have some role in verbalizing the lament.[15] This is also in keeping with near eastern practice.[16] The means by which the divine response is given is not so clear, though the prophetic nature of the book would appear to suggest a means in keeping with that seen above. It is also possible that the prophet has a role in the lamentation proper here (cf. 1:19), a possibility which may also be seen in Habakkuk.[17] In all of these cases of prophetic lamentation, the first person singular is used.

---

[12] See Mowinckel, *Psalms*, I, 42-61.

[13] On the first person singular of the ancient near eastern psalms, see Gunkel-Begrich, *Einleitung*, 123; also George Widengren, *The Accadian and Hebrew Psalms of Lamentation as Religious Documents* (Stockholm: Bökforlags Aktiebolaget Thule, 1937). The Israelite counterparts are the so-called royal laments. On these, see the views of Erhard Gerstenberger, "Psalms," in *Old Testament Form Criticism*, ed. by John H. Hayes (San Antonio: Trinity University, 1974) 199, 205-206, who correctly sees Mowinckel's finding of this genre in almost all the individual laments (*Psalms*, I, 225-246) as an exaggeration.

[14] On the basis of the "fear not" and the direct address, one might see this speech as more in line with the *Heilsorakel* and its priestly agent. (See Joachim Begrich, "Das Priesterliche Heilsorakel," *ZAW*, N.S. 11 (1934) 81-92; also Claus Westermann, *Isaiah 40-66* (Philadelphia: Westminster, 1969) 79. However, the situation here is clearly communal rather than the individual situation usually associated with the *Heilsorakel*. This may be an indication that the account in Chronicles has conflated what were earlier more distinct elements. However, it may also be the case that these elements do not by themselves indicate a priestly mediator. In support of this possibility, one may note the fact that the Zakir inscription has both the expression "fear not" and more specifically "prophetic" intermediaries. The same is also true of the Neo-Assyrian oracle collections. See the discussion in Wilson, *Prophecy*, 111-119, 130-132.

[15] See Joel 1:9, 13; and, especially, 2:17 which quotes part of a lament.

[16] One thinks especially of the *kalû* priesthood, whose ritual functions included, but were not restricted to, the singing of laments. See *CAD*, K volume, 91-94 for bibliography.

[17] Though a setting in a national ceremony is not clear here.

A slightly different pattern may be seen in a passage such as Jeremiah 14. This passage recounts a communal lament in the first person plural (vv 2-9, 19-22), together with a conversation between God and Jeremiah. This conversation not only describes the ceremony surrounding the lament (v 12) but also the mechanics of the response (vv 13-16). In this case as well, the response appears to have been given through prophetic agency![18]

Unfortunately, the means by which the prayer is verbalized is a bit more difficult to determine. The people are, of course, implied by the first person plural, but, as was seen above, this does not necessarily mean that they actually verbalized the prayer in the cult. Instead, one may consider whether Jeremiah himself is conceived of as the one who does this verbalizing, since in v 11 he is specifically ordered not to pray for the people. One may also note the response in 15:1 to the second lament of vv 19-22, where again prophetic intercession is implied and rejected. Such prophetic intercession is, of course, known from elsewhere and is even to be seen as particularly at home in the Ephraimite tradition stream of which Jeremiah is a part![19] One has thus at least to reckon with the possibility that prophets also had a role in the verbalizing of the lament in public ceremonies of that nature.[20]

The above examples have established a range of possible functionaries who could verbalize the communal lament in the Israelite cult. It is difficult to determine which of these possibilities actually was involved in the performance of the communal laments found in the Asaphite psalms. It is also at this point difficult to determine whether the performers of the latter differed from the performers of the other communal laments of the psalter. Some further clues, however, will emerge in the tradition-historical analysis at the end of this section.

In contrast to this range of possible functionaries responsible for the lament proper, the means by which the divine response is mediated to the community seems to be much more unequivocally prophetic. Thus, while a priestly oracle was apparently the response to the individual lament in Israel and the ancient near east,[21] the answer to the communal lament was more likely mediated by prophets, through whom God spoke—usually in the first person. Hints of such prophetic divine speech may be seen in psalms with elements of the collective lament,[22] though the exact status of these pieces as prophetic parallels will have

---

[18] See also vv 17-18.

[19] On the intercessory function of the Ephraimite prophet, see Wilson, *Prophecy*, 301 and passim. On the presence of such a function in Jeremiah, see especially Jer 7:16; 11:14. On the subject in general, see Mowinckel, *Psalms*, II, 62-63.

[20] The literary character of Jeremiah 14 should, of course, be taken into consideration here, though it is probable that this chapter was shaped in conformity with cultic possibilities known to the shapers, who were probably of the same Ephraimite tradition stream in which Jeremiah himself stood.

[21] Again, see Begrich, "Heilsorakel," Westermann, *Isaiah*, 79, as well as n. 14 above.

[22] For first person speech, see Psalms 12, 60, and possibly 90-91. Contrast the third person speech of Psalm 85. On the type of first person speech present in the former psalms,

to await further analysis in the next section of this chapter.

In all that has gone before, it has been assumed that the collective laments of the Asaphite corpus are similar enough to their non-Asaphite counterparts so as to share with them a common setting. This assumption seems especially valid since the Asaphite psalms provide some of the classic examples of the form and thus would seem to be those most appropriate to any setting that can be isolated on the basis of the form. However, given the existence of these laments within a single identifiable locus, it becomes important to discuss the possibility that these laments differ in their formal details from those examples of the general form found outside that locus. Such a discussion is also perhaps prompted by the possibility that the communal lament had a number of options in terms of its performance by a variety of cultic functionaries. Further analysis of any formal peculiarities present in these psalms is necessary to determine if the latter favor one of these options.

One may perhaps begin where the previous analysis left off, with the prophetic response which was seen to be a common element of ceremonies of communal lamentation and a possible element of certain communal laments themselves. It is noteworthy that none of the Asaphite communal laments contains such an element of divine response. This is perhaps especially striking in view of the fact that the Chronicles account cited above details just such a speech delivered by an Asaphite. It should be noted, however, that four of the remaining Asaphite psalms are psalms in which such divine speech has a prominent role. It is thus possible that these psalms fulfill just this function of divine response and, as such, explain how such sections of divine response could be missing from the corpus' collective laments. If this should be the case, it would provide additional evidence for the internal coherence of the corpus. These examples of divine speech must, however, be examined further in the next section of the present chapter.

In terms of the communal lament itself, it is difficult to determine whether those differences that may be found between the Asaphite communal laments and the other examples of this form are sufficiently distinctive in view of the demonstrated flexibility of forms in ancient Israel. One may point to the striking simplicity of these psalms' invocations,[23] which contrast not only with the more elaborately hymnic invocations of the ancient near eastern laments[24] but also with the historical preliminaries of such psalms as 44, 85, and 90. The fact that this simplicity can, however, also be found in such non-Asaphite psalms as Psalm 60 may indicate the presence of a simple stylistic variant rather than one with any tradition-historical significance. Similarly, one may note the relative

---

see the following section on the prophetic psalms.

[23] The invocation is simply "God" in Psalms 74, 79, and 83. It is slightly more elaborate in Psalm 80.

[24] See Widengren, *Psalms*, 41.

prominence of the lament section proper, as compared with such later psalms as 123, 125, and 126 which are more collective prayers than laments. Once again, however, there are other examples where the lament has a similar prominence,[25] thus rendering doubtful any claim of tradition-historical significance here.[26]

Of possibly more significance is the comparative length of the petition or *Bitte* in these psalms. This would be of some importance if the intercessory nature of these psalms were to be emphasized in accordance with their ties to the Ephraimite tradition stream. However, while the petition is clearly prominent here, it seems impossible to maintain any rigid distinction from the usage of other laments.

Although it is not technically a formal distinction, one may perhaps also note the fact that the Asaphite collective laments are uniform in their concern with military, as opposed to natural, disasters. Thus, on the basis of the available evidence, one may speak of a role in this type of lamentation for the tradition group behind these psalms. This would fit with the picture of Asaphite activity in 2 Chronicles 20. Because of the limitations of the evidence, however, there does not seem to be a firm basis for distinguishing between different lamentation ceremonies and the different functionaries involved in them.[27]

One final individual aspect of certain of the Asaphite communal laments should be noted here, namely the apparent connection of Psalms 74 and 79 with the destruction of the temple. As might be expected, this information has often been seen as an indication of these psalms' possible historical setting in the exilic period.[28] Taking a somewhat different approach, Willesen has noted the ancient near eastern parallels for such "temple lamentations."[29] The latter have their cultic situation in either the New Year's festival or those ceremonies connected with the restoration or re-purification of a temple. Willesen favors a similar ritual interpretation of the destruction detailed in these psalms (specifically in connection with the New Year's festival), though he does admit the possibility of a more historical interpretation. Ringgren has furthered this argument by noting the common reference to creation myths present in both Psalm 74 and some Babylonian texts of this category.[30] Such myths are felt to be especially appropriate to the new beginning of the temple's rededication.

---

[25] See, for example, Psalm 44; Lamentations 5.

[26] It is, on the other hand, possibly significant in terms of the history of the form in general. It might, for example, point to the potentially seditious nature of the lament section proper in those times when the nation (and even the temple) was dependent on a foreign power such as the Persians.

[27] One may also note the non-military nature of the Ephraimite laments in Jeremiah 14 and Hos 6:1-2 in this connection.

[28] See Kraus, *Psalmen*, II, 514-515 and 550-551.

[29] Folker Willesen, "The Cultic Situation of Psalm LXXIV," *VT* 2 (1952) 290-306.

[30] Helmer Ringgren, *The Impact of the Ancient Near East on Israelite Tradition* (VTSup 23, Leiden: Brill, 1972) 41.

It is perhaps a bit too speculative to describe the role of these psalms in an Israelite New Year's festival without more explicit biblical support. Nevertheless, the connection of these psalms with the restoration of the temple or even the rededication of a temple somehow defiled may be accepted as theoretical possibilities. One thing that make such possibilities especially interesting for the present psalms is the explicit Asaphite involvement in laying the foundation for the new temple.[31] It should be noted, however, that the singing at this time was said to include praise and thanksgiving rather than lamentation, again more in the style of the deutero-Asaphite psalms than the superscripted Asaphite psalms.

It is, on the other hand, possible that these psalms were part of a restoration ceremony connected with the rededication of a defiled temple, rather than a literal restoration of one that had been destroyed. If this is the case, one is certainly justified in thinking of the various pre-exilic temple reforms such as those of Jehoash, Hezekiah, and Josiah. At least some of these settings would fit well with the dominant Ephraimite tendencies of these psalms. Again, however, these possibilities are a bit too speculative to bear much weight.

The one sure point in all this is the fact that the presence of such communal laments among the Asaphite psalms indicates some connection between such laments—together with their lamentation ceremonies—and the *traditio* group behind the Asaphite psalms. As has been seen in the last chapter, however, this *traditio* group can be described on the basis of its linguistic usage as having some links with the larger Ephraimite tradition stream. This in turn makes possible some connection of the latter stream to the ceremonies of communal lament. This is especially the case since all the Asaphite communal laments have specific linguistic links with this Ephraimite stream.

Such an Asaphite-Ephraimite connection receives some corroboration from the fact that communal laments are present in sources of the Ephraimite tradition stream. One may note both the already mentioned laments of Jeremiah 14 and the further lament of Hos 6:1-3. In contrast, one finds no such lament in the work of Isaiah of Jerusalem or Ezekiel.[32] It is also interesting that the communal laments of these Ephraimite sources are of the first person plural variety, in contrast to the predominantly singular form of such Southern sources as Habakkuk and Joel.[33] This use of the plural is significant because it nicely corresponds to the dominant form of the Asaphite communal laments.[34] It also,

[31] Ezra 3:10.
[32] Certain traces of the communal lament (especially in the form of a communal petition) do occur in the book of Isaiah (Isa 26:7-19; 33:2; and especially 63:15-64:12), but these are clearly not from the hand of Isaiah of Jerusalem. As such, their tradition-historical links may lie in other directions, as is obviously the case with Isaiah 63-64.
[33] See also Micah 7, though this is not a clear lament form.
[34] One must note the use of the singular pronoun in Ps 74:12 MT (Greek versions have the plural) and 83:14. The former is an exception to the otherwise plural usage of the psalm. The latter, on the other hand, is the only first person reference in the psalm and so more significant, though the concern here is clearly communal throughout.

however, corresponds to those examples of communal laments verbalized by the king,[35] as well as to communal laments found elsewhere in the psalter.[36] Thus, while the correspondence between the communal laments of the Asaphite corpus and those found elsewhere in the Ephraimite literature is real and worthy of note, it should not be overemphasized, since it is not an exclusive link.

On a more general level, however, one may note the appropriateness of such a correspondence in view of the high value placed on intercession in the Ephraimite tradition stream. Ephraimite prophets in particular are involved in intercessory behavior, often acting as the conversational link between the people and their God.[37]

Although certainty is impossible here, the connection of these psalms with the Ephraimite tradition stream might lead one to posit a prophetic role in the performance of these psalms. Interestingly, one possible objection to this is to be found in Ps 74:9 which laments just this lack of a prophet and so would seemingly not be able to be verbalized by the same. Nevertheless, the same verse also contains the phrase, "We do not see our signs . . . there is none among us who knows how long." This could be very appropriately verbalized by a prophetic figure or a chorus of such figures. Thus, the lack of a prophet here may be seen more in terms of the prophet's predictive gifts (or his contact with God in general) than his intercessory functions. Of course, to the extent that the lament situation has been long-standing, the intercessory function may be seen to have broken down as well, thus indicating a prophetic lack in both senses.[38]

Some of these psalms contain other indications which seem to speak against a royal role in their performance. As noted above, Psalms 74 and 79 may stem from a time after the destruction of the temple, and so from a time when a royal figure was lacking. However, even if one locates such psalms in a time of pre-exilic rededication, one must also reckon with the fact that the near eastern parallels for such rededication ceremonies do not indicate their performance by a royal figure. Instead, they are performed by a special class of priests, for whom there is little biblical parallel.[39]

Whether or not one sees a prophetic role in the actualization of these communal laments, the fact remains that such laments seem to be quite at home in Ephraimite circles, especially in their first person plural form. As such, they constitute a significant formal affinity which tends to confirm the proposed linguistic link between the Asaphite psalms and the larger Ephraimite tradition stream.

---

[35] Such as 2 Chr 20:6-12 and 2 Kgs 19:15-19, as considered above.
[36] See Psalms 44, 60, 90, 12:8; also Lamentations 5.
[37] Again, see Wilson, *Prophecy*, 301 and passim.
[38] In this connection, it is interesting that Isa 64:7, which stands in the midst of a communal lament, can say that there is no one who calls on the name of God!
[39] Willesen, "Situation," 296.

THE "PROPHETIC" PSALMS

In addition to the communal laments, the Asaphite corpus is usually seen to contain another block of formally distinct psalms, namely, the prophetic psalms. However, unlike the communal lament, with its set pattern of formal elements and its readily ascertainable setting, the prophetic psalm is not as clear a formal entity. Indeed, on the whole, it would make more sense to speak of prophetic elements which appear in a number of different psalm genres, since the psalms which contain such elements are clearly not of the same form.[40] Nevertheless, it is obvious that these elements do distinguish the psalms which contain them in an important way. As a result, it is possible to consider them as a whole at least on some level — provided that one is constantly aware of the ramifications that accompany the formal variety surrounding such usage.

The Asaphite corpus contains four psalms which can be classified as "prophetic" or, more accurately, which may be seen to contain prophetic elements. These are Psalms 50, 75, 81, and 83, psalms which otherwise belong to a number of different genres. However, even before investigating the significance of these diverse formal links, one needs to attempt some finer definition of what constitutes the prophetic element in these and related psalms.

Such prophetic elements have been variously conceived in the past. Gunkel, for example, described as prophetic not only the use of speech patterns common to the prophets but also the use of imagery and eschatology that he felt to be at home there as well.[41] In the case of the Asaphite psalms, these latter characteristics have been dealt with to some extent in the previous chapter on the language of the psalms.[42] To go beyond this into more abstract categories is to go beyond the methodological caution of this work, and it is doubtful whether such categories have either any form-critical or any tradition-historical significance. The former criterion of patterns of prophetic speech is much more significant in both of these respects, and so to these it is necessary to turn.

On one level, prophetic speech may be defined as the communication of the will of the deity to an interested party through a third party. Such a definition, however, would not separate the prophet from other types of intermediaries, such as diviners, who also make known the will of God to an interested party. A more positive indication of prophetic status is, of course, the presence of a prophetic speech formula, such as *kōh 'āmar yhwh*. However, although this formula is sometimes to be found in cultic contexts,[43] it is not present in the book of Psalms. This may be a coincidence, or it may indicate that this formula is to be connected with a different sort of prophetic function (and functionary). In any event, it cannot help to further specify the nature of the so-called prophetic psalms.

---

[40] Such psalms are often called "prophetic liturgies" in the literature. This is convenient, though not as specific and informative as one might like.
[41] Gunkel-Begrich, *Einleitung*, 329ff.
[42] As in the case of the "cup" of Ps 75:9.
[43] See, for example, 2 Chr 20:15, though this is quite possibly a later conflation.

In addition to such formulae, prophetic intermediation has at times another aspect which distinguishes it from other forms of intermediation. This is the tendency for the prophet to communicate with the interested party as if he or she actually were the deity. In sociological terms, such intermediation would seem to be of the "possession" type.[44] In this, the intermediary is "possessed" by the deity who then makes use of the former's physical being to communicate with others. In formal terms, this mode of intermediation is most clearly indicated by the general use of the first person to indicate the deity.[45] Such a usage distinguishes the prophet from a more priestly or diviner type of intermediary, since the latter usually reports on the will of God in the third person. Nevertheless, while the use of the third person may be proper to other intermediaries, it is also to be found among prophets. Such a use of the third person would, of course, indicate a different style of prophecy than would the use of the first person — possibly not possession, or if possession, then a different type than possession by the deity so as to become an embodiment of that deity for the purposes of speech. In terms of a cultic ceremony, such third person speech would not allow its speaker to actualize the deity in a way that first person speech would. Accordingly, the use of the divine first person clearly indicates prophetic speech and may indicate prophecy of a particular type. Third person speech, on the other hand, has a more general usage and, as such, would require more evidence to determine whether its speaker is a priest or a prophet, and, if either, of what type.

Such a distinction is especially helpful in the case of the Asaphite psalms, since all of the "prophetic psalms" in this corpus contain a divine speech in the first person. However, even such a characteristic is by itself insufficient to distinguish the different formal possibilities here. Thus, for example, one may note such a case as Ps 2:7-9, where first person divine speech is certainly present, but where, almost as certainly, no direct divine presence is indicated for the performance of the psalm. The reason, of course, is that the first person divine speech occurs in a quotation introduced by *'āmar 'ēlay*. This may indeed indicate some form of prophetic activity, but, if so, it is an activity of a different type than that indicated by those psalms in which the divine speech is not of this quotation variety. More specifically, the latter would seem to indicate the possibility of a direct cultic actualization of the divine reality, while the former would appear to exclude this possibility, since the use of a quotation seems to set the divine presence at a distance. Only in the non-quotation type of psalm does one have a real possibility of a direct cultic actualization of the divine reality.

When one considers the various "prophetic psalms" with these formal criteria in mind, one arrives at some interesting results. Thus, while many of the

---

[44] For the use of this terminology as applied to Israelite prophecy, see Wilson, *Prophecy*, 144-146.

[45] Though, of course, an occasional third person self-reference is not to be ruled out in conjunction with a dominant first person usage.

psalms may be considered prophetic because of their inclusion of first person divine speech, the quotation nature of this speech in some of these psalms would seem to indicate that one is not dealing with a present divine encounter but rather with one that has taken place in the past or even with one that is hoped for in the future. Such psalms include Psalms 2, 60, 68, 108, 110, 132, and possibly 12 and 89 as well. Thus, as seen above, Ps 2:7-9 introduces its divine speech with the quotation formula *'āmar 'ēlay*. The speech of vv 5-6 in the same psalm is a similar (though apparently future) quotation introduced by *'āz yĕdabbēr 'ēlêmô*. Psalm 60 introduces the prophetic speech of vv 8-10 (or 8-11) with *'ĕlōhîm dibber*, and because of this the speech now functions in the lament as a motive which reminds God of past divine promises. Similar observations hold true for the parallel Ps 108:8-10 (or 8-11), although the hymnic introduction moves the quotation more in the direction of a divine act to be celebrated. In Ps 68:23-24 one again meets with a past promise introduced by *'āmar 'ădōnāy*. Ps 110:4 is a similar past promise introduced by *nišba' yhwh*. In view of this, v 1 of that psalm is probably to be interpreted in such a way as well.[46] A similar past promise is to be found in Ps 132:11b-18 introduced by the *nišba'-yhwh lĕdāwid* in the first half of v 11.[47]

The divine speech of Psalm 89 is difficult to evaluate because of a textual problem in v 3. The MT of this verse's introductory phrase reads *'āmartî*, thus apparently continuing the psalmist's address in a different tense, while possibly implying a present divine speech (rather than a quotation) for vv 4-5. However, most of the versions assume an *'āmartā*, possibly implying a divine quotation.[48] Both the MT and the versions are difficult here, though the former is possibly the *lectio difficilior*, since it radically shifts the tense of the psalmist's direct address. On the other hand, it is easy to see how a change from *'āmartā* to *'āmartî* could have occurred in view of the three first person verbs which follow. In

---

[46] The *nĕ'um yhwh* of that verse could indicate a present oracle as pointed in the MT, though it is at least possible that it should be repointed to indicate a past oracle (cf. the Greek versions) or that in view of v 4 it indicates a past oracle even as pointed.

[47] Vv 14-18 continue the first person speech after the third person interruption of v 13. This interruption thus deprives the former verses of any introductory phrase which would mark them as a quotation. However, in view of the past nature of the previous promise, it is likely that these verses too are to be seen as a quotation of a previous divine speech rather than as a speech then actualized in the cult. The traditional character of this promise may also point in this direction as well, though this is certainly not a decisive argument against a present actualization in the cult.

[48] This includes all the Greek versions and both translations of the psalm in the Vulgate, though there is some support for the MT in the old Latin (La^G). One should, however, note the awkward second person in the second half of the verse in these versions, which renders any interpretation difficult. This has prompted some interpreters to move the introductory phrase to v 4. This both makes sense of the passage and eliminates the direct divine speech in favor of a quotation, but it has no support in any of the versions.

connection with this question, one should note the definite quotation status of vv 20-38, which begin with '*āz dibbartā-bĕḥāzôn laḥăsîdĕkā watō'mer.* Significantly, the divine speech was apparently not delivered to or through a prophet, but rather came to the king himself in a vision.

Psalm 12 is, if anything, even more difficult to classify with respect to its divine speech in v 6, since the crucial phrase is neither in the past nor does it introduce the divine speech. For this reason, it may indicate an actual present encounter with the Deity in the cult. Nevertheless, the presence of the *yō'mar yhwh* immediately following the divine first person does allow one to think of either an affirmation for the future or even a jussive corresponding to that of v 4.[49] Either of these would fall within the quotation type of divine speech.

In contrast to these "quotation" examples are those cases of divine speech which seem to imply a present encounter with the Deity. In formal terms, one sign of such a present encounter is the lack of any introductory phrase which would categorize the following speech as a quotation. Thus, in Psalm 46, the transition from the preceding descriptive verses to the divine speech of v 10 is totally abrupt, with nothing to prepare the audience for such a shift in perspective. This is not a mere quotation used to buttress an ongoing argument. Rather, it is only by envisioning a cultic situation in which the speech of the Deity is a present reality that one can explain such a verse. Put in another way, it is the expectations of the original cultic audience which allow such a transition to be meaningful. Only the setting makes sense of the text. The actual mechanics of the performance of such a piece are important and will be discussed further when the question of life setting is considered below.

Other psalms are similar to Psalm 46 in their treatment of divine speech. Thus, Psalm 91 abruptly shifts its promise language from the third person of most of the psalm to the first person of the concluding verses. As was the case in Psalm 46, there is no introductory phrase which would indicate that these latter verses are a quotation. As such, one can only envision some sort of cultic activity as the reason for the shift.

The concluding verses of Psalm 85 also seem to contain a shift which would indicate a cultic reality of some sort. Since these verses, however, do not contain a first person divine speech but rather speak of God in the third person, one cannot equate the cultic reality with that found in Psalms 46 and 91. The shift in Ps 87:4, on the other hand, is in the first person, though the present order of the psalm seems to be in some disarray and the verse may be either a quotation or the speech of a personified Zion.

A clearer example of this type of divine speech may be found in Psalm 95, a psalm which was seen in the previous chapter to have a number of linguistic links to the Asaphite psalms. This psalm begins as a hymn (vv 1-7a) but shifts

---

[49] This latter possibility would require repointing and is an interpretation with little support in the versions.

with the admonitory ending of v 7.[50] The first person divine speech which ends the psalm is clearly not a quotation. It would thus appear to indicate a cultic reality similar to that implied by Psalms 46 and 91.

The remaining examples of first person divine speech occur in the Asaphite corpus. It is important to note that all of the examples of such speech which occur in the Asaphite psalms belong to the cultic rather than the quotation type. Thus, in Psalm 50, the long first person speech which constitutes most of the psalm is prepared for by the theophanic description which precedes it, but it in no way can be described as a quotation of a past speech.[51] The shorter speech in Psalm 75[52] likewise has no introductory phrase, following directly upon the opening verse of the communal thanksgiving.

Psalm 81 is more complicated in this respect. In the present MT,[53] its lengthy divine speech is preceded by the phrase *śĕpat lō'-yāda'tî 'ešmā'*, whose first person is clearly not the first person of the following divine speech. If such a reading reflects a cultic reality, it would seem to indicate the presence of just such an intermediary as has been hypothesized above, an intermediary who then verbalizes the divine speech which follows.[54] In any event, the latter clearly cannot be seen as a quotation, especially since it is a "voice previously unknown." Rather, it only makes sense as a present cultic reality.

The final Asaphite psalm with divine speech, Psalm 82, is perhaps the one closest to the quotation type. In accord with the first verse, the divine speech of vv 2-7 is evidently to be seen as taking place in the heavenly council. In such a way, the whole psalm could be a report of what has taken place in that council in the past. Such a report would still be a prophetic event, as seen from the parallels found elsewhere in the Bible,[55] but it would not indicate a direct encounter with the Deity. However, the context does not support such an interpretation of this psalm as a report. Thus, while God has arisen (*niṣṣāb*) in v 1a, the actual judging is not to be relegated to the past, as the *yišpōṭ* of 1b shows. Accordingly, this would seem to be a cultic actualization of God's activity in the heavenly assembly, similar to the judicial activity of Psalm 50. The fact that the

---

[50] Because of the third person suffix, it is difficult to tell whether this latter part of the verse is part of the divine speech which follows. It may be a transition statement of the intermediary similar to that found in Ps 81:6. See further below.

[51] The divine first person of v 5 is probably a quotation, following the *yiqrā'* in the preceding verse. The unanimous Greek witness has a third person here.

[52] How long this divine speech extends is a bit unclear. It certainly includes vv 3-4, but probably not vv 5-6.

[53] The Greek witnesses have the third person here.

[54] Such a phrase may mark the transition from the normal consciousness of the intermediary to the trance state of possession by the Deity, as is known from elsewhere in the anthropological literature.

[55] Namely, 1 Kings 22 and Isaiah 6, though one should also note here the beginning of Job. It might, of course, be prophecy of a different type than that indicated by direct speech, perhaps more in a visionary vein.

divine speech lacks any formal introduction is yet another indication that it is not of the quotation variety.

In such a way, these four Asaphite psalms join with Psalms 46, 91, 95, and possibly 87,[56] to constitute a group of psalms containing first person divine speech of a type different from that contained in the first group of psalms considered above. It is interesting to note that in this group, Psalm 46 and the similar but questionable Psalm 87[57] are Korahite psalms, while Psalm 91 is an untitled psalm which almost immediately follows the Korahite corpus. Since Psalm 95 has been linked with the Asaphite corpus, most of the psalms of this type seem to have some connection with the singer psalms.

In what has gone before, the prophetic dimension under consideration in this section has been narrowed to the presence of first person divine speech. Further, that divine speech has been analyzed into subcategories, each of which contains various formal markers and has its own potential form-critical and even tradition-historical significance. Despite these detailed preliminaries, one is still not ready to make the move from such formal categories to their possible settings in life. The reason for this, as was noted in the opening paragraph of this section, is the fact that the prophetic elements with which one is dealing here are not full-fledged forms in themselves but rather formal elements which are part of a variety of other more complete forms. Thus, even though the ability to point to common traits among these elements is a good indication of the presence of a fairly standard element of Israel's psalmody, such elements must still first be considered in the context of the larger forms of which they are a part.

What then are these larger formal units in which one finds the prophetic elements listed above? By way of background, one may perhaps first consider the quotation type of first person divine speech. As was to be expected, this type of divine speech is not limited to any one formal entity but is instead to be found in a wide variety of the same. Thus, Psalms 12 and 60 locate such speeches in communal laments, while in the second half of Psalm 89 such a speech is to be seen as part of an individual royal lament.[58] In the first half of the latter psalm, such a divine speech is part of a hymn. Such is also possibly the case in Psalm 68, though this psalm is difficult to categorize form-critically. A clearer example of such a hymnic connection is to be found in Psalm 108.[59] As with Psalm 89a, the hymnic Psalm 108 is couched in individual terms. Psalms 2, 110, and 132 are

---

[56] Possibly Psalm 89 as well, depending on one's reading of the text-critical problems involved. Again Psalm 85, while direct speech, is third person throughout.

[57] As well as the different, though related, Psalm 85. The difficult Psalm 89 belongs to a singer as well, Ethan the Ezrahite.

[58] Where it forms a contrast to the complaint which follows and so functions as a motive for God to act in the present.

[59] Though the psalm does end with the communal lament also found in Psalm 60. It is interesting that some medieval Hebrew manuscripts attribute Psalm 108 to Asaph— perhaps because of its divine speech and comnunal lament aspects?

also all psalms of the individual, comprising various types of royal psalms.[60] One may thus find such divine speech quotations in a wide variety of formal units. Nevertheless, most of the psalms so listed are psalms of the individual, though many of these are royal and so in a certain sense communal. Psalms 12 and 60 are more strictly collective in nature.

The situation is somewhat different with the second type of divine speech considered above. Psalms 46, 81, and 95 are all communal hymns of various sorts, while Psalm 75 at least begins as a similar communal thanksgiving.[61] Psalm 87 is indefinite in terms of its being either individual or communal, though its status as a Zion hymn (like its fellow Korahite psalm, Psalm 46) would seem to point to a communal setting. Psalm 91 begins as a wisdom psalm but moves into a psalm of assurance for an individual. Psalms 50 and 82 are difficult to place form-critically, but the former at least is clearly communal in nature, while a good case can be made for such a setting in the latter as well.[62] The only example of a lament that uses this direct type of speech is to be found in Psalm 85, though, as noted above, the fact that the first person is not used there probably places it in a somewhat different category.

Thus, while the first type of divine speech considered above could be found in a variety of formal units with perhaps a certain tendency towards the more individual categories, the second type is almost never to be found in psalms of lament and only rarely in psalms of the individual. Such a distribution may, of course, be due to the coincidence of tradition and preservation. Nevertheless, the strong communal tendency of the latter type is significant in terms of the life setting in which such elements were used. If, as suggested above, the non-quotation first person divine speech is a reliable sign of a present encounter with the Deity in the cult, the latter would seem to have been especially at home in those ceremonies of a communal nature in which hymns played a role.

From such general observations, it is now necessary to turn to the specific examples of prophetic elements in the Asaphite psalms. In contrast to the relative uniformity of the communal laments, the Asaphite psalms containing prophetic elements are much more diverse. Because of this, it will first be necessary to consider each of the psalms separately. Then, in keeping with the usual form-critical methodology of this chapter, one may compare them (both individually and as a group) with the other psalms seen above to contain similar elements. Finally, one might then attempt to correlate them with similar aspects found in the Ephraimite tradition stream.

[60] Psalm 2 places this divine speech in the context of a *Völkersturm*. Psalm 110 is a restatement of a divine promise. Psalm 132 begins as a petition, for which the promise may function as a motive of sorts.

[61] The use of the first person singular following the divine speech will be discussed further below.

[62] Psalm 50 uses the first person plural (v 3) and is addressed to the entire community. The ritual drama of Psalm 82 would seem more at home in a communal setting. This would fit the petitionary ending as well.

The four Asaphite psalms involved may be divided into two groups, according to the ultimate addressee of the divine speech in each. Psalms 50 and 81 clearly have an inner-Israelite addressee, while Psalms 75 and 82 are most likely to be seen as directed against the nations.[63] The latter psalms, of course, have an immediate Israelite audience for whom they are an indication of salvation or a reason for assurance. In such a way, these two groups of psalms may be classified in terms of their stance towards Israel itself, since Psalms 50 and 81 warn and exhort Israel, while Psalms 75 and 82 provide grounds for its assurance and salvation.

The first of these psalms, Psalm 50, is perhaps the most difficult to characterize form-critically. It is often described in general terms as a prophetic liturgy, though there are some important dissenting voices to such a characterization.[64] In any event, such a description does not in itself allow for an adequate specificity in terms of its life setting. Accordingly, many scholars have attempted to further specify both the form and the setting. Kraus, for example, has called it a *prophetische Gerechtsliturgie* and assigned it to a covenant renewal ceremony.[65] Zimmerli, on the other hand, denies any prophetic involvement and connects it with a ceremony of the communal reading of the law.[66] A third possibility is raised by Phillips who sees the psalm as part of a cultic *rîb* in which God appears in response to the complaint of the people in order to justify past divine actions.[67]

Unfortunately, it seems impossible to choose among these alternatives on the basis of the evidence. The reference to the covenant in both the theophanic introduction and the following divine speech[68] is indeed suggestive, but it does not necessarily require a covenant renewal ceremony as its setting. Similarly, even if one were to describe this psalm with Phillips as a cultic *rîb*, one still would not be able to go further, since such a ceremony is otherwise unknown.[69] In the

---

[63] On the latter, see both the linguistic analysis of the previous chapter and the further analysis below.

[64] Thus, Gunkel included this psalm under his prophetic liturgies, though he also noted its Torah aspects (*Einleitung*, 329); see also his *Psalmen*, 214-218. One should also note here the work of Ernst Würthwein who saw in Psalm 50 the clearest example of prophetic judgment within the cult. See his "Der Ursprung der prophetische Gerichtsrede," in *Wort und Existenz* (Göttingen: Vandenhoek & Ruprecht, 1970). For a dissenting view concerning the prophetic nature of this psalm, see Walther Zimmerli, "Ich bin Jahwe," in *Geschichte und Altes Testament*, ed. by Gerhard Ebeling (BHT 16, Tübingen: Mohr, 1953) 204-209. On Zimmerli, see further below.

[65] Kraus, *Psalmen*, I, 371-372; see also Weiser, *Psalms*, 393.

[66] Zimmerli, "Ich," 204-209.

[67] Phillips, *Significance*, 72.

[68] Verses 5, 16.

[69] Though see Phillips' attempt to outline such a ceremony in his *Significance*. The opposite view of Zimmerli will be dealt with in an excursus below.

absence of further evidence concerning such ceremonies, it is perhaps better to leave the exact nature of the ceremony open. This is not to say, however, that the psalm does not offer real clues as to the mechanics of its actualization in the cult. One may, for example, note the very basic, yet important, fact that the setting was a communal one. Further, the community involved is in some sense representative of the people.[70] Of similar importance is the fact that the manifestation of the Deity is clearly an expected part of the ritual here, since it is anticipated by elements in the theophanic introduction.[71] Such elements also mandate the identification of the following speaker with God, an identification also dictated by the self-predication formula in v 7[72] and the general character of the speech. The judicial aspect of the speech is also anticipated as well, though the phrase *lādîn 'ammô* in v 4 should not be interpreted as an indication that a negative speech was anticipated.[73]

As important as any of these is the simple fact that such a psalm of warning, correction, exhortation, and conditional promise was actually a part of Israel's cult. Such elements are, of course, usually seen to be proper to the prophetic, rather than the psalmic, literature.[74] As such, they combine with the other prophetic elements surrounding the divine speech to suggest a prophetic means of delivery for that speech. Even more specifically, these elements may indicate a form of possession behavior, though one which is controlled both by communal expectation and by the demands of the ritual occasion. The possibility of such behavior will be discussed further below in the context of the comparative data.

Psalm 81 shares many of the elements of Psalm 50, and it too has been classified as a prophetic liturgy. It also belongs to a communal setting and contains a divine first person speech of warning, exhortation, and conditional promise. It has a similar divine self-identification,[75] and a similar command for the people to hear.[76] It is, however, slightly different from Psalm 50 in its more historical emphasis, both in the introduction and in the divine speech itself.[77]

Of more formal concern are certain differences in the introductions of the two psalms. As noted above, the introductory verses of Psalm 50 basically constitute a theophanic description. Those of Psalm 81 are, for the most part,

---

[70] See v 7.
[71] Especially the first part of v 3.
[72] On this formula, see the excursus which follows.
[73] It may simply mean that judicial activity was expected, without prejudicing the outcome of that activity.
[74] Though again see Würthwein, "Ursprung," on this issue.
[75] In v 11; note the historical grounding here.
[76] See the linguistic analysis in the previous chapter.
[77] See, for example, vv 6, 7-8, 11, 12-13. The imagery of Psalm 50 is centered more on nature than on history.

a hymnic summons.⁷⁸ This difference in introduction may be significant in terms of the question of how necessary the divine speech of Psalm 81 was to the ritual of which it was a part. Thus, whereas the speech of Psalm 50 was clearly anticipated and prepared for by its introduction, that of Psalm 81 comes as more of a surprise, since such a speech is obviously not the necessary conclusion of a hymn. One wonders if this implies a less ritually controlled prophetic impulse here, although it is unlikely that it was completely contrary to the expectations of the community, either in its manifestation or its message.⁷⁹ One indication that such a prophetic impulse might not be entirely out of place is the already noted connection of divination activity with the new moon in the ancient near east.⁸⁰

A singular speaker is indicated in the second half of v 6, in contrast to the plural of the introductory verse. This speaker is not, however, the Deity, as it is in the verses which follow. This appears instead to be the individual "I" of the intermediary through whom the Deity's speech is verbalized. As such, it is of some interest as a possible example of the transition to the trance state.⁸¹

The various critical attempts to locate this psalm in one of Israel's major festivals (such as the autumn festival) have been mentioned in the previous chapter.⁸² If any of these were to be accepted, it would indicate a connection between the Asaphite *traditio*⁸³ and that festival. This would not necessarily imply a continual connection throughout all of Israel's history, but it would imply a connection at some point in that history. More cannot be said without further evidence.

EXCURSUS: FORM-CRITICAL AND TRADITION-HISTORICAL IMPLICATIONS OF THE PHRASE "I AM THE LORD YOUR GOD"

One should perhaps comment a bit more fully on the phrase, "I am the LORD your God," which occurs in both Psalm 50 and in Psalm 81. This phrase (and certain variations on it) was, of course, the subject of Walter Zimmerli's famous article, "Ich bin Jahwe."⁸⁴ In that article, Zimmerli took note of the frequent use of this phrase in the Holiness Code and other priestly-legal material and proposed on this basis an original setting in the priestly pronouncement of the law.⁸⁵ Such a setting would, of course, have both form-critical and tradition-

---

⁷⁸ Vv 2-4. These summons are historically grounded in vv 5-6.

⁷⁹ Its preservation also would seem to imply a multiple usage, although if preserved by Ephraimites, with their regard for prophecy, this may or may not be the case.

⁸⁰ See the analysis of Psalm 81 in the previous chapter.

⁸¹ See n. 54 above.

⁸² See, among others, Kraus, *Psalmen*, II, 563-565; Weiser, *Psalms*, 553; Gunkel, *Psalmen*, 357.

⁸³ And possibly the Ephraimite tradition stream as well.

⁸⁴ Zimmerli, "Ich."

⁸⁵ One should also note the similar work of Karl Elliger, "Ich bin der Herr—Euer Gott,"

historical implications for the psalms under consideration here. It is, however, significant that Zimmerli himself distinguished somewhat between the above priestly usage of this formula and its function in Psalms 50 and 81.[86] In contrast to the explicitly mediated nature of the former, the latter is seen to reflect a direct interchange between God and the people—as was the case with the formula's use in the Decalogue. This difference is in keeping with the additional function of divine self-presentation found in the formulae of these texts. Naturally, in the context of the cult, both this divine self-presentation and the mediation of the commandments are spoken representatively through "*bevollmachtigten Menschen.*"[87]

In the context of Zimmerli's article, it is apparent that he would identify such a personage with a priest.[88] However, in spite of the phrase's frequent usage in the priestly literature, there is some reason to doubt whether such a conclusion is correct for these psalms. The most significant of such reasons is the aspect of direct communication between God and the people already cited by Zimmerli himself for these psalms and the Decalogue.

It is perhaps not unreasonable to argue that the distinction so consistently preserved in the Hebrew Bible between the direct communication of the Decalogue and the mediated communication of the rest of the law in fact reflects a real distinction between how these were actualized in the cult. The fact that the former direct communication is often surrounded by theophanic elements would also seem to point to such a different setting, a setting in which not only the word of God but also God's actual manifestation in some form plays a major role. The presence of this formula in the theophanic stories of the Pentateuch would also seem to support such a possibility.

How then is this direct manifestation of God to be envisioned? More specifically, in the case of Psalms 50 and 81, how is this manifestation to be conceived of as having taken place in the cult? One such possibility is that of prophetic means. Zimmerli, of course, is correct that, despite its use in the prophetic literature, this formula is not a specifically prophetic formula, at least not in such a way as *kōh 'āmar yhwh* or *nĕ'um yhwh*. Nevertheless, as has been noted above, the fact that these formulae are almost non-existent in the psalms material may mean that one should not expect prophetic activity in the cult to be indicated by these means. According to the above analysis, however, one way

---

Kleine Schriften zum Alten Testament (TBü 32; München: Chr. Kaiser, 1966) 211-231, which attempts to distinguish the different theological backgrounds of the variations of this phrase. More specifically, it sees this phrase as having a background connected to the *Heilsgeschichte*. This analysis does not, however, seem to challenge Zimmerli's determination of the setting, which is of crucial importance here.

[86] Zimmerli, "Ich," 207-209.
[87] Ibid., 207.
[88] Ibid., 204, 209.

that such activity may be indicated is by first person divine speech. Obviously, the formula under consideration here would be quite at home in such speech. This possibility draws some support both from the larger near eastern context and from within the Hebrew Bible itself. It is significant that this self-predication formula occurs in conjunction with a number of those comparatively rare cases where prophecy is to be found in the ancient near east. It is, for example, present in the Mari texts, where it is part of a message sent to the king by a prophet.[89] It is also found among the oracles delivered to Esarhaddon by means of various prophetic figures.[90] In neither of these cases does it appear to be connected with a formal recitation of the law.

The evidence from within the Hebrew Bible is suggestive as well. Again, the fact that this formula is to be found within the prophetic corpus is not necessarily indicative of an original prophetic setting, since the Israelite prophets are known for adapting originally non-prophetic forms to their prophetic purposes.[91] The question is instead whether one can determine from the usage in the prophets the original setting from which the prophets have taken the form. In such a way, Zimmerli is able to trace the use of this phrase in Ezekiel back to its original priestly and legal setting.[92] Still, as Zimmerli is aware, not all the occurrences of this phrase in the prophets or the other biblical literature necessarily point in the same direction. What needs to be brought out further, however, is the fact that some of these other occurrences can also be distinguished tradition-historically from that priestly-Ezekiel material.

The possibility that there is a tradition-historical distinction to be made between the different occurrences of this form is suggested by certain linguistic data. Thus, Zimmerli himself has noted that the material from the "priestly circle" (Ezekiel, H, P) uses the pronoun *'ănî*, while other sources, such as that of the Elohist, use the variant *'ānōkî*.[93] Nevertheless, he has not pursued this to its conclusion. To do this, one must also note that both the Decalogue and the Hosea occurrences of this formula join the Elohist in the use of *'ānōkî*.[94] Significantly, this usage is the same as that which is to be found in both Psalms 50 and 81.

---

[89] See A 2925, where an interrogative form of this formula is voiced by an *āpilu*; also see Herbert B. Huffmon, "Prophecy in the Mari Letters," in *The Biblical Archaeologist Reader* vol. 3, ed. by Edward F. Campbell, Jr. and David Noel Freedman (Garden City: Doubleday, 1970) 203-206.

[90] See the collection in K4310 and Wilson, *Prophecy*, 117.

[91] Though it does at least show it to be a prophetic possibility at some point.

[92] Zimmerli, "Ich," 192.

[93] Ibid., 193 n. 2.

[94] See Exod 20:2; Deut 5:6; Hos 12:10; 13:4; as well as Gen 31:13; 46:3; Exod 3:6 (all E). Significantly, almost all of the J and P usages of this formula use *'ănî*. See Gen 15:7; 28:13 (J); and Gen 17:1; 35:11; Exod 6:2, 6 (P). The only possible exception to this is Gen 26:24 which Zimmerli attributes to J but notes that it may be secondary ("Ich," 193).

A similar distribution appears when one considers the number of the second person pronominal suffix attached to the word God. Here again, the priestly and Ezekiel material line up on one side with their use of the form 'ĕlōhêkem, while the Hosea and Decalogue passages line up on the other with their use of the form 'ĕlōhêkā.[95] Once again, Psalms 50 and 81 contain the usage of the Hosea/Decalogue passages rather than the priestly/Ezekiel passages. The reason for the use of the 'ānōkî / 'ĕlōhêkā form in these cases is not entirely clear.[96] Nevertheless, this form does appear to be tradition-historically distinctive for Northern or Ephraimite circles. It is rarely, if ever, used in the usual priestly or Jerusalemite sources.[97] Conversely, the opposite form has its almost exclusive reference in Southern or Jerusalemite circles, though it is found once in the Ephraimite literature in Judg 6:10. Even here, however, it is significant that while the non-Ephraimite form is used, this passage has prophetic as well as legal aspects.[98] Thus, all the Ephraimite examples (including even the variant Judg 6:10) involve in some way a direct or prophetic encounter with the Deity. In keeping with their Ephraimite linguistic usage, the same would seem to be true of Psalms 50 and 81 as well.

It must, of course, be noted that both Psalms 50 and 81 do contain references to the law, and, more specifically, to the Decalogue. In at least the case of Psalm 50, however, this legal reference is not the same as what is to be found in Zimmerli's examples of priestly mediation. As noted in the last chapter, the "accusatory list" found in verses 17-20 has its best parallels in the similar lists of Hosea and Jeremiah. Such parallels are noteworthy in that they are both prophetic and Ephraimite.

The legal aspect of Psalm 81 is perhaps a bit closer to Zimmerli's examples, though it is even closer to the beginning of the Decalogue. It also, however, leads directly to an accusatory section similar to that found in a number of Ephraimite passages, as was also noted in the previous analysis.[99]

In this way, both the accusatory nature of these psalms and the particular shape of their accusations give some clues as to how these psalms were actualized in the cult. Again, this is not to deny the legal aspects of these psalms, especially

---

[95] The Elohist also has the singular but this is unavoidable in the context.

[96] One wonders whether the use of 'ānōkî is due to Northern dialect or metrical preferences. The topic needs more research.

[97] See n. 94 for Gen 26:24. This usage is to be found in the Korahite Ps 46:11, in a divine first person speech ('ānōkî 'ĕlōhîm). It is also the minority usage in second Isaiah (cf. especially Isa 51:15), but this is certainly not an unmixed Jerusalemite source.

[98] The fact that it is now a part of a prophetic address may explain why it is found in the present Ephraimite passage. On the other hand, the fact that there are possibly original legal aspects here (see Zimmerli, "Ich," 203-204) may help to explain the present non-Ephraimite form.

[99] The previous analysis also showed the Ephraimite links of the verses in question.

in terms of their connection to the Decalogue. It is, on the other hand, to emphasize that what is involved here is not simply a mediation of the law, as implied in Zimmerli's priestly use of this formula. Rather, it is a use of the law as a basis for an indictment of the people. Considering the similar use of the law throughout the prophets—especially the Ephraimite prophets—a prophetic role in the actualization of these psalms is surely not to be dismissed.

This excursus provides a good example of the way in which tradition-historical observations can affect even such technically form-critical conclusions as the determination of the life setting. Even in the case of such a brief formula as the one under consideration here, one can distinguish between two linguistic formulations, each of which appears to be at home in a different tradition stream and, further, in a different setting in that stream. In such a way, the present analysis allows one to link Psalms 50 and 81 with prophetic and Ephraimite circles rather than with priestly and Jerusalemite circles, as might have been suggested by a purely form-critical analysis.

Unlike Psalms 50 and 81 which involve the relationship between God and Israel, Psalms 75 and 82 deal with the wider divine relationship with the entire earth. In such a vein, certain elements were noted in the linguistic analysis of the previous chapter which indicate that these psalms were concerned with the status of the "nations," despite their being phrased in more general and symbolic terms. To the extent that these nations may be seen to be under the judgment of God, these psalms may also be seen as psalms of salvation or assurance for Israel, in a way similar to the oracles against the nations of the prophetic books. Not incidentally, these psalms were found to share many elements with the latter formal units.

On the basis of these psalms, then, the Israelite cult may be seen to have been involved with "national" concerns. Further, these psalms indicate that the Asaphite *traditio* was involved in the delivery of prophetic oracles relating to these concerns. Both of these facts are in some agreement with the already discussed account of 2 Chronicles 20, in which a similar oracle is delivered by an Asaphite under the guidance of the Spirit of the Lord. The location of this oracle in a ceremony of national lamentation in answer to a communal lament is especially interesting for determining the life setting of these psalms. Before accepting this as the setting, however, it is necessary to examine the psalms themselves in a bit more detail.

Like Psalm 81, Psalm 75 has been classed as a prophetic liturgy which opens in a hymnic style![100] The opening verse is especially noteworthy since it provides the main rationale for seeing a communal setting here. It also indicates a real degree of assurance on the part of the community, and as such may even anticipate the salvific nature of what follows![101]

---

[100] See Gunkel, *Psalmen*, 327.
[101] If this psalm were to be connected to the communal laments in some way, this verse

This hymnic introduction is followed by the divine speech of vv 3-4. This speech affirms the divine sovereignty, as well as the certainty of the divine judgment. These verses are in themselves only a general assertion of the nature of God, similar to that found in Ps 46:11.[102] However, in the course of the psalm, this speech provides the basis for the more specific image of judgment which follows.

Verses 5-11 are also in the first person, although it does not appear that these verses continue the divine speech.[103] More likely, a community spokesperson of some sort is to be thought of here. It is, unfortunately, difficult to tell whether this spokesperson is the same person as the one who has just verbalized the preceding divine speech. The spokesperson's speech itself is an interesting mixture of a confession of assurance with hymnic overtones[104] and more specifically "prophetic" images.[105] The rebuke of the wicked in v 5 appears to be a mirror image of complaints proper to the psalms of lament.[106]

If Psalm 75 is similar to Psalm 81 in its combination of hymnic and prophetic aspects, Psalm 82 is similar to Psalm 50 in its almost exclusive concern for theophanic description and divine speech. Thus, in Psalm 82, the first verse sets the scene by describing what has happened and what is about to happen,[107] while vv 2-7 constitute the divine first person speech. Only in the final verse does the community make itself heard in a petition combined with a brief hymnic statement.

Certain differences between these psalms should also be noted here. In Psalm 50 the divine speech is directed to the community there present, while in Psalm 82 the heavenly assembly itself is the primary addressee. The former is, of course, a necessary situation, since the direct confrontation of the community is the focal point of that psalm. In the latter psalm, on the other hand, the community overhears an independent "quasi-mythological" drama, a drama which concerns them intimately and which is enacted for their benefit.

The witnessing of such a mythological drama involving the heavenly assembly is not unknown elsewhere, and it is perhaps significant that one such event involves a prophet in the temple.[108] However, these other cases now have the form of prophetic narrations and, as such, do not really illuminate the

---

would almost function as a certainty of hearing, since it precedes the divine response.
[102] Though there the nations are more directly addressed in an imperative.
[103] See Gunkel, *Psalmen*, 327; Kraus, *Psalmen*, II, 522.
[104] Especially vv 5-6; also 10-11.
[105] Especially v 9. See the analysis of the previous chapter.
[106] See, for example, Ps 5:6; 10:3.
[107] The perfect-imperfect sequence of divine activity is similar to that found in Ps 50:1-4.
[108] See Isaiah 6. That such an event is not to be confined to the temple may be seen in 1 Kings 22. Also note the beginning of Job in this connection.

mechanics of how this would be actualized in the cult.[109] It is possible that these prophetic narrations are modelled on a cultic prototype such as that found in the present psalm.

In such a vein, it may be that both the descriptive introduction and the divine speech were narrated by an intermediary.[110] This is, however, unlikely for a number of reasons. One may first of all point to the parallel descriptive introduction in Psalm 50 which is phrased in the first person plural as an expression of the community. It is unlikely, though just possible, that this could be verbalized by an individual speaking for the entire community. It is equally unlikely that both the introduction and the speech in Psalm 82 are to be seen as all part of the same narrative entity, since the sequence of tenses in the first verse indicates a present actuality rather than the narration of a past event. The lack of a phrase to indicate a quotation also appears to tell against the mere narration of a past event here.

Perhaps the easiest way of envisioning how the introductory verse of Psalm 82 was actualized in the cult is to see it as having been sung by a group of singers to set the scene for the divine speech which follows. This would fit most easily with the parallel Psalm 50, though the issue is difficult to decide. The divine speech is less puzzling with respect to the mechanics of its delivery, since it fits the first person pattern which has been seen to be indicative of the activity of a cultic prophet engaged in direct divine speech. Nevertheless, once again it is worthwhile to note that the Deity's speech is on one level strictly in the mythological realm, even though the people are an obviously interested audience on another level.

The practical importance of the mythological confrontation for the community is to be found in the links between this psalm and the oracles against the nations. Such a "national" interpretation is reinforced by the response of the community in v 8 which, in seeming contrast to the heavenly interests of the previous speech, is concerned with the earth and the nations. It is striking that the psalm should end with a petition, since the divine sentence has already been handed down. One may perhaps envision here a communal urging either to carry out that sentence or to complete the judgment by applying it to the rival deities' client nations.

This psalm has obvious theological implications which go beyond such practical concerns. If, however, it did function on some level as an oracle against the nations, this would have real implications for its life setting. It would, for example, again point to the possibility that it could be a response to a collective lament, as discussed above in connection with Psalm 75. Such a setting would

---

[109] Isaiah 6 is a first person narration, while 1 Kings 22 (like Job 1-2) is a third person account.

[110] Such an intermediary would almost certainly be of a prophetic type, in keeping with the above parallels.

fit in well with the large number of collective laments in the Asaphite corpus. It is, however, difficult to be certain in this respect.

One should perhaps mention the fact that, like Psalms 50 and 81, Psalms 75 and 82 have been seen as part of various special ceremonies within ancient Israel. Once again, however, while these psalms would in many ways fit quite well in such ceremonies, they are clearly not a sufficient basis on which to prove their existence. Should such ceremonies be proven to have existed and these psalms to have been a part of them, the presence of these psalms within the Asaphite corpus would argue for a role for the Asaphite *traditio* in such ceremonies at some point in Israel's history.

Despite this uncertainty, one does need to pursue the question of life setting a bit further, though in a slightly different direction. The focus of this section has been on prophetic activity as it is manifested in the Israelite cult. When one defines this activity in line with such formal indicators as the presence of direct first person divine speech, there can be little doubt about its existence in the cult, though, of course, some may wish to quarrel with the designation of such speech as prophetic. However one defines such activity, one has the problem of isolating its distinctive life setting. On one level, this problem exists because of the multiplicity of genres in which such speech occurs. This has been discussed above and an analysis of the possible settings of each of the individual psalms has been presented.

In another way, however, the common formal nature of such speech demands a common "setting" in terms of the mechanics of the cultic activity itself. Concern for this aspect of the setting may be seen throughout this section in the attention given the question of how these psalms were actualized in the cult. It is unfortunately the case that while the biblical evidence permits a good case to be made for the existence of cult prophecy in general,[111] it only rarely provides any detailed description of how such prophecy actually functioned. A passage such as 2 Chronicles 20 is a helpful exception to this statement, and as such has been discussed a number of times above. It is, nevertheless, an exception which is almost unique and somewhat ambiguous in its temporal reference.[112] Because of this, there is a need to supplement the biblical evidence with evidence of an extra-biblical nature, both from the ancient near east and from similar societies elsewhere, as found in modern anthropological studies. A complete survey of such material must, of course, await a separate study of its own. Nevertheless, it is informative to consider briefly at least some of the relevant parallels

---

[111] See especially the classic work by Sigmund Mowinckel, *Psalmenstudien III: Kultprophetie und prophetische Psalmen* (Oslo: Jacob Dybwad, 1923) and the development of tne argument in Aubrey R. Johnson, *The Cultic Prophet in Ancient Israel* (Cardiff: University of Wales, 1944; 2d ed., 1962). See also the latter's *The Cultic Prophet and Israel's Psalmody* (Cardiff: University of Wales, 1979).

[112] See the further discussion of this passage in the next chapter.

[113] See the discussion and extensive bibliography on this material in Wilson, *Prophecy*, 89-134.

from these sources, since these do raise certain possibilities for the biblical texts under consideration here.

Although not especially numerous, significant parallels to the type of cultic activity implied by these psalms do exist in the ancient near east. Most important for our purposes are the prophetic texts from Mari, the Neo-Assyrian oracles concerning Esarhaddon and Assurbanipal, and the Zakir inscription,[113] since all of these contain first person divine speech. Of these, the Mari material is particularly relevant, since it provides the most information about the settings and mechanics of such speech — though the other texts do provide some information along these lines.

These texts clearly show that, at least at certain times, such speech had a definite role in the near eastern cult, where it was actualized by a number of prophetic or quasi-prophetic figures.[114] This speech often seems to have occurred in response to both an inquiry (or prayer) and sacrifice.[115] Such a response could be either positive or negative.[116] In addition, this type of speech could also play a role in the regular monthly festival.[117]

There is some indication that this cultic activity involved trance behavior in which the prophetic figure may have represented the deity in a manner similar to that of a possession type intermediary.[118] Such trances were apparently expected to occur spontaneously at certain points in the ceremony, though such behavior might be induced if spontaneous possession did not occur. It should, however, be emphasized that none of this precludes coherent speech and manners on the part of the possessed figure.[119]

Such ancient near eastern material obviously provides the most relevant parallels with which to interpret the biblical passages under consideration here. However, one should not ignore similar parallels to be found in modern anthropological studies, since these often provide detailed information about the setting and mechanics of such cultic activity. One may, of course, find many examples of ritual spirit possession in a wide variety of cultures. One must, however, distinguish between such possession in general and the more strictly

[114] On the cultic role of such figures as the *muḫḫû*, *assinnu*, and possibly the *āpilu* in the Mari texts, the *maḫḫû* and the *raggimu / raggintu* in the Neo-Assyrian oracles, and the *ḥzyn* and the *'ddn* in the Zakir inscription, see Wilson, *Prophecy*, 98-119, 130-134 and the texts cited there.

[115] For a response to prayer in Mari, see ARM 50; in the Neo-Assyrian oracles, see K 2401 and possibly K 883. The Zakir inscription also details such a prayer and its oracular response. For a connection with sacrifice in Mari, see ARM XIII:23; in the Neo-Assyrian texts, see S. A. Strong, "On some Oracles to Esarhaddon and Ašurbanipal," *Beiträge zur Assyriologie*, II (1891-94), 637-639.

[116] Contrast ARM XIII:23 with A.455 for examples of each in Mari.

[117] See the text cited by G. Dossin, "Un rituel du culte d'Ištar provenant de Mari," *RA* 35 (1938) 6, col. 2, 11. 21-27; col. 4, 11. 34-36.

[118] On the possible trance behavior of the *muḫḫû* and the *assinnu*, see Wilson, *Prophecy*, 103-107.

[119] See especially ibid., 103-104.

defined cases of spirit mediumship, where the emphasis is on communication between the divine and the human, especially as such communication occurs in the cult. This considerably reduces the number of relevant parallels, although these may still be found throughout the world.[120] Perhaps the best example of such cultic mediumship is to be found among the Yoruba of Nigeria and those groups related to them.[121]

Here again, as was the case with some of the prophetic figures of the ancient near east, spirit possession takes place at an appropriate point in the cultic ceremony. That is to say, it takes place at a point where its presence is expected by the community. The possessed person then assumes the personality of the possessing deity and delivers such speeches and performs such actions as would be expected of that deity. These activities are often vital for the course of the ceremony. Such behavior is very disciplined. It conforms to communal expectations and is to some extent under communal control, though this does not mean that the community may not be challenged by it.[122]

An example of such ceremonial possession may be instructive here. In the festival of the Yoruba deity, Shango, one finds the presence of 100-250 "horses" of Shango, or priests able to become the medium of that particular *orisha*.[123] Although all of these (along with the people) are involved in exhorting Shango to come, only one of this group is actually "ridden" or possessed by that deity. Such possession takes place at the exact moment when the sacrifice is offered. At that point, Shango, in the person of his possessed medium, takes the sacrifice in his arms to signify its acceptance.[124]

Such figures speak to the community in the first person and often speak praise in their own behalf.[125] They also can be involved in "if-then" dialogues

---

[120] For example, among the Veddas of Sri Lanka, the Tonga islanders, and the Tamils of India, in addition to the African and American parallels discussed below. On these and other cases of possession behavior, see T. K. Oesterreich, *Possession: Demoniacal and Other* (New Hyde Park: University Books, 1966), and the works cited throughout.

[121] That is, the Fon of Dahomey and the various New World descendants of these groups. On these, see the works cited below. The Yoruba society is actually similar to Hebrew society in a number of ways, especially in the religious sphere with its similar priesthood, prophets, and sacrifices. These similarities have prompted at least one author to see a common (ancient Egyptian) influence on both groups. See J. Olumide Lucas, *The Religion of the Yorubas* (Lagos: C. M. S. Bookshop, 1948), 213-214 and passim.

[122] See Pierre Verger, "Trance and Convention in Nago Yoruba Spirit Mediumship," in John Beattie and John Middleton, eds., *Spirit Mediumship and Society in Africa* (New York: Africana Publishing Corporation, 1969) 50ff. Also his "Yoruba Influences in Brazil" *Odu* 1 (1955) 1-11.

[123] That is, Yoruba deity. The similarity to certain aspects of 1 Kings 22 is suggestive.

[124] See Verger, "Trance," 52, for the ceremony. Such exhortation is also to be seen in "Influences."

[125] See Verger, "Trance," 56-58 and passim; see also Aidan Southall, "Spirit Possession among the Alur," in Beattie, *Mediumship*, 251, for a similar phenomenon among a

with the people, promising benefits if their wishes are followed and warning of destruction if they are not.[126] Such figures are often the voice of very traditional public opinion and are responsible for exposing and condemning scandals and taboo violations which have taken place in the community.[127]

Possession behavior of this type has been characterized by Walker as type one possession.[128] Some of the features of such possession are of interest here. Thus, as we have seen, type one possession is highly structured, often involving a detailed manifestation of the deity's character and behavior. This may sometimes take place in a re-enactment of a mythological event. The personality of the human who is possessed, on the other hand, finds little expression, being almost entirely subordinated to, or even vacated in favor of, the divine reality. Interestingly, the person who undergoes type one possession is often specifically chosen for his or her role and usually undergoes a set initiation period. He or she also serves only one god.

This brief excursion into other cultures has done full justice to neither the ancient near eastern material or the wealth of modern anthropological parallels. Nevertheless, even such a brief survey is a real help in illuminating the possibilities inherent in the biblical passages under consideration here. Thus, it is possible to see the first person divine speech isolated above not as a cultic anomaly or a set piece of some sort but rather as a dynamic living reality of the then manifested Deity. The setting for such a manifestation could be that of a response to a prayer or an inquiry, especially in a time of communal need.[129] It could also be part of the regular sacrificial and festival cult. All these are possibilities suggested by the comparative data which may be seen to have some echo in the biblical material itself.

It is, however, the question of the mechanics by which such a divine manifestation is actualized in the cult that is most aided by this excursion into the comparative material. This material has reinforced the possibility already mentioned above that the first person speech of these psalms is prophetic, possibly involving some form of spirit possession or trance behavior. Significantly, the comparative data has shown not only that such behavior is not foreign to cultic settings but that it can be closely adjusted to both the needs of the ritual and the expectations of the community.

Such possession behavior has also been seen to exist elsewhere in Israelite

---

different people, though here one is not dealing with a "high god" as in the case of the Yoruba but rather with the spirit of a departed chief.

[126] See, for example, Verger, "Trance," 59.

[127] See Margaret J. Field, "Spirit Possession in Ghana," in Beattie, *Mediumship*, 12.

[128] Sheila S. Walker, *Ceremonial Spirit Possession in Africa and Afro-America* (Leiden: E. J. Brill, 1972) 152ff.

[129] Such as was seen above in the discussion on the communal lament.

society,[130] where those who experience it are known as prophets. Given the comparative data and the implications of the formal use of first person divine speech, the presence of some similar form of cult prophecy should be seen as a distinct possibility for the psalms in question.[131]

Such suggestions for the presence of a genuinely prophetic element in the case of the direct first person divine speech in the psalms are, of course, valid for all the cases of such speech as detailed above. However, as was the case with the communal lament, one must also ask whether the specifically Asaphite psalms which contain such an element are in any way distinctive within this larger group. Significantly, the answer here seems to be a qualified yes. A case can be made that the Asaphite corpus contains the only pure theophany among the prophetic psalms. Psalm 50 is, of course, the best example of such a psalm which is almost completely dominated by the theophanic aspect. Psalm 82 is similar in this respect, although the final verse does bring the community into the picture somewhat. This psalm is distinctive, however, in that it very closely resembles the "re-enactment of myth" which Walker saw to be characteristic of type one possession.[132]

Another distinctive quality of certain prophetic psalms in the Asaphite corpus is the presence of an admonition or warning to the community or to certain segments thereof. Most first person divine speech in the psalter may be classified as oracles or proclamations of salvation, taking the form of either a positive word to the addressee or a negative word to the addressee's enemies. Two of the Asaphite psalms, Psalms 75 and 82, seem to fit this latter type, containing various forms of oracles against Israel's national enemies. Psalms 50 and 81, on the other hand, contain indictments or warning speeches against Israel itself. The only other example of such a first person divine warning is to be found in Psalm 95, a psalm which has been seen to have several similarities to the psalms in the Asaphite corpus.[133]

Thus, whether or not one sees Psalms 50 and 81 as representatives of a larger festival, they are significant in that they indicate, along with Psalm 95, a possibly distinctive Asaphite element in the cult. That such an element of warning is not

---

[130] Again see Wilson, *Prophecy*, 144-146, and passim. Also see the recent work of David L. Petersen, *Roles*, 16-34, for a somewhat different view.

[131] Such a possibility goes against many of the traditional Western ways of looking at cultic and ritual activities. It is the great benefit of the cross-cultural parallels that they call into question whether our views were necessarily those of ancient Israel.

[132] The distinctiveness of these psalms is a matter of degree, since their theophanic aspects have some connection with normal hymnic usage. The theophanic aspects of Psalms 50 and 82 differ, however, from normal hymnic usage in that the emphasis is not so much on God's past actions or abiding attributes as on God's present activity which is now manifest in the cult.

[133] See the linguistic analysis of the previous chapter. One wonders whether the location of Psalm 95 next to the deutero-Asaphite Psalm 96 is a further indication of a relationship here.

out of place in psalms of this sort may be seen from the comparative material described above. Several of the Mari first person speeches are concerned with demands for changes in the cult,[134] as is Psalm 50 on at least one level. Similarly, the uncovering of forbidden behavior and the demand for different behavior more pleasing to the deity is a prominent feature of both these psalms and the ceremonial spirit possession seen in the anthropological sources.[135] The conditional possibility of a return to divine favor with which both of these psalms conclude also finds an echo in the comparative data.[136]

The final task of this section is to compare the results of the above form-critical analysis with the possibility of Ephraimite connections suggested by the linguistic analysis of the previous chapter. In such a vein, it is evident that both the formally important first person divine speech and the possession type of prophecy suggested as the vehicle for such speech are attested within the Ephraimite stream. This is, however, not an exclusive connection, since both are to be found among prophets active in other, non-Ephraimite tradition streams. This, of course, fits with the fact that not all first person divine speech in the psalter is to be found within the Asaphite corpus. Still, the prominent place of such prophecy in the Ephraimite tradition stream does fit well with the prominent place such prophecy has in the Asaphite corpus.

Both the warning and promise aspects of the Asaphite prophetic psalms can be mirrored elsewhere in the Ephraimite tradition stream. Of these it is perhaps the warning aspect that is most interesting because of its relatively distinctive status. One may again recall the use of formally similar accusations to be found in both the Ephraimite prophets and these psalms. As such, the psalms may well represent a cultic parallel to the judgment oracles of such Ephraimite prophets as Hosea and Jeremiah. It is difficult to tell whether the psalms are toned down prophecies or whether the prophecies are heightened cultic statements, especially considering the dependence of each on the Decalogue.[137]

Similarly, if these psalms are to be connected with a covenant ceremony of some sort, such a ceremony would not be out of place in the covenant-conscious Ephraimite tradition stream. The Ephraimite Deuteronomic reforms, especially those of Hezekiah and Josiah, certainly provide appropriate settings for such a ceremony.[138] In any event, those reforms would certainly have provided an opportunity for Ephraimite influence in the cult. If one were to imagine how such influence might have taken form, one might do well to think of both prophetic

---

[134] It is not clear whether these demands took place in the cult, although some of them may have (cf. A 1121).

[135] See Field, "Possession," 12.

[136] See Verger, "Trance," 59.

[137] One may again remember the argument of Würthwein, "Ursprung," here.

[138] See, for example, the account of Josiah's reform in 2 Kings 23 and note the presence of prophets in 23:2. See also the Chronicles account of the reigns of both Hezekiah and Josiah.

psalms in general and such prophetic psalms as are now preserved in the Asaphite corpus. Whatever one decides about such Ephraimite connections, the formal evidence clearly suggests that the Asaphite *traditio* of these psalms included cultic prophets. The formal data may thus be seen to confirm the prophetic implications of such external passages as 2 Chronicles 20 and of such internal passages as Ps 74:9.

OTHER FORMS

Communal laments and prophetic psalms are undoubtedly the dominant formal entities in the Asaphite corpus, together comprising eight of the twelve psalms. The four remaining psalms do not form any similarly clear subgroups, and some are even difficult to classify at all form-critically. Nevertheless, despite the fact that the implications are not as strong as in the cases of multiple attestation, the presence of other forms within the Asaphite corpus is still a significant datum which needs to be investigated here. This may, however, be done a bit more briefly than was possible with the more common forms.

PSALM 73

Psalm 73's peculiar mix of wisdom, meditation, personal narrative, and individual lament has already been mentioned in the previous chapter. Such a mix obviously makes it difficult to deal with this psalm form-critically. Nowhere is this difficulty more acute than in the crucial question of life setting. Whereas the cultic setting of the individual lament is widely recognized by scholars, the additional wisdom and narrative elements of Psalm 73 raise questions as to whether this psalm could possibly share such a setting. One may note in this connection that the psalm's complaint is not so much a personal misfortune affecting the speaker as a general dissatisfaction with the working of divine justice. Indeed, even this theological dissatisfaction is dismissed from the start as unacceptable, even by the speaker, and it is seen instead as a source of temptation to the speaker's faith. The latter clearly removes the psalm from the setting of the individual lament, where the complaints are very real throughout. But even the complaint itself, with its explicitly theological and introspective nature, would make such a setting difficult, since it does not readily admit to any cultic resolution of the problem, as in the form of a *Heilsorakel* or the like.[139] For many scholars, these explicitly theological aspects point to a link with the wisdom "tradition." While this is undoubtedly correct to some extent, it only exacerbates the problem of the setting, since no one has been able to isolate a convincing

---

[139] Ernst Würthwein sees an echo of this in vv 17b-20, but this is certainly not a direct oracle as one finds in the usual case of the lament. See his "Erwägungen zu Psalm 73," in *Wort*, 177.

setting for the so-called wisdom psalm.[140] Adding to the form-critical confusion surrounding this psalm is the fact that some scholars see in it a mixture of communal and individual elements.[141] If, for example, the current MT of the first verse is true to the original,[142] this most individualistic of psalms would seem to take on a certain national consciousness.[143] If this were in turn to indicate a cultic setting, one is again faced with the problem of what kind of setting could be appropriate for this psalm.

When one shifts the focus from setting *per se* to the agent by which such a psalm is actualized, one fares a little better, though one is again faced with what is an overabundance of data. Thus, for example, Würthwein has suggested that the speaker of the psalm is the king, who sums up within his person both individual and communal elements.[144] In contrast to this, certain linguistic elements were noted in the previous chapter which would seem to point to a priestly or even, more specifically, a Levitical figure. Such an agent would certainly fit well with a literal interpretation of the speaker's continual nearness to God (vv 23, 28), as well as his telling of God's works (v 28).

The latter "priestly" possibility would also fit well with a non-cultic or "limited" cultic interpretation of the psalm. In this way, the psalm could be seen to have its setting either in more private priestly devotions or, more likely, in the internal education and training of priests. Cultic phraseology would certainly be at home in the latter, but so would a certain wisdom style.

That such an inner-priestly role is not impossible is perhaps indicated by Psalm 42–43 which also combines elements of the personal lament, introspective meditation, and a desire for the sanctuary. The fact that this psalm opens the Korahite psalter in a way similar to how Psalm 73 opens the Asaphite psalter may indicate a similar role for this type of psalm in each group of cultic personnel. The transmission of such a psalm of lamentation as "edifying religious literature" may be seen in the case of the Akkadian *šu-illa* psalms.[145] This would, of course, not rule out an originally cultic role of some sort.

Since Psalm 73 itself does not fit neatly into any one genre, it is difficult to compare it with formally similar psalms, as one could with the Asaphite collective laments and prophetic psalms. One may, of course, note that psalms such as Psalms 37 and 49 have a similar wisdom style and even an interest in the comparative fates of the wicked and the righteous. Nevertheless, the fact that such psalms do not contain such distinctive elements of Psalm 73 as the author's personal uncertainty and self-scrutiny makes one wonder how valid any genre

---

[140] See Gerstenberger, "Psalms," 220.
[141] As does Würthwein, "Erwägungen."
[142] As supported by the versions. On this, see also Würthwein, "Erwägungen," 167.
[143] See also v 15.
[144] Würthwein, "Erwägungen," 173. A presence in the sanctuary (v 17) is not an obstacle to such an interpretation.
[145] See Widengren, *Psalms*, 20–25.

comparison would be here. On the other hand, a psalm such as Psalm 42-43 contains exactly these latter elements, while the wisdom aspect is much less pronounced. In view of such multiple formal ties, it seems best to deal with this psalm on a more individual basis.

The same formal uniqueness makes it difficult to discuss the relationship between this psalm and the Ephraimite tradition stream.[146] The possible linguistic links to the Levites noted in the previous chapter would, of course, fit well with that group's similar links to the Ephraimite tradition stream.[147] Nevertheless, even royal agency would not be impossible for this stream, given the cultic activity of both Hezekiah and Josiah.[148] In terms of the form itself, one might perhaps think of certain of the Jeremianic laments which combine a similar introspective character with a concern about the prosperity of the unrighteous.[149] However, as with the similar psalms cited in the previous paragraph, these parallels are at best partial. Thus, while both the form and the theology of this psalm are not out of place among the Ephraimite tradition stream, in many ways they remain unique.

PSALM 76

Psalm 76 is usually seen as a song of Zion, though in the most technical sense this title is misleading. Like Psalms 46 and 48 with which it is often grouped, Psalm 76 is not so much a song about Zion as it is a song about the God who is manifested in Zion. One might well contrast these psalms with the more strictly Zion-centered Psalm 87, which Wanke has called the purest example of the genre.[150] The former psalms are perhaps more properly hymns in praise of the Deity, who is depicted as calming both international and cosmic disorder. Nevertheless, because of their peculiar connection to Zion, it is both useful to consider them together and convenient to give them a special designation. With the above caution, the title "song of Zion" may be retained for these psalms.

The common grouping of these three psalms is dictated not only by their similar content but also by certain formal similarities. Thus, for example, all three of these psalms open with a non-verbal clause containing a passive participle in which God is described. Similarly, these psalms all end with an admonition of some sort addressed to the community. It is also possible that a refrain

---

[146] It will also be remembered that this psalm had few certain linguistic links to the Ephraimite tradition stream, although it was linked linguistically to its fellow Asaphite psalms.

[147] As may be seen by their favored status in the book of Deuteronomy. On this, see further in the following chapter.

[148] Again see the accounts of those kings' reigns in both Kings and Chronicles.

[149] See especially Jer 12:1-4, with its initial confession of the righteousness of God and its notion of the "end" of the wicked, both of which are to be found in the present psalm.

[150] Gunther Wanke, *Die Zionstheologie der Korachiten* (BZAW 97, Berlin: A. Topelmann, 1966) 22.

or at least some kind of similarly spaced verbal repetition is to be seen as a distinguishing element of these psalms, though this is not equally pronounced in each case.[151] In addition to these structural parallels, one may also note the striking linguistic similarities between Psalms 76 and 46.[152] Together with the generally similar content, such elements point to a clear genre connection for these three psalms.

What then is the setting of these psalms? Given the role of Zion in each, one can only but imagine them in the Jerusalem temple, though there is no theoretical reason why Jerusalem could not be spoken of in such a way from a distance.[153] Their basic hymnic quality makes these psalms appropriate for a number of occasions. As might be expected, they have been placed in the various hypothetical festivals noted above by the advocates of such festivals.[154] Special festivals whose purpose was specifically to extol the virtues of Zion have also been conjectured, as has the possibility of pre-Israelite origins.[155] However, while all of these have certain points in their favor, it does not seem possible to prove any of them on the basis of the available evidence. What does seem certain is that these psalms were at home in a communal festival of some sort, as is indicated by the use of various plurals throughout.[156]

The agent who vocalized these psalms is also difficult to determine exactly. In view of the fact that these three psalms (and Psalm 87) are associated with the singers' guilds by their superscriptions, it is not unreasonable to simply assume their performance by temple singers. However, the fact that Psalm 46 has been seen to contain a prophetic speech is an indication that these singers may be a bit more complex than what is usually meant by that term.[157] There is, unfortunately, no evidence with which to say anything more than this.

Simply on the basis of the presence of Psalm 76 in the Asaphite corpus, one may see a role for the *traditio* behind these psalms in the theological reflection on God's activity with respect to Zion. This, of course, should not be unexpected, considering the place of Zion in such Asaphite psalms as Psalms 50 and

---

[151] In Psalm 46, vv 8 and 12 are an obvious refrain. Verse 1 also has the idea of refuge, though with a different word. There is no such obvious repetition of elements in Psalm 48, though some repetition does occur in vv 9 and 15, a placement similar to that of the refrain in Psalm 46. In Psalm 76, vv 8 and 13 repeat the element *nôrā'*, again a similar placement.

[152] Note the similar language used to describe God (of Jacob), the breaking of the bow, and the melting of the earth.

[153] See J. Maxwell Miller, "The Korahites of Southern Judah," *CBQ* 37 (1970) 62, which locates Psalms 46 and 48 among a community at some distance from Jerusalem.

[154] Thus, for example, Mowinckel places Psalm 76 in the feast of the *Thronbesteigung* of Yahweh (*Psalmenstudien*, II, 58–59).

[155] See Gerstenberger, "Psalms," 217.

[156] There are first person plurals in Psalms 46 and 48, and the second person plural of address is found in all these psalms.

[157] One may note in this connection that such Zion elements are not out of place in the prophetic book of Isaiah.

78. In Psalm 76, however, this theological reflection takes on a specific formal role with all its implications about setting. While the ambiguous nature of the latter does not allow one to characterize the *traditio* too much on this basis, there is still one significant fact which should not be lost sight of here. This is the probable setting of this psalm in Jerusalem. In view of the many Northern elements to be found in the Asaphite corpus, it is not unimportant that such an unambiguous link to the Southern cult center should be found here. This becomes even more important when one considers the possible links to the Ephraimite tradition stream.

Before doing this, however, one needs to consider whether there are any formal differences between this psalm and its fellow songs of Zion. One may note two possibly significant differences. First, it is interesting that, while not really hymns about Zion as much as about Zion's God, Psalms 46 and 48 still offer specific descriptions of the city.[158] Psalm 76, on the other hand, does little more than situate God's dwelling there as a prelude to the divine ordering and peacemaking activity.[159] The second distinctive aspect of Psalm 76 lies in the nature of the concluding admonition to the community. In Psalms 46 and 48, the community is urged to be aware of either the divine activity or of Zion itself.[160] In Psalm 76, on the other hand, the admonitions are more specifically cultic, concerning vows and offerings.[161]

Because of the limited examples of the form, it is difficult to tell whether these distinctive aspects of Psalm 76 fall within the normal limits of formal variation or whether they represent an attempt at a conscious redefinition of the genre. It is interesting, however, that both of these differences have the effect of minimizing the concern with the special nature of the city itself in favor of an extended focus on its God.[162]

As a final task, one must ask how the formal information provided by this psalm corresponds to the possibilities raised by the connection between the Asaphite corpus and the Ephraimite tradition stream. This is an interesting question, especially because of the many ties between such Zion psalms and the *traditio* represented by certain of the Isaianic materials. The latter is, of course, not unexpected, given the close relationship between Isaiah of Jerusalem and the David and Zion material. It is somewhat more surprising to place such materials in the context of the Ephraimite tradition stream with its strong ties to the North. Nevertheless, as noted in the previous chapter, a concern for Jerusalem is certainly not unknown in the Ephraimite tradition stream, a fact clearly illustrated by the repeated Deuteronomic emphasis on "the place where I shall cause my

---

[158] Ps 46:5-6; 48:2-4 (cf. also 13-15).
[159] Compare Ps 50:1.
[160] Ps 46:9-11; Ps 48:13-15.
[161] Ps 76:12; see the similar admonitions in Ps 50:14, 23.
[162] See also Psalm 83 which contains a *Völkersturm* without any reference to the city of Jerusalem.

name to dwell." Given the Ephraimite nature of its language, the present psalm may be seen as a cultic expression of such a theological position.

PSALM 77

The composite nature of Psalm 77 was noted in the previous chapter, where the linguistic evidence was seen to closely mirror the formal division of the psalm into two parts. For the purposes of the present analysis, it would be good to recall the fact that this psalm contains both individual and communal elements. Thus, what begins as an individual lament ends as a communal hymn.[163] The mixture of individual and communal elements goes further than this, however, since it is generally agreed that the cause of the individual's lament is no personal misfortune but rather the ongoing misfortune of the people of which the author is a part. Adding to the mixed nature of this psalm is the combination of historical and mythological divine activity which dominates the second half of the psalm.

This mixed nature makes it difficult to isolate an appropriate setting for this psalm.[164] Nevertheless, even if the psalm is truly a composite in the sense of a combination of two separate blocks of material, such a combination must have been effected for some purpose and have been at home in some setting. Both the psalm's introspective character and its possible recitation at night[165] would seem to speak against a communal setting, though not necessarily against a cultic setting in the temple.[166] Again, how such an individual emphasis is to be reconciled with the psalm's general concern with the communal situation and its specifically communal hymnic section is an open question, especially in terms of setting.

When one moves to the question of the personnel involved in the actualization of this psalm, one meets with a similar ambiguity, even though here the psalm's dual nature becomes something of an asset. Although it is possible that any member of the community would so feel the national plight as to be able to verbalize such a psalm, the latter is perhaps more appropriate to those who were bound up with the national fate in some more official capacity. The king is, of course, the first person of whom one thinks, though he is not the only figure who would have interceded for the nation. One might, for example, also envision a prophetic figure, as was theorized in the case of the collective lament. Similarly, in view of the priestly connection of the introspective lament of Psalm 73, a priestly agent is not to be ruled out. The exact agent by which this psalm was actualized is thus difficult to determine, even while his dual individual/national

---

[163] Note the first person plural in v 14.

[164] Kraus sees it as indicating a special situation for the psalm, though he does not elaborate on this further. *Psalmen*, II, 530.

[165] See vv 5 and 7; also v 3.

[166] Nocturnal priestly rituals are known from elsewhere in the ancient near east. The references here may, however, simply indicate sleeplessness.

nature is clearly indicated by the psalm.

The dual nature of this psalm also makes difficult the usual comparison with others of the same form. While the movement from lament to hymn or thanksgiving is quite common in the genre of individual lament, there are real differences between this and the apparently similar movement to be found here. It is, for example, difficult to imagine the presence of any possible *Heilsorakel* which could effect such a shift, as seen in the other laments. Rather, the movement from lament to hymn appears to be made even without the specific causes of the lament being addressed. Interestingly, while the reference to the previous gracious divine activity is a common motive in standard laments, here it occurs in the hymnic section, almost as an answer to the complaint. It is apparent that both the complaint and the hymn are here parts of the same internal process, the meditation or musing that is mentioned in both parts of the psalm.[167] Such a difference, of course, separates Psalm 77 from the standard laments and brings this psalm closer to such wisdom style laments as Psalm 73. Whether there is a specific cultic setting for such a meditation or whether it reflects a similar, more private situation is difficult to determine.

Given the above ambiguities, little additional information is gained from a comparison with the possibilities found in the Ephraimite tradition stream. As was the case with Psalm 73, all the parallels to the form of this psalm are at best partial because of the individual nature of the psalm itself. There is nothing here that would be completely out of place in that tradition stream, and the linguistic evidence for at least part of the psalm points to a link in that direction. Still, there is little on the formal level which points to a positive link.

PSALM 78

Psalm 78 is another of those psalms which is difficult to classify form-critically. The bulk of the psalm is an extended historical narrative which details the relationship between God and Israel from the exodus to the election of David. This in itself could be seen as one aspect of a hymn. However, the psalm's own introduction describes what follows as teaching, parable, and dark sayings from of old. Above all, it is seen as something to be passed from one generation to the next. In keeping with such terminology and such an instructional function, the psalm has been thought to be in some way related to wisdom.[168] Unfortunately, however, neither its dominant historical interest not its possible wisdom ties clarify its setting.

As was the case with Psalm 73, one of the things which makes any formal discussion of Psalm 78 difficult is its lack of any real parallels in the psalter. Significantly, two of the best parallels are the deutero-Asaphite Psalms 105 and 106, both of which contain extended historical retrospectives. However, it is to be noted that both of these psalms have clear ties to the hymn, while Psalm 106

---

[167] See vv 4 and 13.
[168] Thus, for example, Kraus, *Psalmen,* II, 539.

has additional petitionary and penitential aspects. In contrast, the introduction of Psalm 78 gives it an almost entirely instructional intent. In such a way, it is perhaps even closer to Deuteronomy 32, which also places its historical narrative in an instructional setting (cf. v 2), though there are other aspects present in the latter piece that are not to be found in the former.

The instructional nature of Psalm 78 should not, however, lead one to deny for it a setting in the cult. One may thus first note certain communal indications, such as the address to the people in the opening verse and the first person plural in vv 3-5. Such indications accord well with the specifically communal setting of Deuteronomy 32 and the cultic and communal setting of Psalms 105 and 106 as seen in 1 Chronicles 16.[169]

With respect to the question of who actually performed this psalm in the cult, the suggestion of Kraus that this psalm is an example of Levitical preaching is of special interest.[170] Such a description would, of course, fit the inherently instructional nature of the psalm itself. Even more striking, however, is the way such a Levitical actualization would fit with the Levitical performers of its closest parallels, the Moses of Deuteronomy 32 and the Asaphites of 1 Chronicles 16. It should, of course, be noted that these parallels are seen as songs![171] This is true even for Deuteronomy 32, which was seen above to have instructional aspects as well. One should thus perhaps not distinguish too neatly between Levitical preaching and Levitical song, since both may be actualized by the same personnel and even have something of the same purpose.

Although not strictly a formal distinction, one should also take note of this psalm's polemical aspects, since these too provide information concerning its *traditio*. On the surface, Psalm 78 appears to be a legitimation of David and Judah at the expense of the Northern Joseph tribes. Nevertheless, as was seen in the previous chapters, a linguistic analysis of the psalm would appear to offer strong arguments against placing this psalm in a time as early as the Davidic period. Accordingly, the psalm assumes a more metaphorical aspect, and as such its historical reference is most likely to a period other than the Davidic period to which it refers on the surface.

In this it is helpful to note that it is the Northern kingdom that is rejected and not the exodus and conquest "traditions" themselves (*contra* Coats).[172] Indeed, the latter are elaborated at great length and in such a way as to make the election of David and Judah the natural next step in the unfolding of God's gracious mercy. In addition to being an obvious polemic against the North, the psalm also constitutes a Southern appropriation of the quintessentially Northern exodus and conquest traditions. As noted above, the Ephraimite nature of the linguistic evidence suggests certain situations in which such a polemic and

---

[169] See Deut 31:30; 32:44-45; 1 Chr 16:3, 36.
[170] Kraus, *Psalmen*, II, 539.
[171] See Deut 31:30; 32:44; 1 Chr 16:7.
[172] Coats, *Rebellion*, 219, 223. On this, see also R. P. Carroll, "Psalm LXXVIII: Vestiges of a Tribal Polemic," *VT* 21 (1971) 133-50.

appropriation might have taken place — above all, the Ephraimite reform periods of Hezekiah and Josiah. If this suggestion is correct, it would indicate that the *traditio* behind Psalm 78 was active in Israel's political situation and more specifically, in the process of legitimating the Southern dynasty.[173] As was the case with Psalm 73, this psalm's relatively unique formal status makes it difficult to compare it with form-critical parallels much more than has already been done above. The normal second step of this tradition-historical look at the form-critical data will thus have to be foregone here. The final step, that of comparing the formal evidence with the possibilities raised by the psalm's linguistic evidence, is more productive. If the psalm is indeed some form of Levitical preaching, as suggested by both its instructional nature and the comparison with Deuteronomy 32, Psalms 105 and 106, it would fit quite well with a setting in a period of Ephraimite ascendancy, such as the reigns of Hezekiah and Josiah. Such a setting would also fit both the Ephraimite language and the polemical content of the psalm. On a more formal level, one might also note the similar Ephraimite tendency to historical narration which manifests itself in the so-called Deuteronomic credos. In sum, the form, content, and language of Psalm 78 all combine to indicate a *traditio* compatible with that of the Ephraimite tradition stream.

CONCLUSIONS

In the course of the preceding analysis, a form-critical treatment of the Asaphite psalms was found to have made possible certain characterizations of the institutional and functional status of the *traditio* behind those psalms. A brief summary of these findings may be useful here.

One of the most obvious aspects of the Asaphite forms is their overwhelmingly communal nature. The contrast between the relative paucity of the communal lament in the psalter as a whole and its prominent presence in the Asaphite psalms is perhaps the best indication of this corpus' communal tendencies. These tendencies are, however, indicated in other ways as well. The so-called prophetic psalms may also be seen to have a decidedly communal aspect, whether or not they somehow function in conjunction with the ceremony of collective lament. The same is true of the hymnic Psalm 76 and the instructional Psalm 78. Even the more individualistic Psalms 73 and 77 have their communal side, in some cases as a result of conscious adaptation.

To note this communal aspect is not, however, to deny the role of the individual here. Such individuals may be seen in both the requirements of performance and the occasional presence of the first person singular throughout. Still, these are individuals caught up in the concerns of the nation, and they

---

[173] One might wonder about the audience for which such legitimation was necessary. If the purpose was to legitimate David by means of the Northern traditions, the audience would be most appropriately inner-Ephraimite. Of course, the purpose might simply be that of tying the Northern and Southern theological elements together.

clearly have some functional status in the national cult. It is, unfortunately, difficult to be completely specific about the nature of these individuals. It is, of course, not necessary to assume that the entire Asaphite *traditio* was of the same functional status (*contra* Illman).

On the basis of the form of these psalms, one can say with some degree of certainty that the Asaphite *traditio* had some connection with cultic prophets. However, this does not necessarily mean that all of this *traditio* —which may include the authors, performers, and preservers of these psalms— were cultic prophets. Nevertheless, the prophetic status of the so-called prophetic psalms may make it more likely that such figures were also involved in the verbalization of the Asaphite communal lament. This would fit with the intercessory nature of the prophet in the Ephraimite tradition stream, as well as with certain specific passages within that stream. Nevertheless, even if the prophetic psalms were a part of the same ceremony as the communal laments, such an identity of performers is not strictly necessary![174] Again, functional identity is not necessary to the distinguishing of a *traditio*. Various functional figures may belong to the same *traditio*.

Such a functional diversity is perhaps indicated here by certain hints at Levitical connections contained in such psalms as Psalms 73 and 78. If indeed one has in the latter psalm an example of Levitical preaching, one may speak of the instructional activity for which Levites have been known. However, it is important not to draw too sharp a distinction here, since any such activity most likely took place in the cult, possibly in the form of song. Further, Levites were not adverse to prophecy, as may be seen both by the literature in which they figure and the Ephraimite tradition stream of which they were a part, at least in the preexilic period.

It is also too simple to say with Buss that the Asaphites were involved in the religious education of the people. Instead, the Asaphites are to be seen as involved in a wide range of community religious functions. They also were vitally concerned about the political-religious state of the nation in a manner which goes well beyond the specific functional task of religious education.

There were, however, some aspects of the cult in which the Asaphites were not involved, at least as far as one can tell from the psalms which make up their present collection. They do not, for example, seem to have had much of a role in the ceremony of the individual lament—in either its intercessory or its oracular aspects. There is, of course, always the possibility that they were involved in these rituals and that they used the common treasury of psalms in such a role. They were at least familiar enough with this material to use it for their own purposes in such psalms as Psalms 73 and 77. Nevertheless, what

---

[174] There is, of course, the question of the trance or non-trance state of the performers at each stage of the ceremony which must be addressed in this regard. That such difficulties are not insurmountable may be seen in the Shango ceremony described above.

marked the Asaphites off as a group was not to be found in this area but rather in the more communal affairs of the national cult.

As may be seen from the presence of similar forms elsewhere in the psalter, such communal functions were not unique to the Asaphites, although the exclusivity of their concern with them is somewhat distinctive. It is, however, also necessary to ask whether there was anything distinctive about the way the Asaphites performed these functions, as evidenced by differences in the forms themselves. The clearest example of such a difference was found to be in the prophetic psalms, where Psalms 50 and 81 (and the related Psalm 95) provide the only examples within the psalter of a divine speech of inner-Israelite correction and warning. Such correction and warning may also be seen as implicit in the instructional form of Psalm 78![175] It may even be seen in the formally distinctive cultic exhortation which ends the Zion song, Psalm 76. Even the prophetic salvation oracles of Psalms 75 and 82 are couched in judgment terms, directed here against the nations but also possibly having inner-Israelite implications as well![176]

This is certainly not to imply that such concern for correction serves the function of Illman's "characteristic common content" as a way of uniting these psalms. Such a content would not necessarily indicate a common *traditio* in any case. Such tendencies, however, do appear to be present here both in the forms used and in certain aspects of the content. This may indicate a real theological concern on the part of the Asaphite *traditio,* one which may further indicate an historical setting. In line with previous indications of both a linguistic and a formal nature, one naturally thinks of a setting in a period of reform—though there is no reason why such tendencies could not have been an ongoing part of the Israelite cult.

As a final issue, one may note the formal parallels to possibilities found within the Ephraimite tradition stream, to which these psalms are linked by the linguistic evidence. In particular, the intercessory nature of the communal lament and the prophetic possibilities of other of the psalms were seen to have clear parallels in the Ephraimite literature. The historical retrospective of Psalm 78 has similar parallels, whether or not it is to be taken as an example of Levitical preaching. Even the Zion song, Psalm 76, and the more introspective Psalms 73 and 77 were seen to be not completely out of place in connection with that tradition stream.

A special mention may be made here of two formal or formulaic units of less than genre status which show a certain Ephraimite tendency. The first of these is the Decalogue-based "accusatory list" of Psalm 50 which was seen to have its best parallels in the Ephraimite prophetic literature. Similarly, the phrase

---

[175] See especially vv 7-8. Such elements may also be present in the parallel Deuteronomy 32.
[176] Thus, the "wicked of the earth" (Ps 75:9) could also have an inner-Israelite echo, although the language on the whole points in an international direction.

"I am the LORD, your God" was seen to have Ephraimite links in its Psalms 50 and 81 usage, despite its presence in a rival stream in an alternate formulation.

In sum, the formal analysis of the present chapter may be said to have filled out the description of the *traditio* established on the basis of the common superscription and the common linguistic elements. It now remains to compare this description to those facts which can be discovered about the Asaphites from the evidence external to the psalms. This is the task of the chapter which follows.

5
Asaph and the Asaphites: A Tradition-Historical Analysis of the External Evidence

The previous two chapters of this work have been concerned with those internal aspects of the Asaphite psalms which might indicate their tradition-historical connections. In contrast, the present chapter is a consideration of the external evidence which may be brought to bear on the psalms on the basis of their common superscription. Primary among this external evidence are those biblical texts in which either Asaph or one of his "descendants" figures. As indicated by the history of research outlined in the second chapter, these texts have often been the subject of critical inquiry in an attempt to illuminate either the authorship or the setting of the psalms. Rarely, however, have these texts, like the psalms themselves, been examined in a tradition-historical way — that is, with a view towards understanding how they fit into the larger religious movements in Israel's history. Similarly, just as the psalms had first to be considered on their own without reference to the Asaphite links indicated by their superscription, so now the Asaphite texts indicated by that superscription must be considered on their own in an attempt to better understand their tradition-historical connections. After this has been done, the attempt can be made to consider how well the internal and external evidence cohere to provide a complete picture of the *traditio* of the psalms.

Most of the texts which deal with Asaph and the Asaphites are contained within the work of the "Chronicler."[1] In fact, the only time the name Asaph is to be found outside that work and the psalms is 2 Kgs 18:18, 37 (= Isa 36:3, 22),

---

[1] That is, 1 and 2 Chronicles, Ezra, and Nehemiah. These books are usually seen as connected to each other as the result of an extended period of compositional and redactional activity within the same tradition circle. The main level of this activity — whether it be that of an individual or a "school" — may be conveniently referred to as belonging to "the Chronicler." Similarly, the entire work may be referred to as the "work of the Chronicler," provided that it is understood that this is a mere convenience which does not prejudge the complexities of the tradition process here.

where reference is made to Joah, the son of Asaph, the recorder.[2] Leaving the psalms aside, this is also the only reference to an Asaph to be found in the pre-exilic literature.[3] There is, of course, no guarantee that this Asaph has anything to do with the Asaph of either the Chronicler or the psalms, and, in fact, the passage has rarely been considered in this context. Nevertheless, there are some aspects of this passage which prompt a closer look.

The obvious reason for the neglect of this passage is that the Joah, son of Asaph, mentioned here has nothing to do with singing or even the temple service. He is apparently a completely secular official in the service of King Hezekiah, one of the three officials who met with the Assyrians during the latter's siege of Jerusalem. His formal title is *mazkîr*, which de Vaux translates as "herald" in accordance with Egyptian parallels.[4] In Egypt, the herald had the dual role of reporting to the king on what concerned the people and passing on the commands of the king to the people. He was also in charge of palace ceremonies, such as introducing people to an audience with the king.

Although it is difficult to tell whether this royal official has any connection to the more liturgical Asaphites one meets elsewhere, some points are intriguing. First of all, one must note the treatment of this Joah in Chronicles. While there is no exact parallel to 2 Kgs 18:18, 35 in the latter work, one does find a "Joah" of some importance in its account of the reign of Hezekiah. 2 Chr 29:12 describes a Gershonite Joah, the son of Zimmah, as well as an Eden the son of Joah. It is indeed tempting to read this data in light of the genealogy found in 1 Chronicles 6 and to see the first figure as the same Gershonite Joah son of Zimmah found in 1 Chr 6:5-6 — and further to see the Eden as his son Iddo, as found in the same place.[5] In any event, one meets in 2 Chr 29:12 with a Gershonite Joah in the time of Hezekiah who is not a descendant of Asaph in a way that the Joah of the Kings account is.

The situation becomes even more interesting, however, when one compares the Joah genealogy of 1 Chronicles 6 with the Asaph genealogy of that same chapter. Both Asaph and Joah are Levites, and, even more specifically, Gershonites. Further, in the generations immediately following Gershom, both Joah and Asaph have many similarly named ancestors. This may be seen as follows:

---

[2] Or herald, as suggested by Roland de Vaux, *Ancient Israel*, (New York: McGraw-Hill, 1965) 132. See further below.

[3] That is, if one sees the Deuteronomistic history as having existed in two editions, in which case the present chapter would almost certainly have belonged to the pre-exilic (Josianic) edition rather than the later exilic edition. If one opts instead for a single edition, the written form of this passage would be early exilic. In either case, the material preserved here has a good claim to pre-exilic status, and is even possibly simultaneous with the events.

[4] See de Vaux, *Israel*, 132, where de Vaux also notes that the three officials of this passage are named in the same order in an Egyptian text.

[5] This would require only a minor change in the reading of the final letter.

Levi
Gershom
Jahath
Shimei
Zimmah
(9 generations)
Asaph

Levi
Gershom
Libni
Jahath
Zimmah

Joah
Iddo
(2 generations)

This may, of course, be sheer coincidence. However, the similar order and multiple nature of the overlap would seem to argue for more than this.

At the very least, then, the Joah of 1 Chronicles 6 and 2 Chr 29:12 shares substantial segments of the Asaphite genealogy. And, while he is nowhere held to be a son of Asaph, as he is in the account of Kings, the Joah of the Chronicles tradition[6] may be seen to have retained a substantial genealogical connection with the lineage of Asaph. In this way, it seems likely that, at least for this tradition, the Asaph of 2 Kings 18 was not seen to be unrelated to the Asaph found elsewhere in the Chronicler's work.

The real question raised by the treatment of Joah in the Chronicler's account is that of why he has dropped the explicit designation of Joah as a son of Asaph. The answer to this is certainly not because Asaphites were felt to be out of place in the mission of Joah. On the contrary, they are mentioned in the next verse as also involved in that mission. Instead, the most probable explanation would seem to lie in the fact that in the tradition of Chronicles, Asaph was the eponymous ancestor of the singers' guild of the same name. While the connection of Joah with Asaph would be preserved through other, more indirect, genealogical means, the actual name of Asaph was reserved for the ancestor of the singers' guild. Indeed, because Joah was obviously not a member of a singers' guild, he could not even be listed as a descendant of such an ancestor.

Another question remains. Does the Asaph of 2 Kgs 18:18, the only Asaph of which we know from the pre-exilic literature, have anything to do with the singers' guilds which are later associated with that name? Given the extreme scarcity of the data in the Kings account, it is impossible to say. The fact that Joah was a herald and an apparently learned man capable of understanding Aramaic does not seem to provide any useful information in this respect. Nevertheless, it may not be insignificant that the only pre-exilic mention of Asaph should occur in association with the Ephraimite reformer king Hezekiah.[7] This

---

[6] 1 Chr 6:16-33 is a later edition to the chapter and does not stem from the hand of the Chronicler himself. See Wilhelm Rudolph, *Chronikbücher* (HAT 21, Tübingen: Mohr, 1955) 58; also Hartmut Gese, "Zur Geschichte der Kultsänger am zweiten Temple," in his *Vom Sinai zum Zion* (BEvT 64, München: Chr. Kaiser, 1974) 150. Because of this, it seems best to refer to the more inclusive "Chronicles tradition" here.

[7] Note that 2 Chr 29:12-13 preserves the involvement of both Joah and the Asaphites

is especially the case since it is in this reign and in other such reform reigns that Asaphites are seen to be active in the tradition of the Chronicler. These latter texts will, of course, be discussed further below.

From the pre-exilic reference of 1 Kings 18, one moves to the early postexilic mention of Asaph in Ezra 2:41 and Neh 7:44. This twice-repeated text is part of the larger census of those who first returned from exile. Although this verse is a mere head count of "the singers, the sons of Asaph," it does provide some information for the history of these singers. First of all, as has been noted by others, the fact that singers were included in the return implies that they were an integral part of the worship in the pre-exilic temple.[8] Secondly, this text also shows that as early as the last part of the sixth century such singers were to be identified with the sons of Asaph—and apparently exclusively with these, since no other singer families are mentioned. Thirdly, the fact that the singers are listed separately from the levites (v 46) shows that at this time—in contrast to a later time—the singers were not considered to be a "levitical" group.[9] Finally, one may note the small number of singers[10] in comparison with the considerably larger number of priests in the preceding verses.

To these commonly accepted observations, one may raise a few questions. First of all, one might ask whether the Asaph here is an actual historical personage or whether he already has the status of eponymous ancestor which he undoubtedly has elsewhere in the work of the Chronicler. If one is to take Asaph as parallel with the other names of these lists, it would not appear that this is a reference to the Davidic Asaph, as it is elsewhere in the Chronicler's work. However, even if the Davidic Asaph is not indicated, such eponymous ancestor status cannot be completely ruled out, either for Asaph or for the other figures in this census list. Whatever his historical status, the Asaph of this list is representative of the singers in such a way that the Chronicler could later use this name for his Davidic prototype as well. Again, it is important to take note of the exilic and possibly pre-exilic status of this figure.

Further questions are raised by the non-levitical status of the Asaphites here, especially in view of their attainment of this status in the next level of tradition. Various authors have made much out of this distinction between

---

with this reign. Interestingly, one meets with another recorder by the name of Joah in connection with the reform of Josiah in 2 Chr 34:8.

[8] This conclusion is not absolutely necessary since an exilic origin for these singers is possible at least in theory. However, a pre-exilic origin seems much more likely. See Justus Köberle, *Die Tempelsänger im Alten Testament* (Erlangen: Fr. Junge, 1899) 24; also Gese, "Geschichte," 147.

[9] See also Ezra 10:23-24 which again separates singers from levites. There is no mention of Asaph or the Asaphites here, however.

[10] The difference in the exact number of singers between the two lists (also see the versions) does not appear to be significant here.

levites and Asaphites. Illman, for example, sees this as an argument against Buss' attribution of the Asaphite psalms to Levites.[11] Nevertheless, it may be that the intricacies of the relationship between the singers and the Levites have not been fully explored. The problem would seem to have its roots in the vexed issue of who or what exactly is a Levite. This is, of course, not the place to unravel the full complexities of this much debated issue. Some discussion is, however, important to any understanding of the tradition history of the Asaphites. In particular, it is necessary to keep in mind the fact that "Levite" is used in the Hebrew bible in at least two different senses which are neither identical nor mutually exclusive. The first of these is genealogical — that is, it refers to anyone who traces his or her lineage back to the eponymous ancestor Levi. Whether this originally referred to a "secular" tribe of Levi or whether the genealogical Levite always had a priestly status cannot be gone into here.[12] It is, however, clear that throughout much of the history of Israel those who traced their lineage to Levi were involved with the priesthood in some special sense.

The converse statement is not as easily made. That is, one cannot as easily assert that all those who were involved with the Israelite priesthood always claimed Levitical lineage. Thus, for example, while Abiathar is clearly linked with Levi through the Elide line,[13] the same claim is not explicitly made for his fellow high priest, Zadok, until after the exile.[14] After the accession of Solomon, of course, priestly status — at least at the Jerusalem temple — was denied Abiathar. In this connection, the priestly aspiration of the entire tribe of Levi is a key element of the Deuteronomic reform, though one which was destined to be frustrated, at least in part.[15]

In other words, a claim of Levitical lineage, at least at some times in Israel's history, also implied a claim to the priesthood, even at the temple itself. Conversely, however, not all those who were of priestly status were necessarily accounted of Levitical lineage,[16] at least in the pre-exilic period. In the post-exilic

---

[11] Illman, *Thema*, 63.

[12] For a fuller treatment, see among others, Kurt Möhlenbrink, "Die levitischen Überlieferungen des ATs," *ZAW* NF 11 (1934) 184-231; Antonius H. J. Gunneweg, *Leviten und Priester* (Göttingen: Vandenhoeck & Ruprecht, 1965); de Vaux, *Israel*, 358-371; Aelred Cody, *A History of Old Testament Priesthood* (AnBib 35, Rome: Pontifical Biblical Institute, 1969); Leopold Sabourin, *Priesthood* (Leiden: Brill, 1973); Menahem Haran, *Temples and Temple-Service in Ancient Israel* (Oxford: Oxford University, 1978).

[13] See 1 Sam 22:20; 14:3; 2:27-36; 1 Kgs 2:26-27. See also Wilson, *Prophecy*, 170-172, 302-304.

[14] For this Levitical claim, see the Zadokite glosses of Ezekiel 40-48 (such as 44:5 which identifies the sons of Zadok as Levitical priests) and the genealogies of Chronicles (such as 1 Chr 5:27-41; 6:35-38). Compare Haran who sees Zadok as of Levitical ancestry from the start (*Temple*, 77-78).

[15] See Deut 18:1-8, but also 2 Kgs 23:9.

[16] At least they were not given this lineage by the circles responsible for the

period, however, all those who claimed the priesthood also came to claim descent from Levi.[17]

This genealogical usage is, however, not the only use of the term, "Levite." It is also used to refer to a certain cultic office of sub-priestly rank. These "levites"[18] are involved in the operation of the temple and its liturgical service but are usually barred from such specifically priestly functions as the offering of sacrifices and the burning of incense.[19] Their function is often seen to be that of service to the priests, and they are correspondingly a part of the stereotypical phrase, the priest and the levites. It is important to note that the levites of this functional type are usually seen to be genealogical Levites as well.[20] Obviously, however, not all genealogical Levites are functional levites, since some of the former are priests. In the post-exilic period, the priestly Levites are distinguished genealogically as sons of Aaron.[21] To the other genealogical Levites belong the functional levites.

In light of the above, it is interesting to speculate on how the minor temple functionaries received the name levite. That there is some connection with the earlier genealogical Levites would appear to be reasonably certain. Nevertheless, it is striking that whereas the genealogical Levites of the pre-exilic period are usually either connected with or aspiring to the priesthood, it is precisely that office which is denied the functional levites of the post-exilic literature. Thus, in the post-exilic period most Levites become levites, even while the priests become Levites. In terms of the history of the priesthood, it seems likely that what one finds in the office of functional levite is a post-exilic institutionalization of the demotion of Abiathar, a demotion that even the Deuteronomic reforms could not fully overcome. The post-exilic levites are neither totally excluded from the now centralized cult nor are they awarded full priestly status.

This distinction between genealogical and functional "Levites" has often

---

Deuteronomistic history who apparently reserved this for themselves.

[17] See n. 14 above.

[18] In an attempt to keep separate the two different uses of this term, Levites of the genealogical type will be capitalized, while the functional levites will not be.

[19] This is most explicitly stated in the Zadokite glosses, such as Ezek 44:13, but is also to be found in Numbers 3. See also the polemical Numbers 16-17 in this connection.

[20] This is explicit in Numbers 3, 16-17, but it is implied by the Zadokite glosses as well. The genealogies of Chronicles trace out this Levitical lineage in detail.

[21] Of both the Ithamar and Eleazar lines, according to P and Chronicles, although the Zadokites had earlier made an attempt at an exclusive priesthood (see the Zadokite glosses in Ezekiel 40-48). In the course of the struggles over the priesthood, the Zadokites apparently came to claim Levitical lineage through Aaron. The later compromise reserved the high priesthood and a greater number of priests to the Zadokite line. This was expressed genealogically in terms of a descent through the more prestigious Eleazar and his son Phinehas.

been noted,[22] though its implications for the passage at hand have not been appreciated as much as they might. While Ezra 2:41/Neh 7:44 certainly shows that the Asaphite singers were not counted among the functional levites, this does not rule out their inclusion among the genealogical Levites. In fact, the placement of the singers immediately following the priests and the functional levites may indicate a certain affinity to those groups which at least later were given Levitical genealogies.[23] As will be seen, the singers too are given Levitical genealogies at that time.

Accordingly, one cannot go as far as Illman with respect to the significance of the distinction between the Asaphite singers and the levites here. One can only say that at the time of the census of the returnees, singers were distinguished from the functional levites in the temple hierarchy.[24] This in no way prejudices the question of whether these singers at that time traced their lineage back to Levi, as one finds elsewhere in the work of the Chronicler. If they did, this would indicate a certain relationship with Buss' pre-exilic Levites, though this does not mean that all Buss' comments about the nature of these Levites can be accepted.

The next time that one meets with the name Asaph is in another census list, the so-called list of inhabitants. This list has been incorporated into the Nehemiah memoirs (in Nehemiah 11), and a form of it is also to be found in 1 Chronicles 9. Since the genealogical nature of this list can be plausibly connected to the reforms of Nehemiah, it can be dated to the middle of the fifth century.[25] In this list, one learns of a Mattaniah, the son of Mica, son of Zabdi, son of Asaph who, at least in Nehemiah, was the leader to begin the thanksgiving in prayer.[26]

A number of points are worthy of note here. While Mattaniah, at least in the Nehemiah version, is still to be connected with the "sons of Asaph, the singers" of Ezra 2/Nehemiah 7, he is here listed under the levites. There has thus been a change in status from the previous list where the singers were distinguished from the levites. Given the descending order of official status in these lists, the inclusion of the singers among the levites would appear to be a promotion of some sort. Nevertheless, the significance of this move is not entirely clear, and it should be noted that the singers are still listed in a secondary position among the levites.

---

[22] Thus, for example, Köberle has distinguished between a narrower and wider sense of the term. *Templesänger,* 48 and passim.
[23] Though the *nĕthînîm* and the servants of Solomon which follow may present some problems for this view.
[24] As will be seen below, this distinction does not remain for long.
[25] See Gese, "Geschichte," 148-149, as well as the bibliography cited there.
[26] See Neh 11:17 and compare 1 Chr 9:15 which omits the latter information. There is also a difference between these lists in the name of Asaph's son—Neh 11:17 having Zabdi and 1 Chr 9:15 Zichri (see also G^L for Zichri in Neh 11:17).

A second change from Ezra 2/Nehemiah 7 may be found in the fact that others who are not sons of Asaph are here included among the singers. While Bakbukiah, "the second among his brethren," is apparently also an Asaphite, Abda, the son of Shammua, son of Galal, son of Jeduthun is obviously not.[27] This addition is of some importance for the history of the singers in the post-exilic period,[28] since it is the first of many additions to the ranks of the singers. It also marks the first appearance of the figure of Jeduthun who will remain among the singers until almost the end of the Chronicles tradition. However, despite the addition, one should note the priority of the Asaphite Mattaniah in this passage.[29]

It is unclear whether the Asaph (or the Jeduthun) whom one meets here is to be understood as the eponymous ancestor of the Davidic period whom one meets later in the Chronicles tradition. Certainly, if one takes the number of generations from Mattaniah to Asaph literally, it would in no way allow for such an ancient reference. It would, in fact, scarcely allow for a pre-exilic date for Asaph. In addition, the parallel with the other figures of this list also make an identification with an eponymous Davidic Asaph difficult. Once again, however, one should not rule out all eponymous possibilities.

A final element which deserves further comment here is the designation of Mattaniah as the leader to begin the thanksgiving and prayer. As noted above, the priority of this Asaphite figure is clearly a part of the list. However, the attribution of a more specific leadership role is less certain, since it is missing from the Chronicles parallel. At any rate, the involvement of the Asaphites in thanksgiving and prayer is something that will recur throughout the later Chronicles tradition. The stage at which this aspect of their ministry was spelled out in the present text is difficult to determine.

A few verses after the Nehemiah passage just considered, one meets a certain Uzzi the son of Bani, son of Hashabiah, son of Mattaniah, son of Mica, of the sons of Asaph, the singers, who was overseer of the levites in Jerusalem over the work of the house of God (Neh 11:22). The Mattaniah-Mica-Asaph part of this genealogy is clearly similar to that which was found in the previous passage.[30] This, however, causes certain chronological problems, because, while the genealogies make Uzzi the great grandson of Mattaniah, the placement of this verse here also makes him his contemporary and superior. This verse seems

---

[27] There are many minor differences between the versions of the names of each list, though they are for the most part clearly related.
[28] See Gese, "Geschichte," 149, as well as the entire article for a good discussion of this history in general.
[29] This is especially the case in the Nehemiah passage, though such priority is also to be seen in the Chronicles parallel, with its listing of Mattaniah first.
[30] Note that Zabdi/Zichri is missing in this passage and that the specific end point in Asaph has become the more general "sons of Asaph." There are also some similarities to Neh 12:35, especially if Mica and Micaiah are to be seen as related.

to be out of place in its present position on other grounds as well.[31] The other two verses having to do with overseers (*pāqîd*) in the list immediately follow numerical summaries of those who are to be supervised.[32] Neh 11:22, however, is separated from its appropriate numerical summary in v 18 by a census of the gatekeepers (v 19), an overall summary statement about the rest of the people (v 20), and an account of the temple servants and their overseers (v 21).[33] Although the presupposition is that the levites too once had an overseer immediately following their census, in analogy with 11:9, 14, all of these factors point to a peculiar status for v 22. More specifically, v 22 would seem to reflect a later period than the original list of inhabitants. Indeed, it may plausibly be seen to stem from the Chronicler himself, since the three additional generations beyond the Mattaniah of Nehemiah's time would place it near the time of the Chronicler.

In this verse, an Asaphite singer has not only risen to the office of levite, but has also become overseer of the levites with respect to the work of the house of God. A further indication of a solidifying of the singers' status may be seen in the following verse, where daily provisions are provided according to the command of the Persian king.

Some additional comment should be made concerning the phrase "the sons of Asaph, the singers" which appears in this passage. This phrase has already been seen in Ezra 2/Nehemiah 7, where it was part of a series of similar genealogical notations. It will be remembered that because of these similar listings, it was difficult to determine how much this phrase was to be taken in a professional-eponymous, rather than a literal-genealogical, way. In the present case, however, there does not appear to be much doubt about the professional character of the phrase. In comparison with the similar v 17, the literal genealogical connection has been broken. No longer is Asaph merely the end point of the genealogical lineage, as in v 17. Instead, the more general plural, sons of Asaph, is used, in distinction from the rest of the chapter. The transition to professional eponym has clearly been made.

Neh 12:35 is another passage with ties to 11:17. Here, in the midst of the account of the dedication of the wall, one meets with a Zechariah the son of Jonathan, son of Shemaiah, son of Mattaniah, son of Micaiah, son of Zaccur, son of Asaph. Once again, the last four names of this genealogy have obvious links with the genealogy of 11:17.[34] Mattaniah, Micaiah, and Asaph also link this passage to the genealogy in 11:22, though the post-Mattaniah lineage is completely different in each case.

As with the previous two passages, this verse is to be found in the Nehemiah

---

[31] It is, for example, not to be found in 1 Chronicles 9.
[32] Neh 11:9, 14.
[33] The latter does not use the term *pāqîd* as found in 11:9, 14, and 22.
[34] Thus, Zaccur appears to represent the 1 Chronicles 9/G^L alternative (Zichri) of the Zabdi in Neh 11:17, while Micaiah appears to be an alternate form of the Mica found in both versions.

memoirs. As with 11:22, however, there are certain aspects which render an original setting in these memoirs problematic. Thus, for example, v 35 is the only place in the entire account of the dedication where a genealogy of one of the participants is given. Further, the verse sits awkwardly in its present position, where it is uncertain whether Zechariah is to be taken with the *bĕnê-hakkōhănîm* of the first part of the verse or with those figures which follow in v 36. Although the natural translation would be to link Zechariah with the former, this is difficult on a number of grounds. First of all, the expression *mibbĕnê-hakkōhănîm* would appear to anticipate more than one figure, especially when it is combined with the plural *baḥăsōṣĕrôt*. Yet, if *mibbĕnê-hakkōhănîm* refers to what follows, Zechariah is the only candidate, since Shemaiah etc. are clearly to be connected with the instruments of David and not the trumpets. Further, the inclusion of an Asaphite among the priests raises certain tradition-historical problems in itself, since this would be a unique instance of such an inclusion.

For these reasons, it would seem that the *mibbĕnê-hakkōhănîm* should be taken with those names which precede it in vv 33-34, in spite of the difficulty raised by the *waw*. In support of this is the parallel list in v 41, where seven trumpet-playing priests are named. This would also be the case if the names of vv 33-34 are considered as priests.[35] In such a vein, v 36 may also be seen to be parallel with v 42, since each contains a list of eight names who would then be associated with the singers. Neither Jezrahiah, the leader of the singers in v 42, nor the Asaphite Zechariah would be counted in this list of eight. They would then be parallel to each other, with the Asaphite as the leader of "his brethren" (v 35). The two halves of the dedication ceremony would then look like this:

Hoshaiah	Nehemiah
Half the princes (*śārê*)	Half the officials (*hassĕgānîm*)
7 priests	7 priests
Zechariah	8 singers
8 singers	Jezrahiah

In spite of the fairly exact parallel thus obtained, the difficulties in the text and the obtrusive extended genealogy of Zechariah would seem to argue for a later hand here. Once again, as with 11:22, the post-Mattaniah genealogy would appear to extend to the time of the Chronicler. Both the concern with musical instruments and the priority of Asaph are at home in that time as well. If this is the case, it is important to note that this later hand saw nothing out of place with an Asaphite presence in the time of Nehemiah.[36]

---

[35] See also 1 Chr 15:24, in which the names of seven trumpet playing priests are enumerated as well. However, in other places the number of such priests can vary from two (1 Chr 16:6) to twenty (2 Chr 5:12).

[36] Before leaving the book of Nehemiah, one should note the presence of a certain Asaph, the keeper of the king's forest, in Neh 2:8. Unlike the other references to Asaph in the Bible, there does not appear to be any relationship to the singer Asaph in this case.

The next Asaphite passages to be considered take one more clearly beyond the sources of the Chronicler into the main body of his work. It is, of course, generally accepted that this history is not a one-dimensional work, and this is abundantly clear when one looks at those passages which have to do with Asaph. Fortunately, these passages are, for the most part, fairly clear in their relationship to each other. In such a vein, one may start with the Asaph material which may plausibly be seen to stem from the hand of the so-called Chronicler—that is, the editor-author responsible for the main body of that work. The Asaph material which is contained in the additions to the main body will be considered afterwards.

Pre-eminent among the Asaph material in Chronicles is what might be called the "foundation story" of 1 Chronicles 16. This chapter details the Davidic establishment of the singer cult, an establishment that will figure prominently throughout the rest of the Chronicler's history. As might be expected, the foundation story is full of a number of significant tradition-historical elements.

In 1 Chronicles 15–16, the ark is brought into Jerusalem and arrangements are made for its maintenance there. Of prime importance in both of these activities are the levites. The levites carry the ark on their shoulders, and in 16:4 they are appointed as "ministers before the ark." More specifically, this ministry entails an invoking, thanking, and praising of the Lord. In other words, their new ministry is the ministry of the singers.

Several points should be noted in this scenario. First of all, this passage assumes the development that has taken place from Ezra 2/Nehemiah 7 to Nehemiah 11/1 Chronicles 9. The singers are here clearly of levitical rank, and are explicitly seen to have always been of such rank. In such a way, the levitical standing of the Chronicler's own day is given a Davidic etiology.[37] Further, in a clear anachronism, the levitical nature of the singers is seen here as functional rather than genealogical. This is evident from their repeated mention alongside the priests.[38] On the other hand, nothing is said directly about the genealogical standing of these levitical singers, as will be done later in the Chronicles tradition.

Among the levitical singers, Asaph has the clear pre-eminence, and he is given the title *hārō'š*. With him in v 5 are nine fellow singers of secondary rank.[39] These are referred to as the brethren of Asaph in vv 7 and 37. A relationship of some sort is also indicated by their common ministry before the ark. In contrast, the singers Heman and Jeduthun are explicitly linked, not with the ark in Jerusalem, but with the tabernacle in Gibeon (16:41).

It is perhaps significant that this name should show up in a post-exilic context here. Still, the name does have a pre-exilic usage in 2 Kings 18. More cannot be said about this passage.

[37] For the slightly different etiology of 1 Chr 15:16–24, see below.

[38] See 15:4, 11, 14, though compare 15:12.

[39] Note the partial overlap with 15:18, 21. Implicit here is a certain fluidity between the gatekeepers and the singers, a fluidity which may be seen elsewhere as well.

Important here is the special connection of Asaph and his brethren with the ark, a connection which even sets them apart from other levites. The fact that this passage makes such a distinction within the levitical singers is clearly tradition-historically significant. Since the ark was no longer in existence at the time of the Chronicler, the latter cannot simply be attempting to provide an etiology for a contemporary liturgical situation. Instead, he appears to be offering an explanation for the differences between Asaph and some of his fellow singers. This distinction is somehow related to the connection of Asaph with the ark.

The special connection of Asaph with the ark, then, offers a real clue towards a description of the Asaphite singers, at least as they were seen by the Chronicler. In tradition-historical terms, the Asaphites—again, at least for the Chronicler—can be put into a relationship with those other figures who can lay claim to a special connection with the ark. The identity of these figures is a very significant tradition-historical datum.

In the Chronicler's own source book, the Deuteronomistic history, the ark is first of all connected with the temple at Shiloh and, consequently, with the Elide priesthood. This connection continues even after the ark has been brought into Jerusalem, in the person of the Elide Abiathar.[40] In such a way, the Chronicler would appear to have first of all linked the Asaphites with the Elide priesthood and its Jerusalem descendants.

To say only this, however, would be to ignore both the other textual evidence and the larger tradition-historical significance of the Elide line. Thus, one may note that there do exist in the Deuteronomistic history scattered references to Levites carrying the ark.[41] These are usually taken as later glosses, since they appear to reflect the post-exilic office of the functional levite. It is, however, at least minimally possible that some of them could be accepted as pre-exilic,[42] if the Levitical references are taken in a genealogical rather than a functional vein. Thus, for example, in 1 Sam 6:15, the genealogical connection is made at least plausible by the fact that Beth-Shemesh is elsewhere seen as a Levitical town.[43]

Equally interesting is the usage of Joshua 3-8 where the ark is said to be

---

[40] See 1 Samuel 1-4; 1 Kgs 2:26; also 1 Sam 14:18 MT where the ark is again in the possession of an Elide, though some Greek versions have ephod for ark here. This would fit better with 14:3 MT which also has ephod.

[41] See 1 Sam 6:15; 2 Sam 15:24; compare 1 Kgs 8:4.

[42] The dual "priests and levites" of 1 Kgs 8:4 would not allow for such an interpretation, though this phrase is missing from most Greek manuscripts and its presence in the MT is a clear overload. As such, it seems likely that it is a later addition of the post-exilic period.

[43] See Josh 19:11; also 1 Chr 6:44; though note that these cities are given to Aaron among the Levites. It is difficult to say how 2 Sam 15:24 is to be taken. Here the Levites are clearly connected with the carrying of the ark, but so is Zadok. Abiathar comes later in the verse and the syntax is difficult with respect to how they all fit in. Note the different implications of vv 25 and 29 in this regard.

carried by priests. Significantly, however, the first and last references to priests carrying the ark in these chapters (MT 3:3, 8:33) speak of the "Levitical priests." This inclusion of sorts is apparently an attempt to make the Deuteronomic claim of the priesthood for the entire tribe of Levi explicit even in the older narrative material. This claim also may be seen in connection with the ark in Deut 10:8, where the commission of the Levites to carry the ark is accompanied by a commission to priestly duties as well.[44] Deut 31:9 explicitly refers to the priests, the sons of Levi, who carried the ark of the covenant.[45]

Accordingly, within the Ephraimite tradition stream as manifest in Deuteronomy and the Deuteronomistic history, those who carry the ark are usually seen as either Elides or Levites—that is, genealogical Levites. Since the Elide line may plausibly be seen to be connected with the Levitical circles responsible for the Deuteronomic works,[46] a clear tradition-historical picture emerges here. Notably, in this tradition stream, the carrying and care of the ark is seen as a priestly function, connected with either Elides or specifically Levitical priests.

Account must also be taken of two passages outside the Ephraimite tradition stream which connects others with the ark. The first of these is Num 3:31, which connects the ark with the Kohathites. This would actually fit better with the later Chronicles tradition reflected in 1 Chr 6:16 which sees all the levitical singers in charge of the service of song in the house of the Lord after the ark comes to rest there. In contrast to the earlier 1 Chronicles 16, Heman the Kohathite would be included in this and would even be preeminent, since he is listed before Asaph. One can only conclude that this constitutes a rival tradition to that reflected in 1 Chronicles 16 and the Ephraimite stream.

A similar tendency might also be seen in the overloaded addition to Judg 20:27-28, where Phinehas is said to be ministering before the ark. The exact nature of this ministry is not certain, however, and it is difficult to be sure of the tradition-historical direction here. It is, however, interesting that Phinehas is the ancestor of Zadok, who is explicitly excluded from ministry before the ark in 1 Chronicles 16.

In light of these tradition-historical observations, one may see 1 Chronicles 16 as establishing a clear link between the genealogical Levites of the Ephraimite tradition stream and the ark-connected Asaphite singers. The fact that the non-Ephraimite figure Zadok is not connected with Asaph but with the alternate

---

[44] Standing before the Lord, ministering to God directly (as opposed to ministering to the priests or the congregation), and blessing in God's name, all of which are priestly prerogatives elsewhere.

[45] One might also mention Jer 3:16, the only reference to the ark in the prophets, which reflects the concern over the ark in Ephraimite circles. 1 Kgs 8:3, 6 also sees the carrying of the ark as a priestly function, though it does not specify these as Levitical priests. (On v 4, see n. 42 above.)

[46] See Wilson, *Prophecy*, 302-304, and n. 13 above.

singers and shrine at Gibeon is a further confirmation of this tradition-historical link. Significantly, what was once seen as a priestly function belonging to the Levitical priests has now become a levitical function belonging to the Asaphite singers. This change is also reflected in 2 Chr 5:4, where the priests of 1 Kgs 8:3 have been changed to levites.[47]

Once again, for the Chronicler, those who were once genealogical Levites (with priestly functions, at least at one time) have now become functional levites, and, even more specifically, Asaphite singers. In such a vein, it is of interest that this priestly function of the levites re-emerges at various times in the Chronicler's work—usually during the reform movements of Israel's history.[48]

In the present passage, Asaph and the levitical singers under him do not appear to have any priestly functions. Neither do the opposite singers under Heman and Jeduthun who are left with the tabernacle at Gibeon. However, these other singers do not need any such priestly powers, since Zadok the priest and his brethren are also connected with that sanctuary. In contrast, no priest is explicitly left with the ark in Jerusalem, even though one should have expected Abiathar (but cf. v 6). In view of the above tradition-historical observations, it may be that Abiathar is in some way represented by Asaph here. In any event, the placement of Zadok in the opposite shrine with the opposite singers is yet another indication of Asaphite links with the Ephraimite tradition stream.

The function of the Asaphites before the ark is to "invoke, to thank, and to praise the LORD, the God of Israel." The latter two functions (ydh and hll) are often joined together in the Chronicles tradition as attributes of the levitical singers.[49] Interestingly, each of these verbs is used frequently throughout the psalms, though only rarely in parallel with each other.[50] As such, the Chronicler's use of these terms together seems to be an attempt to refer in a summary way to the singing of psalms. The additional reference to invocation is unique in the Chronicler's work, though the purpose appears to have been the same, since this activity is also commonly named in the psalms. It should, be noted, however, that despite this summarizing tendency, the reference to invocation, thanks, and praise is not all-encompassing in terms of Israel's psalmody. In fact, it appears to exclude some of the very aspects of Israel's psalmody which have a prominent place in the Asaphite psalms. This discrepancy will be dealt with at the end of this chapter.

In 1 Chronicles 16, however, Asaph and his brethren do exactly what they

---

[47] Though 2 Chr 5:7 retains the reading "priests."

[48] See, for example, 2 Chr 29:34 and 35:14, though in the latter case the singers were not involved. On the priestly aspects of the levites in Chronicles, see Adam C. Welch, *The Work of the Chronicler* (London: Oxford University, 1939) 77 and passim.

[49] And of David as well. See 1 Chr 16:4; 23:30; 25:3; 29:13; 2 Chr 5:13; 7:6; Ezra 3:11; Neh 12:24.

[50] See Ps 35:18; Isa 38:18.

have been commissioned to do; they sing psalms of thanksgiving and praise.[51] More specifically, they sing sections from Psalms 105, 96, and 106,[52] psalms which by virtue of their Asaphite performance here have been referred to as deutero-Asaphite throughout this work. In this collection are included many variations of hymnic and confessional statements, almost all of which fulfill the description of thanks and praise. The only possible exception is v 35a (= Ps 106:47a) which is a communal petition. Even this, however, quickly moves into a statement of thanks and praise in the second half of the verse.

Verse 34 is noteworthy since it recurs throughout the Chronicler's work as a fixed refrain of the levitical singers. It is, as such, not restricted to the Asaphites, and it even finds an echo among Heman and Jeduthun in v 41 of this chapter. It is also the standard opening of many psalms.

The concerns found in 1 Chronicles 16 also dominate the rest of the Asaphite passages which may be attributed to the Chronicler himself. Thus, 2 Chronicles 5 picks up from 1 Kings 8 the account of the transfer of the ark into the Solomonic temple and adds to this account some special features concerning the cultic officials involved in the transfer. Not surprisingly, the levites figure prominently in the revised account, replacing, as has already been seen, the original priests in the carrying of the ark. The levitical singers also have a prominent place in this ceremony, especially after the ark has come into the temple. In fact, it is during the performance of the song of praise that the glory of God made itself present in the form of a cloud.

One variation from 1 Chronicles 16 may be seen in the fact that here Asaph, Heman, and Jeduthun (together with their sons and kinsmen) all perform together. This is, of course, only appropriate since this passage recounts the centralization of Israel's cult in the Jerusalem temple. Nevertheless, the fusion of these circles in the temple is a tradition-historically significant occurrence, probably reflecting the usage of the Chronicler's own day. As in 1 Chronicles 16, the role of the levitical singers is to praise and thank God, again using the standard refrain in 5:13.

2 Chr 29:12-14 has already been discussed to some degree in connection with Joah the son of Zimmah and his role in 2 Kings 18. This enumeration of the levites involved in the reform of Hezekiah is, however, interesting in other ways as well. This passage not only details a list of participants from the classic

---

[51] Rudolph (*Chronikbücher*, 127), following J. Wilhelm Rothstein (*Kommentar zum ersten Buch der Chronik* [Kat 18, Leipzig; A. Deichersche, 1927] 297), sees this psalm as a late addition to 1 Chronicles 15-16, though the grounds for this are not entirely compelling. Still, even while Rudolph places its incorporation into this text as late, he does note that in itself it probably had an earlier setting, since it is Asaph and not Heman who is featured prominently here. Such a connection would make its tradition-historical value similar to that which it would have if it were original to this passage. In any event, it may be considered here.

[52] Vv 8-22 = Ps 105:1-15; vv 23-33 = Ps 96:1-13a; v 34 = Ps 106:1 (also 107:1; 118:1; 136:1); vv 35-36 = Ps 106:47-48.

Levitical families[53] but also includes two participants from each of the levitical singers, Asaph, Heman, and Jeduthun.[54] This is indeed fitting, since in the following account of Hezekiah's reform, the major role is taken by the levites and the levitical singers.

In vv 25-30 there is an extended description of the musical ceremony performed by these figures.[55] A number of elements are interesting here. First of all, one may note the co-ordination of song and sacrifice. The song begins when the sacrifice is offered on the altar (v 27), continues throughout (v 28), and finally concludes the entire ceremony (v 30). The latter musical conclusion is specified as the words of David and of Asaph the seer, though the actual words are not given. This introduces the second feature worthy of note, namely, the twofold Davidic grounding of the musical ceremony (v 25, 30). Along with this Davidic grounding is a prophetic grounding—through "Gad, the king's seer and Nathan the prophet" (v 25) and through "Asaph the seer" (v 30).

The exaltation of the levites in this chapter goes beyond a highlighting of the musical cult. In some places, it even means an encroachment on the priestly prerogative. Specifically, the greater righteousness of the levites in sanctifying themselves allowed them to take over the priestly sacrificial function. Other priestly functions had apparently already been given to them in 29:11.[56] In view of the special connection of the levitical singers with thanksgiving, it is perhaps appropriate that the levites are specifically involved in the offering of the thanksgiving sacrifices here.[57]

From all of the above, it is obvious that for the Chronicler the levites—and the levitical singers—occupied a special place in the reform of Hezekiah. This is often explained by saying that the Chronicler was fond of these functionaries in his own day and was even possibly one of them himself. It is, of course, quite correct to take note of this levitical concern which is undoubtedly present on the part of the Chronicler. However, to do only this is to stop short of the important tradition-historical question of why this concern has manifested itself specifically in the reign of Hezekiah. In other words, one must ask what it was about this reign—and most especially its reform—which lent itself to an expression of the Chronicler's levitical interests. As will soon be seen, this question will repeat itself with respect to the reign of Josiah, a fact which in itself gives a clue to the answer of this tradition-historical question.

---

[53] And of the less well known Elizaphan.

[54] The two Asaphite participants have names familiar from other Asaphite references, namely, Mattaniah and Zechariah.

[55] They are called levites in vv 25, 26, and 30, where they both sing and play musical instruments. One meets with singers proper in v 28.

[56] See Welch, *Chronicler*, 76-77. On P's view of the consequences of non-priestly burning of incense, see Num 17:5.

[57] See further Jer 33:11 which combines the bringing of thank offerings with the standard levitical refrain. Note also the specific call for thank offerings (as opposed to other kinds of sacrifices) in Ps 50:14, 23.

These reigns are, of course, the only reigns which are given the full Deuteronomistic blessing in the Chronicler's source, 2 Kings. Further, these reigns are the prime examples of Ephraimite influence in the Southern monarchy and its cult. Part of this expression of Ephraimite influence was the reassertion of old Ephraimite claims to the central priesthood from which this group had been barred since the expulsion of Abiathar. The Deuteronomic phrase, "Levitical priests, all the tribe of Levi," is an example of this Ephraimite aspiration to the central cult. How thoroughly this aspiration was realized is difficult to determine,[58] but it is undeniable that it was at these times that Ephraimite influence in the Jerusalem cult was at its highest.

It is indeed striking that it is at these points that the Chronicler gives his most exalted accounts of levitical participation in the cult. Once again, it would seem that the functional levites of the Chronicler's day are in some way a reflection of the Ephraimite genealogical Levites of the pre-exilic period. This, of course, does not resolve the question of whether the cultic functions which the Chronicler narrates here are reflective of his own day or that of Hezekiah (or even whether it is an ideal plan advocated by him and never implemented). It does, however, address the larger tradition-historical question of how the Chronicler saw the relationship between the characters of his own day and those of the past.

It is thus not clear from this passage whether the levites of the Chronicler's day had attained or even aspired to the priestly rights of sacrifice, incense burning, and blessing. What is clear is that the Chronicler saw such levites as in some way related to those figures in the past who had either attained or aspired to those rights at the time of the great Deuteronomic reforms. That is, the Chronicler sees the levites of his day as in some way related to the Ephraimite circles connected with the Deuteronomic literature.

One final question remains, that of why the Chronicler is so concerned to undergird both the musical set-up and the actual words of praise by prophetic means. Petersen has suggested that the Chronicler was using this device to argue for the prophetic status of the levitical singers of his own day.[59] While a complete discussion of Petersen's position is best left until 2 Chronicles 20 is considered, it is at least necessary to note here that this does not do justice to the present passage. Indeed, the latter makes no claims for any prophetic activity by the singers in the time of Hezekiah. By extension, no such claim is made for the singers' activity in the Chronicler's own day. Rather, it is only claimed that the foundation of the musical aspect of worship is to be attributed to prophetic means. Asaph is the seer, not those levitical singers who use his words. The point seems to be not that the singers are prophets but that their performance here was not only according to Davidic specifications but also according to a direct divine

---

[58] Again see 2 Kgs 23:9; also Wilson, *Prophecy*, 243, 304.
[59] David L. Petersen, *Late Israelite Prophecy: Studies in Deutero-Prohetic Literature and in Chronicles* (SBL Monograph Series 23, Missoula: Scholars, 1977) 84, 87 and passim.

command, as is emphasized in v 25. It is, however, interesting that for the Chronicler this implied a prophetic legitimation.

Most of the points made in connection with the Hezekiah reform may also be made with respect to the Josianic passover in 2 Chronicles 35. Once again, one meets with the prominent role (and expanded prerogatives) of the levites. Again, one finds the singers at their appointed places during the service (v 15). Again, the musical aspect of the cult is given both Davidic and prophetic grounding,[60] though again no specific prophetic activity is attributed to the singers at this time.

The tradition-historical observations made concerning these points in connection with the Hezekiah passage are all applicable here. Here too one should emphasize the important tradition-historical connection which the Chronicler has made between the levites and the levitical singers of his own day and the Ephraimite circles of the pre-exilic period.

The only additional point that requires comment in this passage is the simple apposition of singers with sons of Asaph in v 15. In view of the standard reference to Asaph, Heman, and Jeduthun in the same verse, it is somewhat surprising that the singers involved in Josiah's passover could be grouped under the ancestry of the first of these figures alone. Implicit here are the hierarchical primacy and the chronological priority of the sons of Asaph, both of which have been seen above. The hierarchical primacy was probably still a feature of the Chronicler's own day.

The hand of the Chronicler is also evident in two other Asaphite references found in his larger historical work, namely, Ezra 3:10-11 and Neh 12:46. Ezra 3:10-11 recounts the foundation of the temple under Zerubbabel. Here one finds many of the same elements which characterized the Chronicler's description of the singers elsewhere. Thus, for example, the singers are here identified with the functional levites (opposite the priests). More specifically, these singers are referred to as the sons of Asaph who perform their task according to Davidic direction. This task is to praise and thank God with the standard refrain seen above.[61]

The importance of this passage does not lie in this fairly standard description of the Asaphites. Rather, it lies in the fact that the Chronicler associates the Asaphites with the re-establishment of the temple. This fits well with the inclusion of the sons of Asaph in the list of returnees. Of course, the latter list sees the Asaphites as separate from the levites, while the Chronicler has all but identified them. It is also well to remember that whereas the list's mention of the sons of Asaph probably has a very specific denotation, the Chronicler is capable

---

[60] The latter by means of Asaph, Heman, and Jeduthan, all called seers by most versions, though not the MT as it now stands.

[61] One may ask whether the priests are also involved in this singing. They are certainly involved in the ceremony, but their role as trumpeters would seem to preclude any involvement in the singing proper.

of using this phrase to refer to the singers in general.[62] Still, the association of the sons of Asaph with the temple here is a point of some tradition-historical significance.

A similar association of the sons of Asaph with a critical period of restoration is to be found with reference to the time of Nehemiah. This association has already been noted with respect to Neh 11:17 in the list of inhabitants, as well as with 11:22 and 12:35. As has been seen, the latter two passages probably stem from the Chronicler. So does Neh 12:46 which specifically relates the singers' involvement in the Nehemianic reform to the command of David (and Solomon). Significantly, part of this Davidic imitation involved the presence of a chief of the singers on the model of "Asaph of old."[63] Both here and in 11:22, the Chronicler has confirmed the primary rank of the Asaphites, as was first seen in the case of Mattaniah in the list of inhabitants.

Two other elements should be noted in this passage. The first is the standard reference to songs of praise and thanksgiving. The second is more significant, namely the specific reference to the economic status of the singers (and gatekeepers) in the time of Zerubbabel and Nehemiah. Aside from the hierarchical position here,[64] the reference to Zerubbabel is interesting, since it ties this passage together with Ezra 3:10.

These references to Asaphites in Ezra and Nehemiah are instructive, since they provide an insight into the way the Chronicler has used his sources. Specifically, the Chronicler has elaborated on the Asaphite presence in the time of both Zerubbabel and Nehemiah which was suggested by his sources. In other words, the Chronicler did not completely invent their presence at these times. If one can apply the same principle elsewhere in this work, one should not explain the Asaphite presence in the reigns of Hezekiah and Josiah as simple invention. Rather, as suggested above, the Chronicler probably had a reason for depicting them as active at these times, a reason which apparently had to do with the Ephraimite nature of both of these reigns.[65]

The references to the Asaphites in the book of Chronicles do not end with the passages which have been seen to belong to the main level of that book. There are other references which, while now interwoven into this main level, clearly stem from another stage in the development of the tradition process. Perhaps the most easily identified of these are those passages which alter the standard triumvirate of Asaph, Heman, and Jeduthun in favor of Heman,

---

[62] See 2 Chr 35:15.
[63] Probably read with the Greek versions, the Syriac, and Aquila *'āsāp* rather than *wĕ'āsāp* as in the MT.
[64] Note the apparently subordinate relationship to the levites here.
[65] One should, of course, also note the Asaphite presence in the reign of David himself, the reign which forms the Chronicler's ideal. This, however, should not be surprising in itself, since the Davidic reign also was a time of substantial Ephraimite influence, as may be seen most obviously in the presence of Abiathar, the priest.

Asaph, and Ethan. The singer lists in 1 Chr 6:16-33 and 15:16-24 are the best examples of this change.[66]

1 Chr 6:16-33 provides a detailed list of the Davidic appointees to the service of song, together with their descendants. Unlike those previously considered passages where Asaph is assigned a certain priority and importance, here he is replaced by Heman who is listed first and who occupies the central position. Asaph moves to second place and stands on Heman's right, while Ethan replaces Jeduthun and stands on Heman's left. The reason for this change is not given. It is simply presented as the action of David, in clear contradiction to passages such as 1 Chronicles 16. Also lost in this change is the special connection of Asaph with the ark. Here Asaph seems to have joined Heman in ministering before the tabernacle, even before the Solomonic construction of the temple.[67]

The primary importance of this genealogical passage lies in its making explicit the Levitical tie of the singers by means of a genealogical connection. In this schema, each of the three singers is a descendant of a different son of Levi. Heman, as befits the most important singer, stems from Kohath, the ancestor from whom Aaron and the priests also spring.[68] Asaph stems from the first born, but secondary, figure of Gershom, and Ethan from Merari.

1 Chr 15:16-24 is in some respect a doublet of the establishment of the cultic service that one finds in 1 Chronicles 16, though with some important differences. Once again the familiar Asaph, Heman, and Jeduthun has become Heman, Asaph, and Ethan, along with various brethren of the second order. Further, in this passage, David is no longer the direct founder of the cult as in 1 Chronicles 16. Instead, he works through the levites who themselves appoint the cultic officials.[69]

These passages apparently reflect a later stage in the development of the post-exilic singers. In this stage, the fortunes of the Asaphites, once the only group of singers worthy of mention, have declined with respect to the ascendant line of Heman. This change apparently took place after the composition of the main body of the book of Chronicles. Occupying a middle position between the two previous levels is 1 Chronicles 25, which presents yet another account of the Davidic organization of the singers. Here the latter are organized into 24 divisions, corresponding to the similar organization of the priests in chapter 24. In this, Asaph remains the first named of the three singers, but his priority

---

[66] See Gese, "Geschichte," 224.

[67] See 1 Chr 6:17 and note the phrase, "tabernacle of the tent of meeting." Is this to be taken as the tent of 16:1?

[68] This line contains the figure of Korah, who is also known from the Psalms and the Pentateuch. On Korah, see further below.

[69] Is this perhaps indicative of a greater cultic autonomy at the time of this passage? Note also that the Chenaniah of v 22 is called śar rather than rō'š, as Asaph was designated elsewhere. Considering the context, one may ask whether this is indicative of a functional leadership rather than a general primacy.

appears to be undercut by the use of another device. Thus, whereas Asaph has only four sons, Jeduthun has six, and Heman fourteen (in addition to three daughters). This disparity seems to be intended to exalt Heman at the expense of his fellows, an exaltation explicitly seen as the fulfillment of a divine promise in v 5.[70] These conflicting tendencies are also present in the second part of the chapter which details the casting of lots for duties among the singers. The first five lots alternate between Asaph and Jeduthun, whereas the remaining lots belong to Jeduthun and (towards the end, exclusively) Heman. Thus, once again, Asaph has a priority of sorts, while in another way the list is heavily weighted towards Heman. The use of lots in the first place is ambiguous as well. It is, on the one hand, a denial of explicit Davidic sanction for this aspect of the organization of the cult. On the other hand, depending on how the lots are to be interpreted, it may be substituting a form of divine sanction.

All of this very likely indicates that 1 Chronicles 25 — at least in its present form — stems from a time of some flux in the post-exilic history of the singers' groups. The sons of Asaph, while still retaining a nominal priority, are clearly either already in decline or at least being severely challenged. As is known from 1 Chronicles 6 and 15, the main challenger, Heman, does indeed finally usurp the position of Asaph. The reasons for this may be related to those which resulted in the Kohathite genealogy — namely, a close relationship to the priests.[71]

Another important aspect of this chapter is that of the prophetic nature of the singers' activity. Thus, in v 1, the sons of Asaph, Heman, and Jeduthun are said to prophesy with lyres, harps, and cymbals. In v 2, Asaph is said to have prophesied under the direction of the king. In v 3, Jeduthun is said to have prophesied with the lyre in thanksgiving and praise to God. Finally, in v 5, Heman is said to be the king's seer. These elements raise some interesting tradition-historical questions which are best treated in connection with 2 Chronicles 20.[72]

Some mention should be made of 1 Chr 26:1 which immediately follows the list of chapter 25. This passage begins the divisions of the gatekeepers with the enigmatic "of the Korahites, Meshelemiah the son of Kore, of the sons of

---

[70] On the artificial nature of the list of Heman's sons from Hananiah on, see Rudolph, *Chronikbücher*, 167–168, where they are seen to form a psalm fragment.

[71] In the case of the Hemanite ancestor, Korah, one can see the furthest reaches of this ambition, namely the priesthood itself. See Numbers 16–17 and further below.

[72] While at one time the terms *nābî'* and *hōzeh* appear to have some tradition-historical implications (again see Wilson, *Prophecy*, 136–138, 254–256; Petersen, *Roles*, 63), by the time of the Chronicler this was apparently no longer the case. Still, one wonders why Heman is called a seer in v 5, in contrast to the use of *nb'* in vv 1–4. With respect to Petersen's larger argument, one may perhaps note that here prophecy is simply identified with what the singers are doing in a musical vein. It will be seen below that this is something very different from saying that the singers were prophets in any strict sense of the word.

Asaph." It is, of course, difficult to see how the same Meshelemiah could be attributed to both the Korahites and the Asaphites. For this reason, the often suggested emendation of Asaph to Abiasaph, in line with the standard genealogy in 1 Chr 9:19 and Exod 6:24, is tempting. This, however, has little support in the versions and poses some other difficulties as well.[73] On the other hand, it is hard to know exactly how to interpret the dual ascription, except perhaps to note that the boundary between the singers and the gatekeepers was fluid and that this apparently held true for the Asaphites as well as the Korahites.

The last passage to be treated in this survey of Asaphite references is 2 Chronicles 20. This passage has been considered to some extent in the previous chapter insofar as it provided a good form-critical parallel for some of the genres found in the Asaphite psalms. As was noted there, what makes these parallels so intriguing is the prominent role of an Asaphite in the present passage. Thus, after the communal lament of the people is spoken by the king, "the Spirit of the LORD came upon Jahaziel, the son of Zechariah, son of Benaiah, son of Jeiel, son of Mattaniah, a levite of the sons of Asaph, in the midst of the assembly." This Jehaziel then delivered a salvation oracle.

An exact parallel to this chapter does not exist in Kings, though there is the possibility that a faint echo is to be heard in 2 Kings 3 which also concerns Jehoshaphat, a (musical) prophet, and approximately the same collection of foreign enemies. It is difficult to determine how much of this chapter reflects an historical occurrence, contemporary usage, or the development between the two. It is even difficult to determine to what level of the Chronicles tradition the present form belongs, though a good case can be made for seeing it as directly antecedent to the Chronicler.[74]

For the purposes of this chapter, the crucial issue is what to make of the prophetic activity of the Asaphite Jehaziel. As he has in every other case of levitical or liturgical prophecy in the book of Chronicles, Petersen has argued that one finds here a reflection of post-exilic contemporary usage. By such means, Petersen sees the levitical singers as claiming prophetic status in order to increase their prestige.[75] An alternate view of these phenomena in the book of Chronicles is that they represent the post-exilic diminution of what was originally pre-exilic cultic prophecy. This is preeminently the view of Mowinckel and those who follow him.[76] Again, the real question is one of what stage in the tradition process is reflected by the institutional phenomenon under consideration here.

To some degree, the issue turns on whether there actually was such a phenomenon as cult prophecy in the pre-exilic period. Petersen has denied this,

---

[73] Thus in G^B, one of the only Greek manuscripts to have Abiasaph here, one still finds the plural "sons," which would fit better with Asaph.
[74] See Gese, "Geschichte," 233.
[75] Petersen, *Prophecy*, 99, and passim.
[76] See especially Mowinckel, *Kultprophetie;* Johnson, *Prophet,* among others.

while Mowinckel is, of course, its great proponent.[77] In attempting to disprove Mowinckel's thesis, Petersen has attacked—with some success—Mowinckel's interpretation of such texts as 1 Chr 15:22.[78] He has not, however, come to grips with the major argument for Mowinckel's theory, namely, the data supplied by the psalms themselves.[79] It is this data which is the primary evidence for Mowinckel's establishment of cult prophecy, while the narrative material provides an additional support for the life setting.

It is obvious from the form-critical analysis of the previous chapter that this author inclines more towards the view that cultic prophecy was indeed a phenomenon of the pre-exilic cult. The possibility of a real cult prophecy—as opposed to the levitical pretense envisioned by Petersen in the post-exilic period—is further strengthened by such ancient near eastern and anthropological materials as were considered in that chapter. However, the mere possibility of such a phenomenon does not settle the tradition-historical complexities of this passage. It does not, for example, settle the question of whether the phenomenon reflected by this passage existed in the pre-exilic period or in the Chronicler's own time—or at any time in-between.[80]

As noted above, this question is difficult to answer. One that may be perhaps a little more susceptible of an answer is that of why an Asaphite does what he does here. As noted above, Asaph does not take on the full eponymous ancestor status that he has here until the later post-exilic period and, more specifically, around the time of the Chronicler. Previous to this, he was most likely a less far reaching genealogical figure.[81] Thus, the fact that in the case of Jehaziel, "sons of Asaph" is apparently to be taken in the professional sense points to a later post-exilic locus.[82] The fact that this son of Asaph is also

---

[77] Petersen, *Prophecy*, 64. Interestingly, Petersen is willing to see "certain cultic procedures" which were often "typologically similar to prophetic performance, i.e., a holy man spoke on behalf of Yahweh" (p. 99). Yet for him these are not authentically prophetic. Perhaps what is needed here is a greater precision in defining prophecy and a greater flexibility in seeing its social possibilities. It is hoped that the form-critical and cross-cultural analyses of the previous chapter have been a step in the right direction in this regard. Petersen himself discusses these possibilities in more detail in his later book, *Roles*.

[78] Petersen, *Prophecy*, 62-64.

[79] Perhaps indicative of the fact that Petersen has not taken the psalms data seriously enough is the fact that Psalm 74, one of the psalms which he claims would have been seen as part of a "prophetic corpus" of the pseudo-prophetic Levites (*Prophecy*, 99), can lament that there is no longer any prophet (74:9). See the previous chapter for a discussion of this verse.

[80] Thus, even if one sees Petersen as mistaken on the question of cult prophecy, he may still theoretically be correct about what was taking place in the Chronicler's own time— that is, the lack of any real cult prophecy and the perception of liturgical song as prophetic.

[81] As in Ezra 2:41/Neh 7:44 and Neh 11:17/1 Chr 9:15.

[82] That this phrase is not to be taken in the more general sense of all the singers (as 2 Chr 35:15) is indicated by the presence of a specific genealogy, and further, one with a number of Asaphite names.

explicitly a levite also points in this direction.[83]

While the Asaphite aspect of the story is clearly post-exilic, there are some decidedly pre-exilic aspects of the story as well. Thus, the presence of a royal spokesman for the communal lament finds no clear parallel in the post-exilic period. The context of a foreign military threat might also be a bit more at home in the pre-Persian period. On the other hand, other elements of the account have a post-exilic ring to them. The explicit and elaborate role of the singers, for example, is not to be found in the pre-exilic literature.

How does the peculiar role of the Asaphite fit into such a context? Interestingly, Jehaziel is not grouped among the singers, although this is undoubtedly assumed. Still, he does have a specific prophetic aspect which distinguishes him from the other singers. This may, of course, be either accidental or incidental, since other singers have all been associated with prophecy at various points in the Chronicles tradition. Nevertheless, this passage does raise the possibility that the Asaphites were seen to have a special connection of some sort to prophecy, similar to their special connection with the ark. This is especially likely since this is probably the earliest association of singers and prophecy in the Chronicles tradition.[84]

In such a way, this account shows something about either the contemporary nature or the tradition-history of the Asaphites—or perhaps both. Curiously, however, the picture of Jehaziel here is at variance with what is known about the Asaphites from elsewhere in the Chronicles tradition. There the function of the Asaphites—as well as the other singers—is to thank and praise God. Even in those cases where the prophetic nature of the singers is expressed, this prophecy is usually thought to consist of thanks and praise.[85] This is not the case here. The speech of Jehaziel is very close to a true prophetic oracle, as may be seen by the use of the standard prophetic opening, "Thus says the LORD." That the passage itself sees this speech as prophecy is clear from the fact that the divine spirit is always associated with prophecy in the Chronicles tradition.[86]

In other words, this passage is saying something different from those passages such as 1 Chronicles 25 where the singers are simply said to be prophets. These latter passages may be plausibly taken along the lines of Petersen in the sense that what the singers do—namely, thanks and praise—is in some way to be taken as prophecy. It is even different from vv 20-21 in the present chapter,

---

[83] Again unlike Ezra 2:41/Neh 7:44.

[84] Especially if, as Gese has suggested, this passage antedates the Chronicler himself ("Geschichte," 233). The other connections between the singers and prophecy stem from the Chronicler or from the later additions to his work.

[85] See 1 Chr 25:1-5, especially v 3. Elsewhere similar musical activity is seen to have been established according to prophetic commands (2 Chr 29:25, 30; 35:15).

[86] See 2 Chr 15:1; 18, especially v 23; 24:20; Neh 9:30 and possibly 9:20 as well. 1 Chr 12:19 is a possible exception to this, though *rûaḥ* here is indeterminate and is certainly not specified as the spirit of God, as are the other Chronicles references cited here.

where, once again, songs of praise and thanksgiving are apparently equated with prophecy. Rather, this passage asserts that the Asaphites have some connection with what is actually prophecy in the strict sense. If this connection is not functional (in the sense that the Asaphites of the time were true prophets), it can only be tradition-historical. Either way, the Asaphites can be seen to have some relationship with those prophets who were at one point active in Israel's cult.

Some of the form-critical observations of the previous chapter are appropriate here. Thus, the type of cult prophecy with which the Asaphites are connected here is that which takes place in the ceremony of the communal lament. Notably, the divine answer is clearly prophetic, including a prophetic speech formula. The fact that this standard prophetic opening is somewhat unusual for cult prophetic speeches probably indicates a certain distance from the actual cultic practice of the author's own day. This is as one might expect, since, according to most of the Chronicles tradition, the dominant duty of the singers was the offering of thanks and praise.[87]

The divine answer itself is clearly out of the holy war tradition, as befits the context. This may be seen in the opening injunction of v 15. However one views the life setting of the "fear not,"[88] one has not done justice to the present case until one also considers the parallel phrase "and do not be dismayed." This parallel usage clearly has its primary locus in the holy war.[89] This connection with the holy war is suggestive, since it has often been noted that the pre-exilic (genealogical) Levites have a special connection with the same institution.[90] This, of course, also fits with the special connection such circles had with the ark, since the latter was at times a symbol of God's presence in the holy war.

Some other aspects of this account need to be mentioned here. First of all, one may note that this episode takes place in the reign of Jehoshaphat. The reason for this is not entirely clear. It may, as noted above, be because this is the Chronicles version of 2 Kings 3. Even if the parallel is not this exact, Jehoshaphat might have been felt to be an appropriate king since he is seen as twice inquiring of prophets in the book of Kings. He is also given a partial seal of approval in that Deuteronomistic work, thus perhaps prompting the display of virtue in the present account. It may also be an authentic but otherwise unknown tradition from the pre-exilic period.

One should also not let the discussion of this passage end without mentioning the Korahites of v 19. Korah, of course, is the other prominent singer

---

[87] Alternately, it might indicate a different style of cultic prophecy about which we know little.

[88] See chapter four, n. 14.

[89] See especially, Deut 1:21; 31:8; Josh 8:1; 10:25; 1 Sam 7:11; also 2 Chr 32:7. Other cases not so clearly linked with the holy war include Isa 51:7; Jer 23:4; 30:10; 46:27; Ezek 2:6; 3:9; 1 Chr 22:13; 28:20.

[90] See especially Gerhard von Rad, *Studies in Deuteronomy*, trans. by David Stalker (London: SCM, 1953), 66–67.

attribution mentioned along with Asaph in the canonical psalter. As such, it is of interest to find the Korahites active as singers in the present passage. Even more interesting is the fact that the present passage is unique in its description of the Korahites as singers. Where the Korahites are met elsewhere, they are either minor temple personnel[91] or defeated aspirants to the priesthood.[92] This diversity raises the likelihood of a complex tradition-history. While this cannot be gone into fully here, there are some ways in which the Korahites are relevant to the history of the Asaphites.

Primary among these is the eventual genealogical connection of Korah with Heman.[93] The latter has been seen to appear alongside Asaph in Chronicles and even to usurp Asaph's primacy in the later tradition process of that book. It is tempting to see this rise of Heman in connection with either the common derivation of Korah and Israel's priests from Kohath[94] or with the priestly aspirations of that group.

The secondary way the Korahites may contribute to an understanding of the Asaphites has to do with dating. Although there have been recent attempts to link the Korahites (and even the Korahite psalms) exclusively to the post-exilic period, there does seem to be convincing evidence to the contrary. Foremost among these is the inscription *bny qrh* found on a potsherd in the sanctuary of the Arad temple. Noting that this temple was destroyed in the seventh century, J. Maxwell Miller has made a good case for the existence of a group of Korahites in the pre-exilic period, a group which can plausibly be connected with a number of the Korahite psalms.[95] The pre-exilic status of the Korahites lends weight to the possibility that the Asaphites as well had some sort of roots in the pre-exilic period. As Miller notes, the destruction of the Arad temple in the seventh century is suggestive in terms of a connection with the Deuteronomic reform of Josiah and the possibility that the Korahites came to Jerusalem at that time, as suggested by that reform.[96] This would parallel certain suggestions made above that the Asaphites are also to be connected with this Deuteronomic movement.

CONCLUSIONS

These passages comprise the evidence about the Asaphites which one finds outside the psalms. In the light of these passages, certain possibilities suggest themselves about the nature and history of the Asaphites. These possibilities

---

[91] Gatekeepers in 1 Chr 9:19; 26:1, 19; bakers in 1 Chr 9:31.
[92] See especially Numbers 16–17.
[93] 1 Chr 6:18–22.
[94] See Exod 6:18–24; Num 16:1; 1 Chronicles 6. Given this relationship between Korah and Kohath, the reference to the levites of the Kohathites and the Korahites in 2 Chr 20:19 is somewhat puzzling. For a discussion of this problem, see Gese "Geschichte," 155, n. 33.
[95] Miller, "Korahites," 59–68.
[96] Ibid., 67–68.

need to be summarized here, and then to be compared with the possibilities suggested by the internal evidence of the Asaphite psalms themselves.

The first and most obvious conclusion is that the Asaphites were a group involved in the liturgical life of Israel. Almost without exception,[97] the Asaphites are depicted as singers and musicians especially involved in the liturgical praise and thanksgiving of God. To this end, they are usually seen to have received a royal and a prophetic commission in the reign of David. This commission was renewed by subsequent kings and rulers.

Although in the Chronicles tradition this commission was seen to take place through the eponymous ancestor Asaph himself, it is actually difficult to describe either an historical Asaph or the exact origins of this group. Nevertheless, the presence of the sons of Asaph on the list of returnees in Ezra 2/Nehemiah 7 does indicate that pre-exilic origins are possible and even probable. The later Chronicles treatment of the Joah son of Asaph of 2 Kings 18 points in this direction as well.

In the early post-exilic period, the Asaphites were the only singers' group. In the mid-fifth century, they were joined by a group associated with the name of Jeduthun. By the time of the Chronicler, there were three major groups, associated with the names Asaph, Heman, and Jeduthun. Throughout this time, Asaph retained a primacy of sorts among the singers, as may be seen from his explicit designation as chief (1 Chr 16:4; Neh 12:46) and his first place in the order of names. Such a primacy may also be indicated by the use of the general phrase, sons of Asaph, to designate all the singers (2 Chr 35:15), although this may also be explained by the Asaphites' historical priority.

This Asaphite primacy, however, did not last much beyond the time of the main body of the Chronicler's work. A threat to this primacy was posed by the aspirations of the group associated with the name Heman, who by virtue of their priestly connections were very upwardly mobile and who had already distinguished themselves from and surpassed the Jeduthun group. At the time of the latest additions to the Chronicler's work, this group had usurped the traditional Asaphite primacy and become the preeminent singing group of the second temple period.

While this appears to be a fairly reliable outline of the history of the Asaphites, it does not answer the more interesting question of who the Asaphites originally were and how they became associated with singing in the first place. Such questions are perhaps ultimately unanswerable, though the texts do provide some suggestive clues. One must, of course, not rely entirely on the genealogies of 1 Chronicles 6, since these represent, for the most part, a formal working out of later post-exilic cult relationships. Even the Levitical origins of the Asaphites cannot be entirely accepted on this basis alone, since this may simply be a genealogical recognition of the inclusion of the Asaphites under the functional

---

[97] The possible exceptions are 2 Kgs 18:18, 37 (= Isa 36:3, 22); Neh 11:22; 1 Chr 26:1; and 2 Chr 20. Only the first of these, however, is unconnected with the liturgical service.

levites which had taken place in the mid-fifth century. Any insight into the origins and peculiar characteristics of the Asaphites must be sought elsewhere.

Fortunately, the way the Asaphites appear in the narrative material of the Chronicles tradition does provide some clues on these counts. Thus, the above analysis has shown that the Chronicler connected the Asaphites with such institutions as the ark, the holy war, and cultic prophecy—most of which appear to have a primary pre-exilic locus. At least from the vantage point of this post-exilic tradition, the Asaphites may be said to have a relationship of some sort with the pre-exilic circles connected with these institutions. As has been pointed out above, these circles appear to be precisely those which have been designated as Ephraimite. The connection of the singers (though not exclusively the Asaphite singers) with the reigns of Hezekiah and Josiah also points in such a direction.[98]

This then is the evidence about the Asaphites that one can gather from outside the psalms. It is certainly meager enough, yet it does allow some tradition-historical conclusions as to the place of the Asaphites in Israel's social and religious history. How well do these conclusions correspond to those gained from the internal analysis of the psalms? In other words, how well do the Asaphites whom one meets in the Chronicles tradition fit as possible tradents for the psalms bearing the Asaphite superscription? On the whole, they fit very nicely, though there are some interesting divergences.

The most important similarity is, of course, the common links to the Ephraimite tradition stream which are to be found in both the internal and the external evidence. In such a way, the Ephraimite linguistic tendencies found in the Asaphite psalms dovetail nicely with the Ephraimite connections attributed to the Asaphites in the Chronicler's account, as seen in such matters as the ark and the holy war. Similarly, some of the form-critical concerns of these psalms, especially those related to cultic prophecy, find an echo in some of the formal activities attributed to the Asaphites in the Chronicler's history. The effect of all these convergences is to underline the probability that the psalms do indeed have a common *traditio* and also to further enable one to describe that *traditio*. In other words, its effect is to validate the ability of the common superscription both to unite these psalms in a common tradition history and to provide valuable information as to the nature of that history.

There is, however, one major divergence between the internal evidence of the psalms and the external evidence concerning the Asaphites. This difference involves the actual nature of the Asaphites' cultic song. According to the work of the Chronicler, the Asaphites are primarily engaged in singing thanks and praise. In general form-critical terms, this means that they were engaged in hymnic activity. Appropriately, the psalms which they are given to sing in 1 Chronicles 16 are almost entirely hymns.

---

[98] The similar connections with the governments of Zerubbabel and Nehemiah raise questions which need to be investigated further. Certainly, Nehemiah's reforms are not dissimilar to Deuteronomic reforms.

This, however, by no means corresponds to the picture that one finds in the case of the Asaphite psalms themselves. As noted in the previous chapter, the dominant genres to be found in this collection are communal laments and prophetic psalms of various types. Only Psalms 75, 76, and 81 may be said to have any hymnic ties. Even here, however, these ties are not terribly strong. Thus, in Psalms 75 and 81, the hymnic elements serve mostly as a frame for the more central prophetic utterance. Only Psalm 76, a Zion song, clearly belongs to a hymnic category. In view of the general agreements between the internal and external evidence in other respects, this discrepancy is striking, especially since it is at the heart of the Asaphite activity.

Since the Chronicles tradition was apparently very well acquainted with the Asaphites, one can only assume that it was also acquainted with the Asaphite psalms. Although one cannot date these psalms with complete precision, certainly at least some of them are pre-exilic,[99] while others possibly date from the early exilic or post-exilic period.[100] There is even some evidence that the Asaphite collection itself was fixed before the time of the Chronicler's activity.

On this question, one may note the fact that the Asaphite psalms are a part of the Elohistic redaction of the psalter which includes Psalms 42-83. It is noteworthy that this redaction does not include the so-called "Korahite appendix," Psalms 84-89![101] In this appendix, one meets for the only time the names of Heman and Ethan, both of whom have been seen to belong to a later stage in the history of the temple singers. The Asaphite collection, therefore, belonged to the main body of what would later become the psalter at a time before the later Korahite psalms with their Heman and Ethan attachments were included. Ethan belongs to the very latest stages of the Chronicles tradition, at which time he takes the place of Jeduthun among the three main temple singers. Heman may also belong to this stage or possibly to the previous stage where he was the secondary figure to Asaph. This would place him in the time of the Chronicler himself at the earliest. Thus, according to this schema of when the psalms were added to the developing psalter, the Chronicler would have been faced with an already closed Asaphite collection of psalms — a collection which did not include much thanks and praise.

Despite this, the Chronicler still portrayed the Asaphites as almost exclusively involved in just this aspect of the cult. The most likely explanation for this

---

[99] Psalm 78 would seem to be the most obviously pre-exilic of these psalms, since it appears to be linked with an ongoing Davidic monarchy.

[100] Psalms 74 and 79 would be strong candidates for this period, though see the previous chapter for the various possibilities of interpretation.

[101] The fact that there are Korahite psalms both within and outside the Elohistic psalter would seem to indicate an extended period of Korahite activity. On these questions of the individual psalters and their relationship to the book of Chronicles, see Gese, "Geschichte," 158, as well as his "Die Entstehung der Büchereinteilung des Psalters," in *Sinai*, 159-167.

dichotomy is that in this case the Chronicler is representing what the Asaphites were doing in his own time![102] The psalms collection would thus be representative of an earlier stage in the Asaphites' history. In such a way, the Asaphites moved from primary concern with communal laments and cultic prophecy to the delivery of thanks and praise.

According to this scenario, Psalms 96, 105, and 106, the deutero-Asaphite psalms attributed to Asaph in 1 Chronicles 16, would be representative of the sort of song sung by the Asaphites known to the Chronicler![103] These could not, however, be added to the Asaphite psalter, since the latter was already closed![104]

Psalm 95 in some ways provides a bridge between the Asaphite and deutero-Asaphite psalms. This psalm has already been seen to have certain linguistic affinities with the original Asaphite collection. It is, however, its form which is of interest here. Like Psalm 81, Psalm 95 is a combination of an introductory hymn and a divine admonition delivered by a prophet. Its introductory hymn is, however, much more developed than in the former psalm. In this respect, it is much closer to the deutero-Asaphite psalms. Especially indicative of this development is Psalm 95's specific emphasis on thanks and praise. On the other hand, a parallel to its prophetic section is nowhere to be found in the deutero-Asaphite psalms. In formal terms, it appears to be a bridge between different stages of a changing tradition![105] Significantly, even while the form of the *traditum* and the function of the *traditio* is changing, at least some of the linguistic ties to the original tradition remain![106]

Thus, instead of pointing to divergent traditions, the difference between the concerns of the Asaphite psalms collection and that of the Asaphites in the Chronicles tradition may simply point to different stages in the life of the same tradition stream. A group which was once chiefly (though not exclusively) concerned with communal laments and cultic prophecy has moved to more hymnic pursuits. This development apparently took place sometime before the

---

[102] As seen above, 2 Chronicles 20 would most likely stem from an earlier time.

[103] Whether its addition to 1 Chronicles 16 stems from his own or a later time.

[104] It is, however, not clear why these psalms could not have been included in an "Asaphite appendix" similar to the Korahite appendix—complete with identifying Asaphite superscriptions. Did the inclusion in Chronicles make this unnecessary?

[105] In view of the similar mix of hymnic and prophetic elements to be found in both places, a time corresponding to that of 2 Chronicles 20 would be very attractive for Psalm 95. This would place the latter before the time of the Chronicler and the more purely hymnic deutero-Asaphite psalms to be found there (the latter corresponding to his emphasis on the singers' role in the offering of thanks and praise). A similar movement to thanks and praise may be noted in a comparison of Psalms 60 and 108, where the same oracle is introduced in the first case by a communal lament and in the second by a hymn. Interestingly, Psalm 108 has an Asaphite superscription in some Hebrew manuscripts.

[106] As seen earlier, this would also be at least partly true for the deutero-Asaphite psalms as well. Both Psalm 95 and the deutero-Asaphite psalms need further analysis from a tradition-historical perspective.

time of the Chronicler, though it is hard to say exactly when. If Neh 11:17 is original as it stands, it would seem to have taken place before the mid-fifth century. On the other hand, if 1 Chronicles 9 reflects the original form of this list and Neh 11:17 reflects the Chronicler's redaction, such original elements as cultic prophecy may have continued to exist a bit further into the post exilic period![107] 2 Chronicles 20 may point in this direction, though this is in itself difficult to date. At any rate, by the time of the Chronicler, cult prophecy had disappeared, or better, had been redefined as the offering of thanks and praise![108] The semantic shift in the hiphil of *šm'* is also perhaps indicative of this change![109]

More interesting than the chronological question, yet even more difficult to determine, is the question why this shift took place. This undoubtedly has to do with Israel's changed historical circumstances and the altered relationships of the various tradition streams. It may also have something to do with the general disappearance of prophecy elsewhere in Israelite society. Beyond this, the evidence will not let us go.

[107] This is, of course, in keeping with certain aspects of such works as Joel and possibly Haggai and Zechariah. That prophets were not seen to be out of place during the time of Nehemiah is suggested by Neh 6:7, 14.
[108] The "prophetic" activity of 1 Chronicles 25 and the prophets to levites shift of 2 Kgs 23:2/2 Chr 34:30 are indicative of this redefinition, as seen above.
[109] See the analysis of this word in connection with the third chapter discussion of Ps 76:9.

6
Conclusions

The dual nature of this study requires two sets of conclusions. The first of these summarizes the results of this work's tradition-historical analysis of the Asaphite psalms and the material related to them. Specifically, it attempts to present a coherent picture of the Asaphite *traditio*, both in itself and as it was involved in the larger social and theological history of ancient Israel. The second set of conclusions focuses on the larger methodological questions raised throughout this work. In particular, it assesses the implications of the exegetical material for the discipline of tradition history and especially for the subdiscipline of *Traditionsgeschichte*.

TRADITION-HISTORICAL CONCLUSIONS

Perhaps the most basic conclusion of this work lies in its assertion that one can, with a fair degree of probability, point to a distinct and discernible *traditio* group responsible in some way for the Asaphite psalms. Such a conclusion is indicated not only by the superscription which the psalms share but also by their common language which to a large degree reaffirms the superscription link. Significantly, this language also links these psalms to a larger theological movement in ancient Israel, referred to here as the Ephraimite tradition stream. In such a way, the linguistic analysis not only confirms the Asaphite psalms as the *traditum* of a distinct *traditio* but also allows for a further description of that *traditio*.

The description of the *traditio* is furthered by both the form-critical analysis of the psalms and the analysis of the external evidence suggested by the Asaphite superscription. Both of these also manifest certain tendencies in an Ephraimite direction, as well as pointing to various functional possibilities for the tradents. In particular, these analyses link the Asaphites with the institutions of cult prophecy, the ark, and the holy war—all of which would be quite at home in Ephraimite circles.

What then can be said about the Asaphites and their place in the theological and social history of ancient Israel? First of all, both the psalms and the external evidence point to the fact that this group existed over a long period of Israelite history. The exact origins of the group are unknown, although the linguistic and functional analysis of the psalms themselves allows one to move back beyond the post-exilic information of the Chronicles tradition into the pre-exilic period. In addition, the Ephraimite nature of these psalms suggests even more specific historical and cultic possibilities. One thinks in particular of the reform periods of Hezekiah and Josiah as times in which these Ephraimite elements could most plausibly have gained access to the Jerusalem cult. These would, of course, also be times in which both royal and cultic concerns would have been especially important to an Ephraimite *traditio*. Such a setting is also suggested by the combination of Ephraimite and more properly Southern elements, a combination found in both the language of the psalms and the external evidence.

Whether or not the Asaphites may be connected with these Deuteronomic reforms, the Asaphite psalms provide an insight into the peculiar concerns and emphases of the Ephraimite cult. These are especially indicated by the psalms' more individual aspects. In such a way, the strong concentration of both communal laments and prophetic psalms clearly points to a concern for these in Ephraimite circles. Even more specifically, the distinctively Asaphite use of prophetic speech for the purpose of warning the people against various legal and cultic abuses indicates how such prophetic warnings found elsewhere in the Ephraimite literature might have been actualized in the cult. This aspect of warning well fits a reform situation, though it should not be limited to such a time.

The Asaphite presence in the central cult might well have been only part of a larger Ephraimite presence there at various times. It is, however, impossible at this time to go into such vexed questions as that of how successful the Ephraimites were in attaining the priesthood, even during the periods of reform. What the Asaphite psalms clearly show is that at some point in the pre-exilic period the Ephraimites did achieve at least something of a presence in the central cult. They resumed this presence in the time of the second temple and maintained it for as long as can be seen into the post-exilic period.

This continued presence does not, however, mean that the Asaphites remained the same throughout this period. Indeed, the analysis of the preceding chapter showed that both the status and the function of this group changed over the course of its existence. With respect to status, the Asaphites evidently went from being the only singers' group of the immediate post-exilic period to a more secondary position in the period after the Chronicler. Since the Ephraimite nature of the Asaphites was still recognized by the Chronicler, it seems safe to see their varying status as at least a partial indication of a similarly changing Ephraimite position within the central cult.

With respect to function, it is precisely the distinctive Asaphite concerns with cult prophecy and the communal lament that seem to have changed over time. While such concerns may very possibly have distinguished the Asaphites into the post-exilic period, they had been lost by the time of the Chronicler. At that time, the Asaphites seem to have joined the rest of the singers in more specifically hymnic pursuits. It is, however, significant that even while they lost their specific functional identity, their distinctiveness from the other singers' groups was still recognized by such contemporaries as the Chronicler. Indeed, the

CONCLUSIONS   195

latter was still both aware of the tradition-historical reasons for making such a distinction and interested in preserving some indication of this in his own work. In summary, then, the above analysis has both related the twelve Asaphite psalms to a single *traditio* and described that *traditio* on the basis of the internal and external evidence. This combined evidence provides us with a coherent picture of the Asaphites as distinctive and durable participants in both the Jerusalem cult and the larger social and theological history of ancient Israel.

METHODOLOGICAL CONCLUSIONS

The first chapter of this work was devoted to a critical examination of the most recent developments in the field of tradition history, namely, those connected with the name *Traditionsgeschichte* (or Tradition history). In the course of this discussion, certain general problems were found to exist in the latter method. These problems were felt to be such as to threaten the method's goal of an accurate reconstruction of Israel's social and theological history.

The second chapter continued the methodological analysis in a more concrete way by examining in some detail Karl-Johan Illman's Tradition-historical study of the psalms of Asaph. This critical examination found Illman's study to illustrate many of the difficulties discussed in the more theoretical analysis of the method. The fact that such a comprehensive Tradition-historical analysis led to generally negative conclusions was seen to be especially problematical, since it ultimately failed to explain these psalms' common superscription. Both the negative conclusions and the methodological problems were such as to merit a new look at the psalms in question.

On the methodological level, the remaining chapters of this work may be seen as an attempt to determine whether a better tradition-historical understanding of the psalms of Asaph might be achieved by using a somewhat different approach. Simply stated, this new methodological stance shifts the criterion for determining the existence of a *traditio* from such abstract elements as motif and theme to more concrete elements as specific language. In one sense, this simply emphasizes an element which is recommended by most advocates of Tradition history. In another sense, however, making such language a primary requirement greatly alters the amount of subjective critical judgment involved in making tradition-historical connections. As such, the language provides more of an internal control than was possible with more abstract elements which may shift according to the perception of the individual scholar.

As noted in the previous set of conclusions, this reliance on language as the determinant of tradition-historical connections resulted in a plausible definition of a single *traditio* for the Asaphite psalms and also allowed for a further description of this *traditio* in terms of the larger tradition-historical movements in ancient Israel. The tradition-historical conclusions gained in this way were found to correspond to both the additional internal evidence supplied by the psalms' forms and the external evidence gained by a similar tradition-historical study of the Asaphites. The success of this alternate tradition-historical analysis may be judged by the fact that it seems to provide a more credible explanation of the common superscription than that which emerged from the Tradition-historical analysis of Illman.

The methodological implications of the exegetical work of the last three chapters correspond to many of the more theoretical criticisms of the first two chapters. Most importantly, one learns from this the need for a less subjective criterion for establishing tradition groups than that of abstract motifs, notions, and themes. In contrast to the latter elements, language has the advantage of being both reasonably objective and sufficiently distinctive. It is reasonably objective because a word or phrase is obviously either present or absent from a certain text, however one might interpret that presence or absence. It is sufficiently distinctive because certain words and phrases do link together some literary works to the exclusion of others. When a distinctive relationship between certain works can be conclusively established, it requires explanation. If such a link is not formal or traceable to genre peculiarities, it can only be tradition-historical. That is, it can only be due to actual social contacts among similarly inclined groups in ancient Israel. In such a way, linguistic analysis can be seen to act as an internal control which leads to tradition-historical conclusions of reasonable plausibility. Again, in the case of the Asaphite psalms, such a linguistic analysis was able to indicate the probable existence of a tradition-historical relationship which was rejected by Illman on the basis of his more conceptual analysis.

The ability of distinctive language to indicate tradition-historical connections has implications for the question of whether Israel's tradition groups were functionally or ideologically based. It was, of course, argued above that formal criteria, while admittedly more objective and concrete than more strictly conceptual criteria, were not able in themselves to determine the existence of tradition streams within ancient Israel. Specifically, it was argued that to base one's tradition-historical conclusions on such formal criteria is to prejudge the question of whether tradition groups were made up of those who shared similar functions or whether they included within themselves a variety of functionaries.

In such a vein, it is significant that the linguistic analysis of the third chapter was able to demonstrate a clear relationship first of all between psalms belonging to different genres and further between such psalms and material of completely different formal types. The fact that such links can be made would seem to indicate that tradition-historical connections are not necessarily to be restricted to those groups which share the same function. Instead, one must envision much more inclusive groupings which contain within themselves persons from a variety of institutions and functions. What binds these people together as a group is not the fact that they are engaged in the same "occupation" but rather that they appear to have a similar view of the world and, as a result, speak a similar language. Such groups would certainly seem to be more theological and ideological than functional in nature.

The inability of form criticism to determine the existence of tradition groups does not, however, mean that form criticism is irrelevant to the tradition-historical enterprise. Indeed, the form-critical work of the fourth chapter may be seen to be indispensable to an understanding of the functional character and institutional connections of the Asaphite *traditio*. Still, it is important to note that the role of such formal analysis is descriptive of the nature of a *traditio* rather than constitutive of its existence in the first place. The same is also true, of course, of the more specifically Tradition-historical units of content.

In summary, then, this work has raised certain questions concerning the ability of Tradition history accurately to reconstruct the social and theological history of ancient Israel. This is not to deny the legitimacy of this method's historical goals, but only to insist that such goals demand adequate safeguards against subjective speculation on the part of modern scholars. To the extent that both *Traditionsgeschichte* and tradition history in general proceed in accordance with such safeguards, they will be on more solid ground in reconstructing the social and theological history of ancient Israel.

One final point should be noted. It is not the purpose of this work to deny the importance of a conceptual analysis which concerns itself with such elements as motifs, notions and themes. This type of analysis can be extremely valuable, though not necessarily in terms of historical or tradition-historical goals. Indeed, such analysis would seem to have its proper place in a more literary interpretation of these texts. Such a move would, of course, fit well with the origins of a number of the terms used. It does, however, mean that one becomes less interested in the historical task of reconstruction and more involved in the specifically literary tasks of appreciation and appropriation.

While only a limited amount of the biblical material may be able to meet the historical controls suggested in this study, all of it is open to thematic interpretation. The same caution applies to language as well. Only a limited number of texts may have a language sufficiently distinctive to allow them to be placed tradition-historically. All language is capable of being appreciated in a literary way.

Both historical and literary analysis have a proper place in the interpretation of biblical texts. Because of this, two things are incumbent on the interpreters of such texts. They must always be aware of which task they are undertaking at any given time. And they must use such tools as are relevant to that task. It is hoped that this work has succeeded in sharpening the tools to be used in the task of tradition history.

Bibliography

Adam, Gottfried; Kaiser, Otto; and Kümmel, Werner Georg. *Einführung in die exegetischen Methoden.* München: Chr. Kaiser, 1975.

Barth, Hermann, and Steck, Odil Hannes. *Exegese des Alten Testaments: Leitfaden der Methodik.* Neukirchen-Vluyn: Neukirchener, 1971.

Begrich, Joachim. "Das Priesterliche Heilsorakel." *ZAW* n.s. 11 (1934) 81-92.

Briggs, Charles Augustus. *A Critical and Exegetical Commentary on the Book of Psalms.* Edinburgh: T. & T. Clark, 1906.

Bright, John. *Early Israel in Recent History Writing.* Chicago: Alec R. Allenson, 1956.

Buss, Martin. "The Psalms of Asaph and Korah." *JBL* 82 (1963) 387-392.

Campbell, Anthony. "Psalm 78: A Contribution to the Theology of Tenth Century Israel." *CBQ* 41 (1979) 51-79.

Carroll, R. P. "Psalm LXXVIII: Vestiges of a Tribal Polemic." *VT* 21 (1971) 133-150.

Childs, Brevard S. *The Book of Exodus.* Philadelphia: Westminster, 1974.

———. "Psalm Titles and Midrashic Exegesis." *JSS* 16 (1971) 137-150.

———. "A Traditio-Historical Study of the Reed Sea Formula." *VT* 20 (1970) 406-418.

Coats, George W. *Rebellion in the Wilderness.* New York: Abingdon, 1968.

Cody, Aelred. *A History of Old Testament Priesthood.* Rome: Pontifical Biblical Institute, 1969.

Cross, Frank Moore. "The Divine Warrior in Israel's Early Cult." *Biblical Motifs: Origins and Transformations.* Edited by A. Altmann. Cambridge, MA: Harvard University, 1966.

———. *Canaanite Myth and Hebrew Epic: Essays in the History of the Religion of Israel.* Cambridge, MA: Harvard University, 1973.

Culley, Robert C. "An Approach to the Problem of Oral Tradition." *VT* 13 (1963) 113-125.

———. *Oral Formulaic Language in the Biblical Psalms.* Toronto: University of Toronto, 1967.

———. *Studies in the Structure of the Hebrew Narrative.* Philadelphia: Fortress, 1976.

Dahood, S. J., Mitchel. *Psalms.* AB 16-17A. Garden City: Doubleday, 1968.

Davies, G. Henton. "The Ark in the Psalms." *Promise and Fulfillment.* Edited by F. F. Bruce. Edinburgh: T. & T., Clark, 1963.

Delitzsch, Franz. *Biblical Commentary on the Psalms.* 2d ed. Edinburgh: T. & T. Clark, 1871.

de Vaux, Roland. *Ancient Israel.* New York: McGraw Hill, 1965.

Duhm, Bernhard. *Die Psalmen.* HKAT 14. Freiburg, Mohr, 1899.

Eissfeldt, Otto. *Das Lied Moses Deuteronium 32:1-43 und das Lehrgedicht Asaphs Psalm 78 samt einer Analyse der Umgebung des Moses Liedes.* Berlin: Akademie, 1958.

———. "Psalm 80." *Geschichte und Altes Testament.* Edited by Gerhard Ebeling. BHT 16. Tübingen: Mohr, 1953.

———. "Psalm 80 and Psalm 89." *WO* 3 (1964-1966) 27-31.

Elliger, Karl. "Ich bin der Herr—Euer Gott." *Kleine Schriften zum Alten Testament.* TBü 32. München. Chr. Kaiser, 1966.

Engnell, Ivan. "The Book of Psalms." *A Rigid Scrutiny.* Translated by John T. Willis. Nashville: Vanderbilt University, 1969.

Field, Margaret J. "Spirit Possession in Ghana." *Spirit Mediumship and Society in Africa.* Edited by John Beattie and John Middleton. New York: Africana Publishing Corporation, 1969.

Fohrer, Georg, et al. *Exegese des Alten Testaments.* Heidelberg: Quelle & Meyer, 1973; 2d ed. 1976.

Freedman, David Noel. "Early Israelite History in the Light of Early Israelite Poetry." *Unity and Diversity.* Edited by Hans Goedicke and J. J. M. Roberts. Baltimore: Johns Hopkins, 1975.

Frenzel, Elisabeth. *Stoff-, Motiv-, und Symbolforschung.* Stuttgart: J. B. Metzlersche, 1963.

Gerstenberger, Erhard S. *Der Bittende Mensch.* WMANT 51. Neukirchen-Vluyn: Neukirchener, 1980.

———. "Psalms." *Old Testament Form Criticism.* Edited by John H. Hayes. San Antonio: Trinity University, 1974.

Gese, Hartmut. "Die Entstehung der Büchereinteilung des Psalters." *Vom Sinai zum Zion.* BEvT 64. München: Chr. Kaiser, 1974.

———. "Zur Geschichte der Kultsänger am zweiten Temple." *Vom Sinai zum Zion.* BEvT 64. München: Chr. Kaiser, 1974.

Graetz, Heinrich. *Kritischer Commentar zu den Psalmen.* Breslau: S. Schott Laender, 1882.

Gunkel, Hermann. *Die Psalmen.* HKAT 2/2. Göttingen: Vandenhoeck & Ruprecht, 1926.

———, and Begrich, Joachim. *Einleitung in die Psalmen.* HKAT suppl. Göttingen: Vandenhoeck & Ruprecht, 1933.

BIBLIOGRAPHY

Gunneweg, Antonius H. J. *Leviten und Priester.* Göttingen: Vandenhoeck & Ruprecht, 1965.

Hanson, Paul D. *The Dawn of Apocalyptic.* Philadelphia: Fortress, 1975.

Haran, Menahem. *Temples and Temple-Service in Ancient Israel.* Oxford: Oxford University, 1978.

Harrelson, Walter. "Life, Faith, and the Emergence of Tradition." *Tradition and Theology in the Old Testament.* Edited by Douglas A. Knight. Philadelphia: Fortress, 1977.

Heinemann, H. "The Date of Psalm 80." *JQR* 40 (1949/1950) 297-302.

Hermann, Siegfried. "Mose." *EvT* 28 (1968).

Huber, Friedrich. "Motiv- und Traditionskritik." *Exegese des Alten Testament.* Edited by Georg Fohrer. Heidelberg: Quelle & Meyer, 1973; 2d ed. 1976.

Huffmon, Herbert B. "Prophecy in the Mari Letters." *The Biblical Archaeologist Reader* vol 3. Edited by Edward E. Campbell, Jr. and David Noel Freedman. Garden City: Doubleday, 1970.

Illman, Karl-Johan. *Thema und Tradition in den Asaf-Psalmen.* Abo: Abo Akademi, 1976.

Jasper, F. N. "Early Israelite Traditions in the Psalter." *VT* 17 (1967) 50-59.

Johnson, Aubrey R. *The Cultic Prophet and Israel's Psalmody.* Cardiff: University of Wales, 1979.

———. *The Cultic Prophet in Ancient Israel.* Cardiff: University of Wales, 1944; 2d ed. 1962.

Junker, Herbert. "Die Entstehungszeit des Psalm 78 und das Deuteronium." *Bib* 34 (1953) 487-500.

Kayser, Wolfgang. *Das sprachliche Kunstwerk.* Bern: Francke, 1968.

Kittel, Rudolph. *Die Psalmen.* KAT 13. Leipzig: 1929.

Knight, Douglas A. *Rediscovering the Traditions of Israel.* Missoula: Scholars, 1975.

Köberle, Justus. *Die Templesänger im Alten Testament.* Erlangen: Fr. Junge, 1899.

Kraus, Hans-Joachim. *Psalmen.* BK 15. Neukirchen-Vluyn: Neukirchener, 1960.

Lauha, Aarre. *Die Geschichtsmotive in den alttestamentlichen Psalmen.* Helsinki: Druckerei der finnischen Literaturgesellschaft, 1945.

Lucas, J. Olumide. *The Religion of the Yorubas.* Lagos: C. M. S. Bookshop, 1948.

McCarthy, S. J., Dennis J. "What Was Israel's Historical Creed?" *Lexington Theological Quarterly* 4 (1969) 46-53.

Miller, James Maxwell. "The Korahites of Southern Judah." *CBQ* 37 (1970) 58-68.

Möhlenbrink, Kurt. "Die levitischen Überlieferungen des ATs." *ZAW* n.f. 11 (1934) 184-231.

Morgenstern, Julian. "The Mythological Background of Psalm 82." *HUCA* 14 (1939) 29-126.

Mowinckel, Sigmund. *Psalmenstudien*. Amsterdam: P. Schippers, 1961.

———. *The Psalms in Israel's Worship*. Translated by D. R. Ap-Thomas. Nashville: Abingdon, 1962.

Mullen, E. Theodore. *The Divine Council in Canaanite and Early Hebrew Literature*. HSM 24. Chico, CA: Scholars, 1980.

Noth, Martin. *Numbers*. Translated by James D. Martin. Philadelphia: Westminster, 1968.

———. *Überlieferungsgeschichte des Pentateuch*. Stuttgart: W. Kohlhammer, 1948.

O'Callaghan, Roger T. "A Note on the Canaanite Background of Psalm 82." *CBQ* 15 (1953) 311-314.

Oesterreich, T. K. *Possession: Demoniacal and Others*. New Hyde Park: University Books, 1966.

Patton, John Hastings. *Canaanite Parallels in the Book of Psalms*. Baltimore: Johns Hopkins, 1944.

Petersen, David L. *Late Israelite Prophecy: Studies in Deutero-Prophetic Literature and Chronicles*. Missoula: Scholars, 1977.

———. *The Roles of Israel's Prophets*. JSOT 17. Sheffield: JSOT, 1981.

Phillips, Morgan Lee. *The Significance of the Divine Self-Predication Formula for the Structure and Content of Deutero-Isaiah*. Unpublished Ph.D. dissertation, Drew University, 1969.

Plöger, Otto. *Theocracy and Eschatology*. Translated by S. Rudman. Richmond: John Knox, 1968.

Rad, Gerhard von. "The Form-Critical Problem of the Hexateuch." *The Form-Critical Problem of the Hexateuch and Other Essays*. Translated by E. W. Trueman Dicken. Edinburgh and London: Oliver & Boyd, 1966.

———. *Old Testament Theology*. Translated by David M. G. Stalker. New York: Harper & Row, 1962.

———. *Studies in Deuteronomy*. Translated by David M. G. Stalker. London: SCM, 1953.

Richter, Wolfgang. *Exegese als Literaturwissenschaft*. Göttingen: Vandenhoeck & Ruprecht, 1971.

Ridderbos, Nic. H. "Die Theophanie in Ps. 11-6." *The Priestly Code and Seven Other Studies*. Oudtestamentische Studien 15. Leiden: E. J. Brill, 1969.

Ringgren, Helmer. *The Impact of the Ancient Near East on Israelite Tradition*. VTSup 23. Leiden: E. J. Brill, 1972.

Roifer, Alexander. "The End of Psalm 80." *Tarbiz* 29 (1959) 113-124.

Rost, Leonhard. *Das kleine Credo und andere Studien zum Alten Testament.* Heidelberg: Quelle & Meyer, 1965.

Rothstein, J. Wilhelm. *Kommentar zum ersten Buch der Chronik.* KAT 18. Leipzig: A. Deichersche, 1927.

Rudolph, Wilhelm. *Chronikbücher.* HAT 21. Tübingen: Mohr, 1955.

Sabourin, Leopold. *Priesthood.* Leiden: E. J. Brill, 1973.

———. *The Psalms: Their Origin and Meaning.* Staten Island: Alba House, 1969.

Schildenberger, Johannes. "Psalm 78 (77) und die Pentateuchquellen." *Lex Tua Veritas.* Edited by Heinrich Gross and Franz Müssner. Trier: Paulinus, 1961.

Schmidt, Hans. *Die Psalmen.* Tübingen: Mohr, 1934.

Smith, Morton. *Palestinian Parties and Politics That Shaped the Old Testament.* New York: Columbia University, 1971.

Southall, Aiden. "Spirit Possession Among the Alur." *Spirit Mediumship and Society in Africa.* Edited by John Beattie and John Middleton. New York: Africana Publishing Corporation, 1969.

Steck, Odil Hannes. *Israel und das gewaltsame Geschick des Propheten.* WMANT 23. Neukirchen-Vluyn: Neukirchener, 1967.

———. "Das Problem theologischer Strömungen in nachexilischer Zeit." *EvT* 28 (1968) 445–458.

———. "Theological Streams of Tradition." *Tradition and Theology in the Old Testament.* Edited by Douglas A. Knight. Philadelphia: Fortress, 1977.

———. *Überlieferung und Zeitgeschichte in den Elia-Erzählungen.* WMANT 26. Neukirchen-Vluyn: Neukirchener, 1968.

Strong, S. A. "On Some Oracles to Esarhaddon and Ashurbanipal." *Beiträge zur Assyriologie* 2 (1891–1894).

Tsevat, Matitiahu. "God and Gods in Assembly: An Interpretation of Psalm 82." *HUCA* 40–41 (1969–1970) 123–137.

Verger, Pierre. "Trance and Convention in Nago-Yoruba Spirit Mediumship." *Spirit Mediumship and Society in Africa.* Edited by John Beattie and John Middleton. New York: Africana Publishing Corporation, 1969.

———. "Yoruba Influences in Brazil." *Odu* 1 (1955) 1–11.

Walker, Sheila S. *Ceremonial Spirit Possession in Africa and Afro-America.* Leiden: E. J. Brill, 1972.

Wanke, Günther. *Die Zionstheologie der Korachiten.* BZAW 97. Berlin: A. Topelmann, 1966.

Weinfeld, Moshe. *Deuteronomy and the Deuteronomic School.* Oxford: Oxford University, 1972.

Weiser, Artur. *The Old Testament and its Formation.* Translated by Dorothea Barton. New York: Association, 1961.

———. *The Psalms*. Translated by Herbert Hartwell. Philadelphia: Westminster, 1962.

Welch, Adam C. *The Work of the Chronicler*. London: Oxford University, 1939.

Westermann, Claus. *Isaiah 40-66*. Translated by David M. G. Stalker. Philadelphia: Westminster, 1969.

———. *Der Psalter*. Stuttgart: Calwer, 1967. English text: *The Psalms*. Translated by Ralph D. Gehrke. Minneapolis: Augsburg, 1980.

———. "Zur Sammlung des Psalters." *Theologia Viatorum* 8 (1961/1962).

———. "Struktur und Geschichte der Klage im Alten Testament." *ZAW* 66 (1954) 44-80.

Widengren, George. *The Accadian and Hebrew Psalms of Lamentation as Religious Documents*. Stockholm: Bokforlags Aktiebolaget Thule, 1937.

Willesen, Folker. "The Cultic Situation of Psalm LXXIV." *VT* 2 (1952) 290-306.

Wilson, Robert R. *Genealogy and History in the Biblical World*. New Haven: Yale University, 1977.

———. *Prophecy and Society in Ancient Israel*. Philadelphia: Fortress, 1980.

Wright, George Ernest. "Archaeology and Old Testament Studies." *JBL* 77 (1958) 39-51.

Würthwein, Ernst. "Erwägungen zu Psalm 73." *Wort und Existenz*. Göttingen: Vandenhoeck & Ruprecht, 1970.

———. "Der Ursprung der prophetische Gerichtsrede." *Wort und Existenz*. Göttingen: Vandenhoeck & Ruprecht, 1970.

Zimmerli, Walther. "Ich Bin Jahwe." *Geschichte und Altes Testament*. BHT 16. Edited by Gerhard Ebeling. Tübingen: Mohr, 1953.

www.ingramcontent.com/pod-product-compliance
Lightning Source LLC
Chambersburg PA
CBHW022100160426
43198CB00008B/296